LEARN
Adobe InDesign CC
for Print and Digital Media Publication

Adobe Certified Associate Exam Preparation

Jonathan Gordon
and Cari Jansen
with Rob Schwartz

ADOBE
PRESS

LEARN ADOBE INDESIGN CC FOR PRINT AND DIGITAL MEDIA PUBLICATION
ADOBE CERTIFIED ASSOCIATE EXAM PREPARATION
Jonathan Gordon (video)
Cari Jansen (book)
with **Rob Schwartz**

Copyright © 2016 by Peachpit Press

Adobe Press books are published by Peachpit, a division of Pearson Education.
For the latest on Adobe Press books and videos, go to www.adobepress.com.
To report errors, please send a note to errata@peachpit.com.

Adobe Press Editor: Victor Gavenda
Senior Editor, Video: Karyn Johnson
Development Editor: Linda Laflamme
Technical Reviewer: Chad Chelius
Copyeditor: Kelly Anton
Proofreader: Patricia Pane
Senior Production Editor: Becky Winter
Compositor: Kim Scott, Bumpy Design
Indexer: Rebecca Plunkett
Cover & Interior Design: Mimi Heft
Cover Illustration: magnia, Fotolia.com

ISBN-13: 978-0-13-439780-1
ISBN-10: 0-13-439780-0

9 8 7 6 5 4 3 2 1
Printed and bound in the United States of America

*To Jennifer, Jacob, and Juliana—my J-crew—thank you for your patience,
love, and understanding, as well as bearing my font snobbery. I don't want
to waste another moment of my life without you in it. I love you all.*

—Jonathan Gordon

To my parents, who instilled in me the passion to learn and teach.

—Cari Jansen

Acknowledgments

This journey would not have been possible without my family. Jacob and Juliana, you are my Captain Toothless and Princess Sourpuss, my Bubba and my baby girl. Jennifer, I know you were just as stressed I was with the book. I have only wanted the best for you and the kids. Whenever I am with you I feel safe. Like I am home. I am glad I am home. I love you so much.

I also have to thank my parents for all the support and encouragement over the years. I appreciated it more than you know.

Thanks goes to Linda Laflamme, my editor, who without her insight and motivation, I could not have gotten through video after video after video after video.

To Rob Schwartz, the brains behind brainbuffet.com and this book series. Thanks for involving me in this endeavor. I owe you a lot—going all the way back to Rickards and McFatter. I admire your tenacity, brilliance, and modesty.

—Jonathan Gordon

It would not have been possible to write the chapters in this book, without the help of the editors and production team. Your input was invaluable. Thank you!

—Cari Jansen

About the Authors

Jonathan Gordon (video author) is a prominent InDesign instructor who has trained students and adults in Adobe products for almost 20 years. Jonathan has lectured at various conventions and media workshops across the United States. An award-winning instructor, he was named Broward County Journalism Adviser of the Year by the *Sun Sentinel* (Broward and Palm Beach) in 2010 and 2015, and was awarded the same distinction by the Florida Scholastic Press Association in 2004 and 2010. Jonathan helped establish the Academy of Journalism at McFatter Technical High School, where students received journalism certificates in digital design and industrial communication. He has also taught Digital Media Technology (Adobe InDesign, Photoshop, Illustrator, and Dreamweaver) through McFatter Technical College. Jonathan earned a Masters degree in Mass Communication from the University of Florida, specializing in online communication and web design. Several of his former journalist students have gone on to be published in the *Columbia Spectator*, *Miami Herald*, *New York Times*, and *Sports Illustrated*. Jonathan presently lives and works in Upstate New York.

Cari Jansen (primary book author) is an Adobe Certified Instructor and an Adobe Community Professional who spends much of her time helping people get the best out of Adobe applications and creative and publishing workflows. Cari is an industry professional with a hands-on production background in print and digital media. As a technical writer and qualified instructor, she provides training and support for a number of Adobe applications, including Adobe InDesign, Illustrator, Photoshop, Muse, and Acrobat and has worked as a technical editor for a number of years. In addition, she has developed many Adobe training courses, including *MyGraphicsLab Adobe InDesign CC Course for Print and Digital Media Publication*.

Rob Schwartz (author of Chapters 8 & 9) is an award-winning teacher (currently at Sheridan Technical College in Hollywood, FL) with over 15 years of experience in technical education. Rob holds several Adobe Certified Associate certifications and is also an Adobe Certified Instructor. As an Adobe Education Leader, Rob won the prestigious Impact Award from Adobe, and in 2010, Rob was the first winner of the Worldwide Certiport Adobe Certified Associate Championship.

Find out more about Rob at his online curriculum website at brainbuffet.com.

Contents

To access your free copy of this book's Web Edition containing more than 10 hours of video, see the instructions on pp. xi–xii.

Getting Started

Welcome to *Learn Adobe InDesign CC for Print and Digital Media Publication*! We use a combination of text and video to help you learn the basics of design with Adobe InDesign CC along with other skills that you will need to get your first job in graphic design. The industry-leading page design and layout program, Adobe InDesign CC lets you create and publish anything from printed books and brochures to digital magazines, eBooks, or interactive online documents.

About This Book and Video

Learn Adobe InDesign CC for Print and Digital Media Publication was created by a team of expert instructors, writers, and editors with years of experience in helping beginning learners get their start with the cool creative tools from Adobe Systems. Our aim is not only to teach you the basics of graphic design with InDesign, but to give you an introduction to the associated skills (like design principles and project management) that you'll need for your first job.

We've built the training around the objectives for the Print and Digital Media Publication Using Adobe InDesign CC (2015) Adobe Certified Associate (ACA) Exam, and if you master the topics covered in this book and videos, you'll be in good shape to take the exam. But even if certification isn't your goal, you'll still find that this training will give you an excellent foundation for your future work in graphic design. To that end, we've structured the material in the order that makes most sense for beginning learners (as determined by experienced classroom teachers), rather than following the more arbitrary grouping of topics in the ACA Objectives.

To aid you in your quest, we've created a unique learning system that uses video and text in partnership. You'll experience this partnership in action in the Web Edition, which lives on your Account page at *peachpit.com*. The Web Edition contains more than 11 hours of video—the heart of the training—embedded in an online ebook that supports the video training and provides background material. The ebook material is also available separately for offline reading as a printed book or as an ebook in a variety of formats. The Web Edition also includes interactive review questions you can use to evaluate your progress. Purchase of the book in *any* format entitles you to free access to the Web Edition (instructions for accessing it follow).

Most chapters provide step-by-step instructions for learning specific techniques. Many chapters include several optional tasks that let you further explore the features you've already learned. Don't stop exploring when you reach the end of the print book. Several valuable chapters and appendices are posted online at *peachpit.com*. There you'll find a chapter dedicated to digital media publishing and several appendices of techniques that expand on the printed chapters. Although they aren't part of the path to learning InDesign itself, two additional online chapters acquaint you with other skills and concepts that you'll come to depend on as you use the software in your everyday work. Here is where you'll find coverage of Domains 1 and 2 of the ACA Objectives, which don't specifically relate to features of InDesign but are important components of the complete skill set that the ACA exam seeks to evaluate. You can find the online chapters posted at *peachpit.com* along with the Web Edition and lesson files.

Each chapter opens with two lists of objectives. One list lays out the learning objectives: the specific tasks you'll learn in the chapter. The second list shows the ACA exam objectives that are covered in the chapter. A printable table you can download along with the lesson files (see instructions below) guides you to coverage of all the exam objectives in the book and videos.

Conventions Used in This Book

This book uses several elements styled in ways to help you as you work through the projects.

Terms that are defined in the glossary appear in bold and in color, such as:

> **Kerning** increases or decreases the amount of space between two characters.

Links to videos that cover the topics in depth appear in the margins.

▶ *Video 5.1*

The ACA objectives covered in the chapters are called out in the margins beside the sections that address them.

★ *ACA Objective 2.1*

Notes, tips, and shortcuts give additional information about a topic. The information they contain is not essential to accomplishing a task but provides a more in-depth understanding of the topic.

> **NOTE** *The default behavior for background images is to tile across and down the container where they are set.*

> **TIP** *You can also show or hide panels by choosing them from the Window menu.*

> **SHORTCUT** *To view your design without seeing all the panels or to eliminate any panel clutter, press Tab.*

Working in InDesign means you'll sometimes need to enter code-like text; this text is listed in a bold monospaced font:

Enter **mailto:** immediately followed by the email address.

Other text that you should enter appears in **bold**.

OPERATING SYSTEM DIFFERENCES

In most cases, InDesign CC works the same in both Windows and Mac OS X. Minor differences exist between the two versions, mostly due to platform-specific issues. Most of these are simply differences in keyboard shortcuts, how dialogs are displayed, and how buttons are named. Where specific commands differ, they are noted within the text. Windows commands are listed first, followed by the Mac OS equivalent, such as Ctrl+C/Command+C. In general, the Windows Ctrl key is equivalent to the Command (or Cmd) key in Mac OS, and the Windows Alt key is to the Mac OS Option (or Opt) key.

In most cases, screen shots were made in the Mac OS version of InDesign and may appear somewhat differently from your own screen. The screen shots in this book show a Light interface, to allow for higher contrast in the print version of the book. Interface elements such as panels and dialog boxes will be darker on your screen.

As chapters proceed, instructions may be shortened with the assumption that you picked up the essential concepts earlier in the chapter. For example, at the beginning of a chapter you may be instructed to "press Ctrl+C/Command+C." Later, you may be told to "copy" text. These should be considered identical instructions. If you find you have difficulties in any particular task, review earlier steps or techniques in that chapter. In some cases when a technique is based on concepts covered earlier, you will be referred back to the specific chapter.

Installing the Software

Before you begin using *Learn Adobe InDesign CC for Print and Digital*, make sure that your system is set up correctly and that you've installed the proper software and hardware. This material is based on the original 2015 release of Adobe InDesign CC (version 11.0) and is designed to cover the objectives of the Adobe Certified Associate Exam for that version of the software.

The Adobe InDesign CC software is not included with this book; it is available only with an Adobe Creative Cloud membership, which you must purchase or which must be supplied by your school or another organization. To install applications from Adobe Creative Cloud onto your computer, follow the instructions provided at *helpx.adobe.com/creative-cloud/help/download-install-app.html*.

ADOBE CREATIVE CLOUD DESKTOP APP

In addition to Adobe InDesign CC, some extended activities suggested in the text require the Adobe Creative Cloud desktop application, which provides a central location for managing dozens of apps and services that are included in a Creative Cloud membership. Although the central lessons in this book and the videos do not require a Creative Cloud subscription, you should explore the ways the Creative Cloud desktop application can be used to sync and share files, manage fonts, access libraries of stock photography and design assets, and showcase and discover creative work in the design community.

The Creative Cloud desktop application is installed automatically when you download your first Creative Cloud product. If you have Adobe Application Manager installed, it auto-updates to the Creative Cloud desktop application.

If the Creative Cloud desktop application is not installed on your computer, you can download it from the Download Creative Cloud page on the Adobe website (*creative.adobe.com/products/creative-cloud*) or from the Adobe Creative Cloud desktop apps page (*adobe.com/creativecloud/catalog/desktop.html*). If you are using software on classroom machines, be sure to check with your instructor before making any changes to the installed software or system configuration.

NOTE

Adobe periodically provides updates to software. You can easily obtain these updates through Creative Cloud. If these updates include new features that affect the content of this training or the objectives of the ACA exam in any way, we will post updated material to peachpit.com.

Accessing the Free Web Edition and Project Files

Your purchase of this book in any format includes access to the corresponding Web Edition hosted on *peachpit.com*. The Web Edition contains the complete text of the book augmented with hours of video and interactive quizzes, as well as three online chapters and other bonus content.

To work through the projects in this product, you will first need to download the lesson files from *peachpit.com*. You can download the files for individual lessons or download them all in a single file.

If you purchased an eBook from *peachpit.com* or *adobepress.com*, the Web Edition will automatically appear on the Digital Purchases tab on your Account page. Click the Launch link to access the product. Continue reading to learn how to register your product to get access to the lesson files.

NOTE

When opening any of the project files, a warning dialog box may inform you that your document contains links to sources that have been modified; click Update Links. You will learn in Chapter 2 how to fix missing links. A Missing Fonts dialog box may also appear. Click Sync Fonts to install missing fonts from Adobe Typekit. For information on Adobe Typekit, see Chapter 2.

If you purchased an ebook from a different vendor or you bought a print book, you must register your purchase on *peachpit.com*:

1 Go to *www.peachpit.com/register*.

2 Sign in or create a new account.

3 Enter the ISBN: **9780134397801**.

4 Answer the questions as proof of purchase.

5 The Web Edition will appear under the Digital Purchases tab on your Account page. Click the Launch link to access the product.

   The lesson files can be accessed through the Registered Products tab on your Account page.

6 Click the Access Bonus Content link below the title of your product to proceed to the download page. Click the lesson file links to download them to your computer.

Additional Resources

Learn Adobe InDesign CC for Print and Digital Media Publication is not meant to replace the documentation that comes with the program or to be a comprehensive reference for every feature. For comprehensive information about program features and tutorials, refer to these resources:

Adobe InDesign Learn & Support: *helpx.adobe.com/indesign* is where you can find and browse Help and Support content on *Adobe.com*. Adobe InDesign Help and Adobe InDesign Support Center are accessible from the Help menu in InDesign. Help is also available as a printable PDF document. Download the document at *helpx.adobe.com/pdf/InDesign_reference.pdf*.

Adobe Forums: *forums.adobe.com/community/indesign* lets you tap into peer-to-peer discussions, questions, and answers on Adobe products.

Adobe InDesign CC product home page: *adobe.com/products/indesign* provides information about new features and intuitive ways to create responsive web page layouts that display beautifully on any screen.

Adobe Add-ons: *creative.adobe.com/addons* is a central resource for finding tools, services, extensions, code samples, and more to extend your Adobe products.

Resources for educators: *adobe.com/education* and *edex.adobe.com* offer information for instructors who teach classes on Adobe software at all levels.

Adobe Certification

The Adobe training and certification programs are designed to help designers and other creative professionals improve and promote their product-proficiency skills. Adobe Certified Associate (ACA) is an industry-recognized credential that demonstrates proficiency in Adobe digital skills. Whether you're just starting out in your career or planning to switch jobs, the Adobe Certified Associate program is for you! For more information, visit *edex.adobe.com/aca*.

Resetting the Preferences to Their Defaults

InDesign lets you determine how the program looks and behaves (like tool settings and the default unit of measurement) using the extensive options in Edit > Preferences (Windows) or InDesign CC > Preferences (Mac OS). To ensure that the preferences of your copy of InDesign match those used in this book, you can reset your preference settings to their defaults. If you are using software installed on computers in a classroom, don't make any changes to the system without checking with your instructor.

To reset your preferences to their default settings, follow these steps:

1 Quit Adobe InDesign.

2 Hold down the Shift+Ctrl+Alt (Windows) keys or the Shift+Ctrl+Option+Command (Mac OS) keys as you startup InDesign.

3 Continue to hold down the keys until the Reset Preferences dialog appears.

4 In the Reset Preferences dialog, click Yes.

5 The file containing your preferences will be deleted.

CHAPTER OBJECTIVES

Chapter Learning Objectives

- Identify and understand different elements of the InDesign CC interface.
- Define common panels and clarify their usage.
- Identify tools and their functionality.
- Navigate through an InDesign document and change zoom levels.
- Organize and customize the InDesign workspace.
- Identify the correct document intent given a job scenario.

Chapter ACA Objectives

DOMAIN 3.0
UNDERSTANDING ADOBE INDESIGN CC

3.1 Identify elements of the InDesign CC interface and demonstrate knowledge of their functions.

3.2 Define the functions of commonly used tools, including selection tools, frame tools, type tools, drawing tools, Line tool, etc.

3.3 Navigate, organize, and customize the workspace.

DOMAIN 4.0
CREATING PRINT AND DIGITAL MEDIA PUBLICATIONS USING ADOBE INDESIGN

4.1 Create a new project.

CHAPTER 1

Getting Started with InDesign

You are about to start your Adobe InDesign journey. As an industry-standard layout application, InDesign is a powerhouse used by graphic designers worldwide to design and produce print and digital media publications.

It's very likely that you've looked at artwork created in InDesign just today. In print format, newspapers, magazines, yearbooks, reports, newsletters, and flyers are commonly designed with InDesign. In digital media format, interactive magazines on your smartphone or tablet might have been designed in InDesign and published with the Adobe Digital Publishing Solution. InDesign is also used for the creation of eBooks, PDFs, and PDF forms.

Whether you end up working as a graphic designer for a design studio; in communications, marketing, advertising, public relations, or elsewhere, there is a high probability that InDesign experience will be a required selection criteria for the job.

So let's step into InDesign, and find your way around the program. In this chapter, you'll learn to recognize and identify commonly used tools and panels, and to customize the look and feel of InDesign based on what works best for the project you're working on.

★ ACA Objective 3.1

★ ACA Objective 3.2

★ ACA Objective 3.3

▶ Video 1.1

▶ Video 1.2

▶ Video 1.3

NOTE

Earlier versions of InDesign will show a Welcome screen instead of the Start workspace.

NOTE

This chapter supports the project created in video lesson 1. Go to the Project 1 page in the book's Web Edition to watch the entire lesson from beginning to end.

NOTE

On Mac OS, the document window opens as a floating window. To combine it with the application frame, as seen in Figure 1.1, choose Window > Application Frame.

Stepping into InDesign

When you first launch InDesign a Start workspace appears with links to recent files, CC Libraries, video tutorials, and Adobe Stock images and videos.

To open an InDesign document (INDD), click Open in the Start workspace or choose Open from the File menu in the menu bar (File > Open). Navigate to an INDD file in the Open A File dialog box, select it, and click Open. The document window you see is your creative work area where document pages are displayed and designed. When you open multiple documents, they appear as tabbed document windows, each displaying its document name on a tab. To display a document in the window, click its document tab. Everything you see on the screen, such as the application with its Tools panel, Control panel, and other panels, is referred to as a **workspace**. The default workspace you see is the Essentials workspace (**Figure 1.1**).

The **pasteboard area** surrounding the pages is used to store design elements that don't appear on a document page. You might use it to place some text that needs to be included in your page designs, to store some design variations, or simply as a work area.

As you progress with your design, you will select different tools from the Tools panel to add new design elements, images, and text to the page, or to modify the appearance of existing objects. The Control panel is a context-sensitive dashboard (**Figure 1.2**). It displays settings for selected objects that you can edit. When you're working on text, for example, the Control panel will show options such as font, font size, or alignment that you can adjust.

The Essentials workspace includes the Pages, Layers, Links, Stroke, Color, Swatches, and CC Libraries panels. Panels are task specific, and you access panels based on the task you want to perform in InDesign. With the Color panel, for example, you can mix colors and apply them to artwork.

The Application bar has buttons that let you change the view options, screen mode, and document arrangement. The Screen Mode setting controls how you view your document.

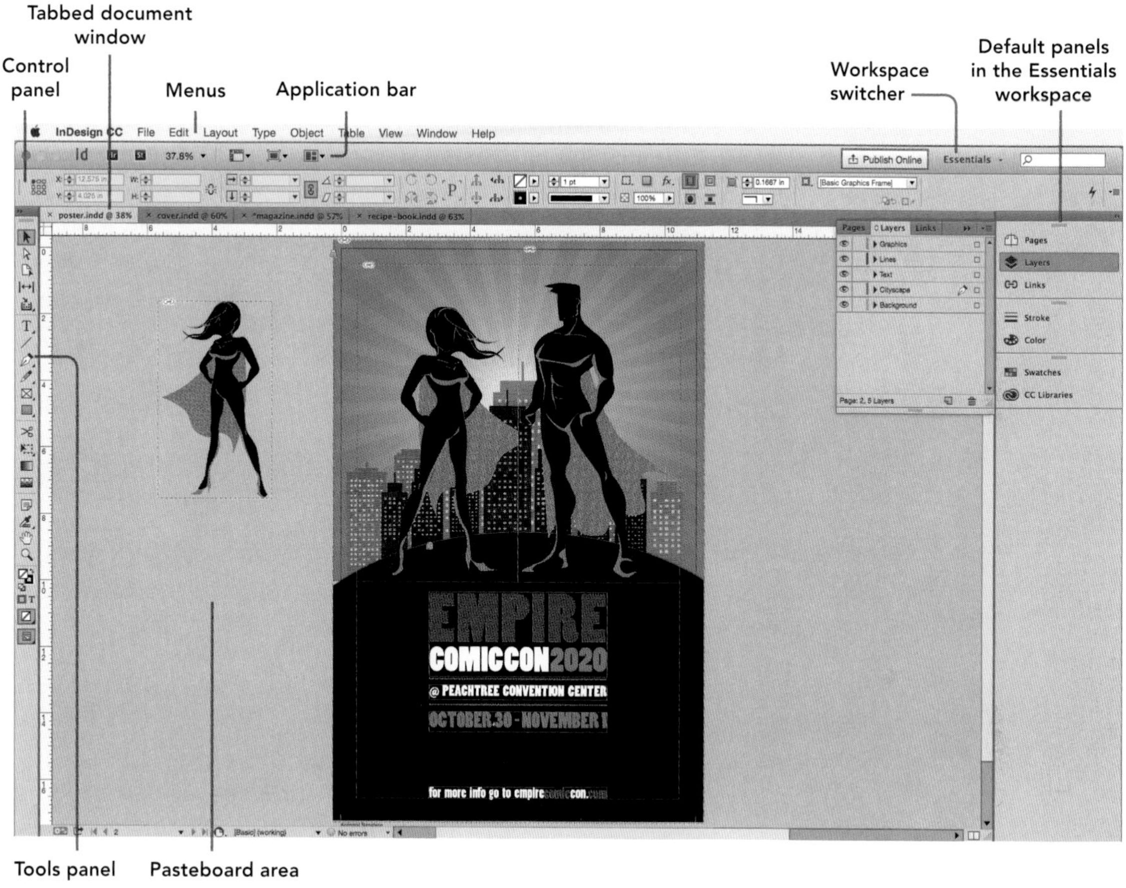

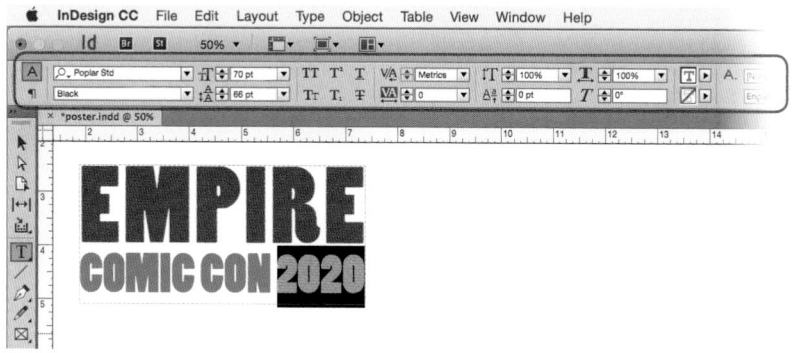

Figure 1.1 The InDesign Essentials workspace, with several documents open

Control panel

Tabbed document window

Menus

Application bar

Workspace switcher

Default panels in the Essentials workspace

Tools panel   Pasteboard area

Figure 1.2 With text selected, the Control panel displays settings for font, font size, and much more.

With the screen mode set to Normal, for example, InDesign displays nonprinting elements (such as guides and frame edges that help you construct your artwork, align objects, and position objects). The elements displayed depend on the settings you enable in the View Options menu on the Application bar. The Preview screen mode hides all of the nonprinting elements as well as objects on the pasteboard. Preview is a great mode to use when you want to see what the finished artwork and pages will look like.

To change the screen mode (**Figure 1.3**):

1   Choose the Screen Mode menu in the Application bar, or choose
    View > Screen Mode.

2   Select the preferred screen mode.

SHORTCUT *To toggle between Preview and Normal Screen modes, press W.
Note that this shortcut won't work when the text insertion point is in text.*

The Application bar also includes the workspace switcher menu that enables you to change from the default Essentials workspace to another workspace, resulting in the display of a different combination of panels onscreen.

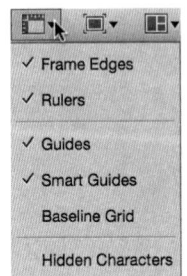

Figure 1.3 Changing from Normal screen mode to Preview screen mode

Tools and Panels

As you start working in InDesign, you'll discover the many different tools and panels that provide you with everything you need to build beautiful layouts.

★ ACA Objective 3.2

▶ Video 1.4

SELECTING THE RIGHT TOOL FOR THE JOB

Think of the Tools panel as your personal toolbox. As you work your way through a layout, you'll select the right tool from it for the task at hand. For example, use the Selection tool (➤) to select, resize, or reposition an object on the page; the Type tool (T) to edit or add text; and the Zoom tool (Q) to look at page content close up.

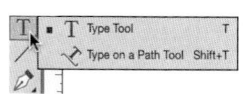

Figure 1.4 The tool name and shortcut for the Type tool

Once a tool is selected in the Tools panel, it remains the active tool until you click on a different tool. To learn the names of various tools and the shortcuts for quick access, move your pointer over each tool in the Tools panel and pause. A tool tip appears with the name and the tool's single-letter shortcut (**Figure 1.4**).

The Tools panel contains a number of hidden tools too. Any tool that includes the tiny triangle in the lower-right corner has one or more hidden tools hidden behind it.

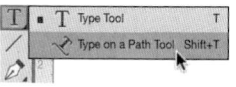

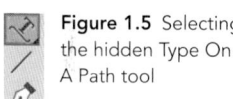

To select and use a hidden tool (**Figure 1.5**):

1 Click and hold the pointer on the tool.

2 From the menu that appears, select the hidden tool you want to work with.

Figure 1.5 Selecting the hidden Type On A Path tool

Let's look at some of the more commonly used tools. This chapter presents the most commonly used tools, but InDesign offers many more. If you ever forget what a tool does or are curious about a particular tool:

- Select the tool in the Tools panel.
- Display the Tool Hints panel (Window > Utilities) for more information (**Figure 1.6**).
- You can also consult the InDesign Help (Help > InDesign Help).

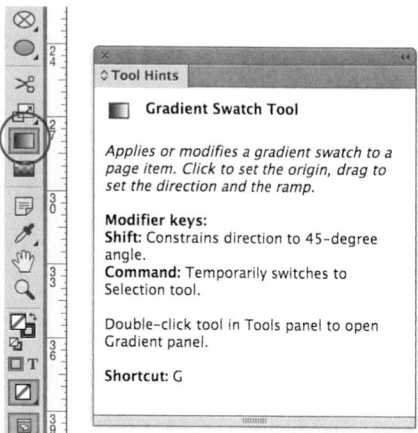

Figure 1.6 The Tool Hints panel provides a short description of each tool's function as well as handy modifier keys and shortcuts.

SELECTION TOOL

The Selection tool ( ) is going to be your best friend. As the name suggests, you use it to select objects. The tool has many other purposes, however, and is a bit of a chameleon. The Selection tool's pointer changes in appearance depending on how and where you use it.

To select an object (**Figure 1.7**):

1   Click the Selection tool in the Tools panel to select it.

2   Position the pointer over an object on the page and click. A bounding box with eight handles appears around the object.

3   Move the object you selected by dragging it into a new position.

Figure 1.7 Selecting (left) and moving an object with the Selection tool

Keep an eye on the pointer: Did you notice it changed appearance as you selected the object and moved it? From a pointer, to a pointer with a dot (for selecting the object), to a small triangle (for moving an object)? Yup, the Selection tool is a multipurpose tool and the pointer will always tell you what it's up to.

To rotate a selected object (**Figure 1.8**):

1   Move the pointer just outside the object's bounding box, near one of the corners. The pointer indicates when you can rotate.

2   Drag in a circular motion to rotate the object.

To resize a selected object, such as the colored background frame in **Figure 1.9**:

1 Move the pointer over one of the handles on the bounding box and click.

2 Drag in either direction that the little arrows indicate.

Figure 1.8 Rotating an object with the Selection tool

Figure 1.9 Resizing an object with the Selection tool

Figure 1.10 Copying an object by Alt-dragging (Windows) or Option-dragging (Mac OS) it

You can also make copies of objects with the Selection tool (**Figure 1.10**):

1 Select the object.

2 Press Alt (Windows) or Option (Mac OS), and drag the object to a new location.

   You can also press Alt (Windows) or Option (Mac OS) after you start dragging the object. Make sure you release the mouse first, then the Alt/Option key in that case to ensure the copy is created.

TYPE TOOL

Typography is an important part of design. Whether it's a poster design, a newsletter, or a digital media publication, text will likely be included and need to be formatted. InDesign has an amazing set of typographic features and controls. To start working with type—including entering new text, formatting text, or editing text—you use the Type tool (T). Text is inserted in box-like elements called **text frames**.

To create a text frame (**Figure 1.11**):

1 Select the Type tool.

2 Click and drag from the upper-left corner to the lower-right corner.

   Once the text frame is created, the text insertion point flashes inside the frame, indicating you can enter text into the frame.

If you need to resize a text frame, use the Selection tool (▶) to select it, then drag any of the bounding box handles.

Figure 1.11 Creating a text frame with the Type tool and adding some text

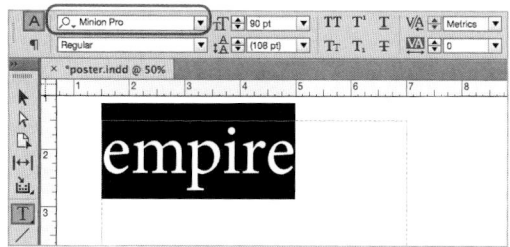

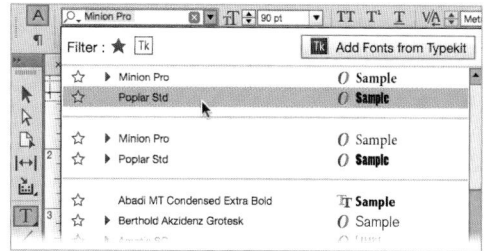

Figure 1.12 Applying a different font to selected text

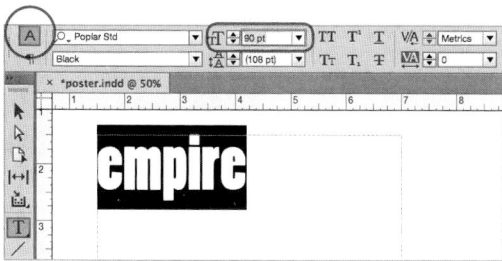

Figure 1.13 Increasing the font size using the Character Formatting controls in the Control panel

To change the font of the text (**Figure 1.12**):

1   With text entered in the text frame, select the text with the Type tool.

2   Click the Character Formatting controls (A) in the Control panel, and choose a font from the fonts list.

To change the size of the text (**Figure 1.13**):

■   Choose a preset size from the Font Size menu, enter a new font size in the Font Size field, or click the increase or decrease size buttons.

When working on commercial InDesign projects, your customer will likely supply you with text that's already final, and it could be that you want to change text from lowercase to uppercase (capital) letters as part of the design. There's no need to retype the text by holding down the Caps Lock or Shift key.

To change text to All Caps (**Figure 1.14**):

- Select the text that needs to be capitalized, and in the Control panel, click the All Caps button.

You'll learn more about InDesign's typography features, adding text to documents, and working with text in the following chapters.

SHORTCUT *When placing and positioning text in a document, you often alternate between the Type tool and the Selection tool. When you have the Selection tool selected, double-clicking in a text frame automatically selects the Type tool. With the Type tool selected, pressing Esc selects the Selection tool again.*

Figure 1.14 Changing text to all uppercase

FRAME AND SHAPE TOOLS

As you start to build your designs, you can use the shape tools to add geometric shapes, such as circles, ellipses, rectangles with rounded corners, starbursts, and more. In InDesign, each design element you add to a page, whether it's a shape, text, a background color, a photo, or a video, is a frame that contains content. Frames themselves can have color applied around their shape border (stroke), or within the shape itself (fill).

There are three different frame types:

- **Graphic frames:** Containers for photos, logos, video, or audio.
- **Text frames:** Containers that hold text.
- **Unassigned frames:** Holds neither text nor graphics.

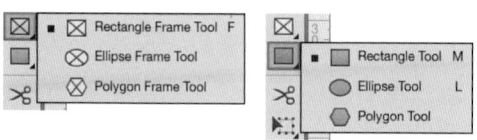
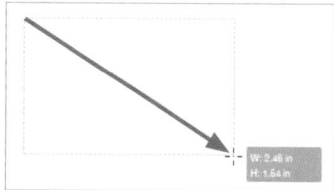

Figure 1.15 Frame tools (left) and shape tools (right)

Figure 1.16 Drawing a rectangle with the Rectangle tool

Two different groups of tools can create frames (**Figure 1.15**):

- The frame tools: Rectangle Frame, Ellipse Frame, and Polygon Frame tools create graphic frames, recognizable by the X within the frame.
- The shape tools: Rectangle, Ellipse, and Polygon tools create unassigned frames.

To create a frame with one of these tools, for example a rectangle (**Figure 1.16**):

1 Select the Rectangle tool (▣).

2 Drag diagonally across the page and release the mouse.

Alternatively, to create a shape with specific tool properties (**Figure 1.17**):

1 Select the Rectangle tool.

2 Click on the page.

3 Enter Width and Height options in the Rectangle dialog box.

4 Click OK.

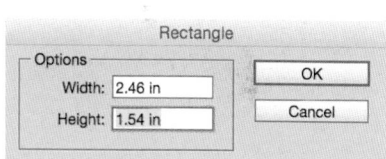

Figure 1.17 The Rectangle dialog box with Width and Height values entered

Once the shape is created, you can adjust its width, height, and other settings from the Control panel, or use the Selection tool to resize the object.

To change the width and height (**Figure 1.18**):

1 Use the Selection tool to drag any of the bounding box handles.

2 Enter Width and Height settings in the Control panel.

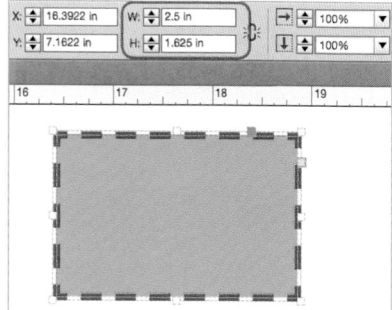

Figure 1.18 Changing the width and height of a rectangle using the Control panel

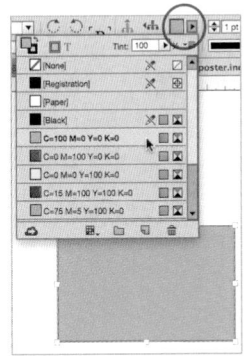

With the shape created, you can now adjust its fill and stroke settings.

To change the fill color (**Figure 1.19**):

1 Select the object.

2 Click the arrow next to the Fill box in the Control panel. Alternatively, click the Fill box in the Swatches or Tools panel.

3 Click to select a swatch color from the Control panel or from the Swatches panel.

To adjust the stroke settings (**Figure 1.20**):

1 Select the object.

Figure 1.19 Applying a fill color using the Control panel

2 Click the Stroke box in the Control panel. You can also click the Stroke box in the Swatches or Tools panel.

3 Select a swatch color from the Control panel (or from the Swatches panel).

4 Select width from the Weight menu in the Control panel (or the Stroke panel.)

5 Select stroke type from Type menu in the Control panel (or the Stroke panel).

We'll discuss various frame and shape tools, as well as working with color, in more detail in the following chapters.

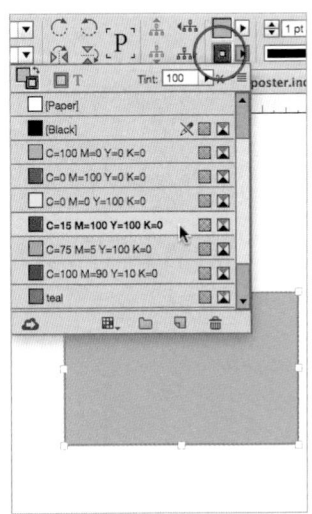
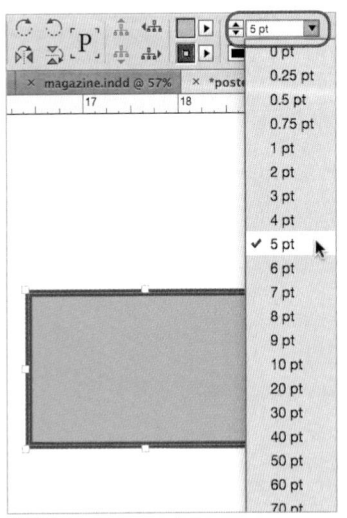
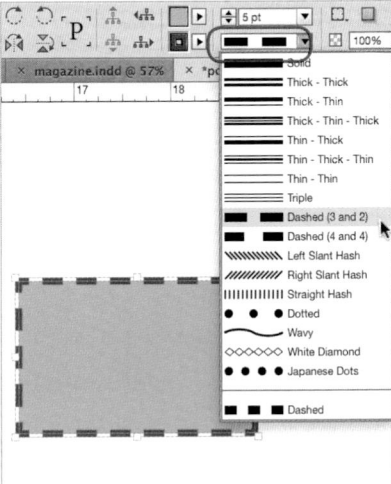

Figure 1.20 Applying a dashed stroke color using the Control panel

PANELS, PANELS, AND MORE PANELS

InDesign has more than 50 different panels that provide access to design and production features. Yikes! When panels are not displayed as part of a workspace, you can access them from the Window menu. For panels that relate to text, such as the Paragraph panel, you can also head to the Type menu. As there are so many panels, the Window menu contains a number of submenus from which you select panels.

Each panel has its own unique usage, for example:

- **Swatches panel:** Manage document colors, including adding, editing, or deleting color swatches.
- **Pages panel:** Navigating pages, adding and removing pages, setting up and applying master pages, and controlling page numbering.
- **Layers panel:** Manage document layers, including adding, editing, showing, hiding layers, locking, and unlocking layers.
- **Links panel:** Manage images and graphics links, flagging any link errors.
- **Text Wrap panel:** Wrap text around an object, such as a graphic.
- **Paragraph Styles panel:** Enable single-click text formatting.

Panels can be expanded or docked on the side of the application window or floating. You can fully customize which panels display and where and how those panels appear. As you start working on more projects in InDesign, you'll discover you have a series of favorite panels that you'd like to access quickly. You'll learn how to save your favorite panels as a reusable workspace later in this chapter.

Panels that are **docked** are attached to the side of the screen. For example, the Control panel is docked to the top, the Tools panel is docked at left, and generally panels specific to InDesign's default workspaces are docked at right. Floating panels can be positioned anywhere on the screen; you might even consider placing them on a second monitor.

To show a panel that is docked (**Figure 1.21**):

- Click the panel icon. Once the panel is shown, you can drag the edges of the panel to make it larger (**Figure 1.22**). To close the panel, click the panel icon again, or click the double arrow at the top of the panel group.

To expand docked panels (**Figure 1.23**):

- Click the double arrow in the top right of the panel. Click the double arrow again to collapse back to the docked panel.

▶ Video 1.5

NOTE

For a complete overview of every panel in InDesign, refer to the InDesign Help.

Figure 1.21 With docked panels, click the panel icon to show the panel.

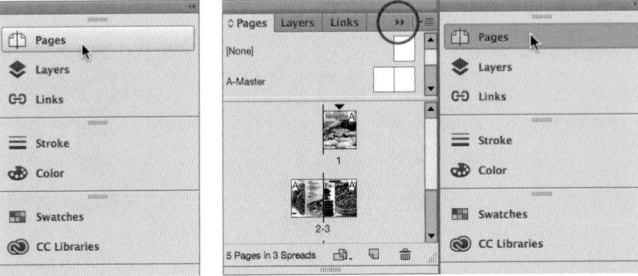

Figure 1.22 Drag the panel edges to change the size of a panel.

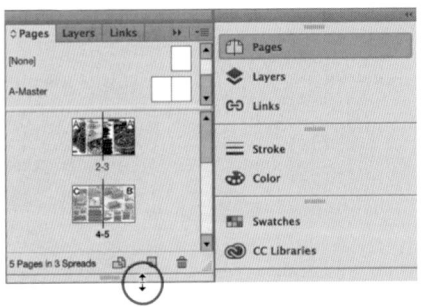

Figure 1.23 Expanding docked panels by clicking the double arrow

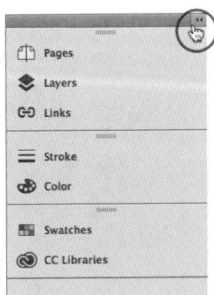
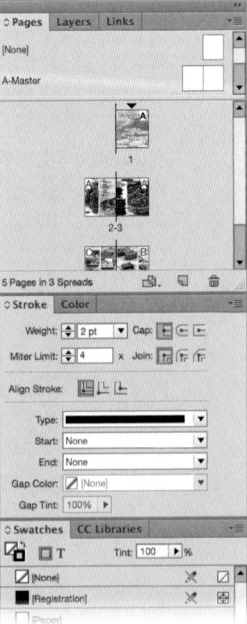

To dock a floating panel (**Figure 1.24**):

1 Select the panel by its panel tab.

2 Drag it to the side, and release the mouse when a blue horizontal or vertical line appears at the insertion point.

Similar to docking panels, you can also drag docked panels by their panel tab out of the dock and turn them into floating panels.

A lot of the panels in InDesign are nested into panel groups. You can create your own panel groups or amend existing panel groups.

To create a panel group (**Figure 1.25**):

1 Drag a panel by its panel tab into the empty area next to a panel tab.

2 Drag a panel into a docked group of panels, and release the mouse when a blue horizontal line appears at the insertion point in the panel group.

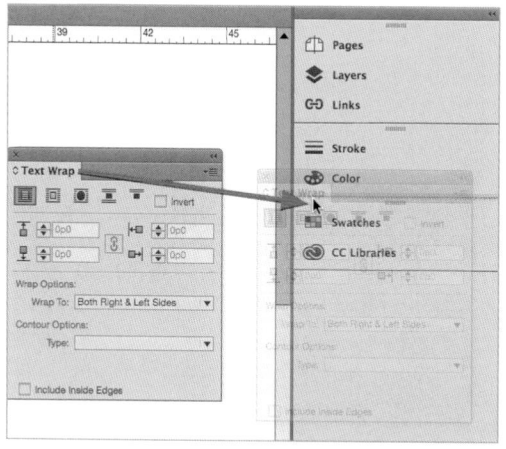
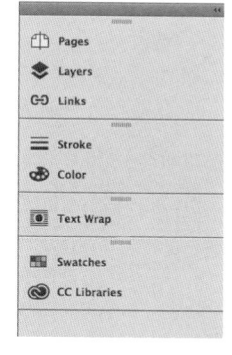

Figure 1.24 Dock a floating panel by dragging it to the docked panels.

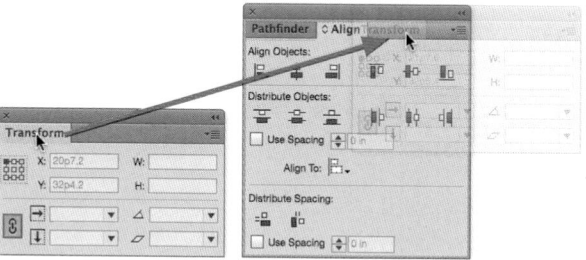
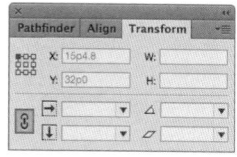

Figure 1.25 Grouping panels

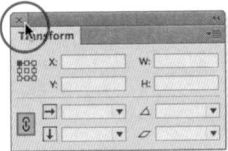

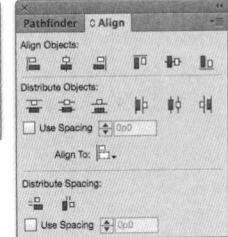

Figure 1.26 Hiding panels

TIP

You can also show or hide panels by choosing them from the Window menu. A checkmark to the left of the panel name means the panel is displayed already.

To hide panels (**Figure 1.26**):

1 Drag the panel by its panel tab out of a group.

2 Click its close box.

Almost all panels have a menu that provides a list of panel-related commands (**Figure 1.27**).

- Click the panel menu to see the commands.

Some commands also appear at the bottom of a panel as a clickable button. A lot of these buttons are similar across panels. For example, the button that looks like a flipping page or notepad ( ) is found in panels such as the Swatches, Layers, and Paragraph Styles panels. In each of these panels, the button does something similar: It makes something new. It creates a new color swatch, new layer, or new style when clicked.

To see what these buttons do in different panels (**Figure 1.28**):

1 Show the panel.

2 Position the pointer over the button.

A tool tip appears.

SHORTCUT *To view your design without seeing all the panels or to eliminate any panel clutter, press Tab. Every panel that was visible onscreen is hidden. Press Tab again to bring the panels back. To show and hide all panels except for the Tools panel and Control panel, press Shift+Tab. (Note that this does not work when the text insertion point is in text.)*

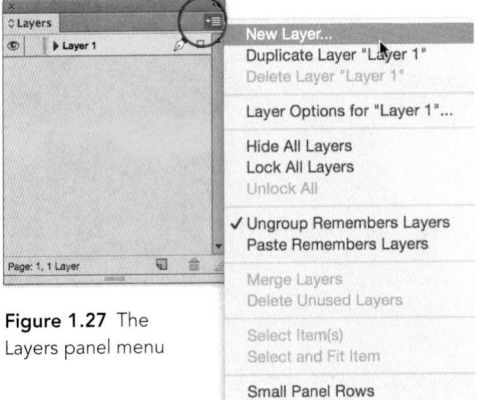

Figure 1.27 The Layers panel menu

Figure 1.28 Tool tips reveal the function of each panel button.

Finding Your Way Around a Document

When working with a lot of content on a single page, the ability to zoom into a smaller section that you are working on is handy. InDesign provides quite a few ways to pan and zoom around a document.

★ *ACA Objective 3.3*

The Zoom tool (🔍) enables you to change the zoom level of the document:

▶ *Video 1.7*

1 Select the Zoom tool.

2 Click an object you want to zoom into.

   With each click, the zoom level increases. It might take several clicks to zoom into a section of the page.

3 To zoom back out, Alt-click (Windows) or Option-click (Mac OS) the Zoom tool.

A more practical way to zoom into an area of the document is to (**Figure 1.29**):

1 Select the Zoom tool.

2 Drag a marquee around the area of the page with the Zoom tool.

   The marqueed area is now centered within the document window.

3 To quickly zoom back out and center the active page in the document window, choose View > Fit Page In Window or press or Ctrl+0 (zero) (Windows) or Command+0 (zero) (Mac OS).

 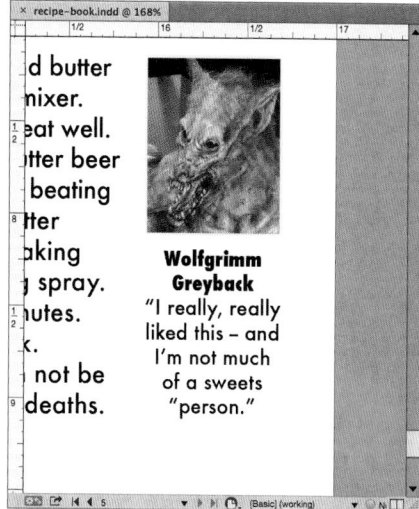

Figure 1.29 Zoom into a section of a page by dragging a marquee around the area with the Zoom tool.

The marquee technique works well when editing InDesign documents from a marked-up proof, such as a PDF with comments. You can see the full page, find the location for the change, and quickly zoom into the text to edit.

The View menu contains a number of other useful ways to view a document.

When you design reports, books, or magazines destined for print, viewing facing pages (with the right- and left-page designs side by side) will help with the placement of design elements and obtaining rhythm, balance, and harmony in your design. Pages that face each other are referred to as a **spread**.

To center the active spread in the document window (**Figure 1.30**):

- Choose View > Fit Spread In Window or press Ctrl+Alt+0 (Windows) or Command+Option+0 (Mac OS).

To set the zoom level to 100%:

- Choose View > Actual Size, or press Ctrl+1 (Windows) or Command+1 (Mac OS).

To increase zoom level using preset increments:

- Choose View > Zoom In, or press Ctrl along with the plus sign (+) on Windows or Command along with the plus sign (+) on Mac OS.

To decrease zoom level using preset increments:

- Choose View > Zoom Out, or press Ctrl along with the hyphen (–) on Windows or Command along with the hyphen (–) on Mac OS. Think of the hyphen as a minus sign to remember this shortcut.

SHORTCUT

To quickly zoom out to 50% zoom level, press Ctrl+5 (Windows) or Command+5 (Mac OS). To quickly zoom to 200%, press Ctrl+2 (Windows) or Command+2 (Mac OS).

Figure 1.30 Fitting a page (left) and a spread (right) in the document window

With the Zoom Level menu in the Application bar (**Figure 1.31**), you can select from any of the preset zoom levels, as well as enter custom zoom levels.

To select a preset zoom level:

- Select a preset option from the Zoom Level menu.

To set a custom zoom level:

- Enter the preferred zoom level in the zoom field, and press Enter (Windows) or Return (Mac OS) (**Figure 1.31**).

When using the commands or shortcuts for incremental zoom and zoom levels, keep in mind that if nothing is selected on the page, the zoom is based on the center of the page or spread. If objects are selected or the insertion point is in text, the zoom level centers on that element.

SHORTCUT *To temporarily access the Zoom tool when another tool is selected, press Ctrl+Spacebar (Windows) or Command+Spacebar (Mac OS). Add the Alt (Windows) or Option (Mac OS) key to zoom out.*

Once you've zoomed into a small section of a page, you can use the Hand tool ( ) to pan to other sections of the page.

To display nonvisible parts of a page in the document window (**Figure 1.32**):

1 Select the Hand tool.

2 Drag to move to other parts of the document.

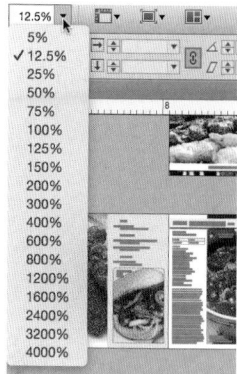

Figure 1.31 The Zoom Level menu in the Application bar

NOTE

Depending on your operating system settings, some shortcuts might conflict with your system.

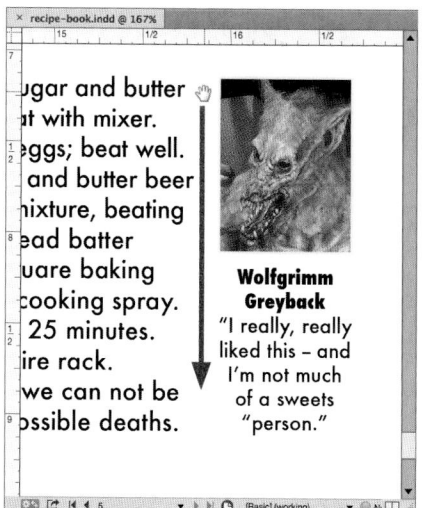

Figure 1.32 Drag with the Hand tool to navigate to a different area on the page.

You can also use the Hand tool as a power zoom tool, offering you zoom controls in combination with panning to different areas of a page or different pages. The area that will be displayed in the document window is marked by a red rectangle.

To use the power zoom (**Figure 1.33**):

1 After zooming in on a page, select the Hand tool, then click and hold with your mouse to access power zoom.

2 Press the Arrow Up or Arrow Down key to zoom.

3 Drag the red rectangle to another position on page.

> **SHORTCUT** *To access the Hand tool, press the Spacebar. If you happen to be editing text with the Type tool, press Alt+Spacebar (Windows) or Option+Spacebar (Mac OS) instead.*

Figure 1.33 Using the power zoom to quickly navigate to other areas of a document

▶ *Video 1.8*

As you zoom into graphics, you might notice that they sometimes appear very jagged. Raster graphics, vector graphics, and transparency effects (such as drop shadows) display according to the View > Display Performance setting, which is set to Typical Display by default. You can change the Display Performance to High Quality, but keep in mind that this might slow the screen redraw as you move from page to page.

Figure 1.34 From left to right, Fast, Typical, and High Quality display applied at the document level

You have three choices for Display Performance (**Figure 1.34**):

- **Fast Display:** Graphics and images are grayed out and transparency effects are not shown. When copyediting a publication, this display performance ensures you'll see the text only.

- **Typical Display:** Low-resolution appearance of graphics and transparency effects. As the default, this display performance works well while you are busy with your designs. It gives you fast previews for placement and image cropping, as well as a faster screen redraw.

- **High Quality Display:** High resolution. Vector graphics appear sharp and detailed, allowing you to position them with more precision in your design. When showing the onscreen design to your client, this display performance provides the best-quality view.

The display performance can be changed at the document or object level.

To change the display performance:

- **For a document:** Choose an option from the View > Display Performance menu.

- **For a selected object:** Choose an option from the Object > Display Performance menu.

When you orient elements sideways on a page, such as a discount voucher placed in a magazine foldout or a wide table that is better placed sideways, working on the element can literally be a pain in the neck. Don't worry! You can keep your head straight, and rotate your work instead. Spreads can rotate 90° clockwise, 90° counterclockwise, and 180° degrees, making it easier to view the content.

To rotate a spread (**Figure 1.35**):

1 Select the spread in the Pages panel.

2 Choose View > Rotate Spread View, and select one of the rotation options.

Figure 1.35 Rotating the spread view 90° counterclockwise to work on the discount voucher design

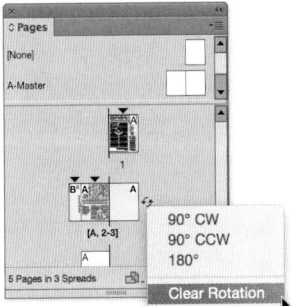

Figure 1.36 Clearing rotation

Figure 1.37 The Pages panel

To clear the rotation, either:

- Right-click (Windows) or Control-click (Mac OS) the spread in the Pages panel, and choose Clear Rotation (**Figure 1.36**).
- Choose View > Rotate Spread > Clear Rotation.

When working with longer documents, such as newsletters, reports, books, or digital magazines, you can use the Pages panel (**Figure 1.37**) to insert new pages, move pages around, or quickly display a page in the document window.

To access a page in a document:

- Double-click a page thumbnail in the Pages panel.
- Double-click the number below a page spread to display both pages of the spread in the document window.

The Pages panel is also used to apply master pages to document pages. **Master pages** add common design elements to pages, such as page numbers, headers, and footers. You'll learn more about working with master pages in Chapter 4.

Aside from the Pages panel, InDesign offers several other ways to navigate to different pages in the document.

To navigate to a different page:

- Use the vertical and horizontal scroll bars.
- Use the status bar, at the bottom of the document window (**Figure 1.38**).
- Choose Layout > Go To Page, enter the page number, and click OK.
- Choose Layout > First Page, Previous Page, Next Page, etc.

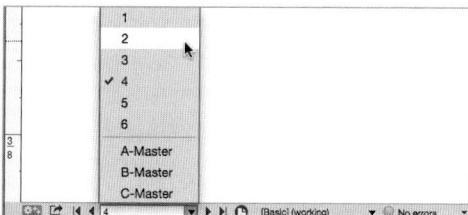

Figure 1.38 Using the status bar to navigate to different pages

Customizing Your Workspace, Shortcuts, and Menus

★ ACA Objective 3.3

▶ Video 1.5

You're about to start working on your first project in InDesign in the next chapter. Before you do, however, take a few minutes to organize InDesign so it works best for you. To do this, you will build your own workspace by creating custom shortcuts, displaying your favorite panels, and even highlighting menus.

Because the panels in InDesign are so task specific, it is only natural that some panels are designed for use when working on projects for different media types. For example, you could be using InDesign to create an interactive PDF or an eBook with animations, which requires the use of specific panels such as Buttons And Forms, or the Animation panel. Adobe has added a number of workspaces based on specific types of jobs or tasks you might work on, making it easier to access the relevant panels.

The workspace switcher in the Application bar makes allows you to toggle between different workspaces, each with their own panel layout.

To switch the workspace, either:

- Click the workspace switcher and select a workspace (**Figure 1.39**).
- Choose Window > Workspace and select a workspace.

Switch to the Interactive For PDF workspace. Can you see any panels you wouldn't be using when designing a product for print?

Figure 1.39 Using the workspace switcher in the Application bar to change workspaces

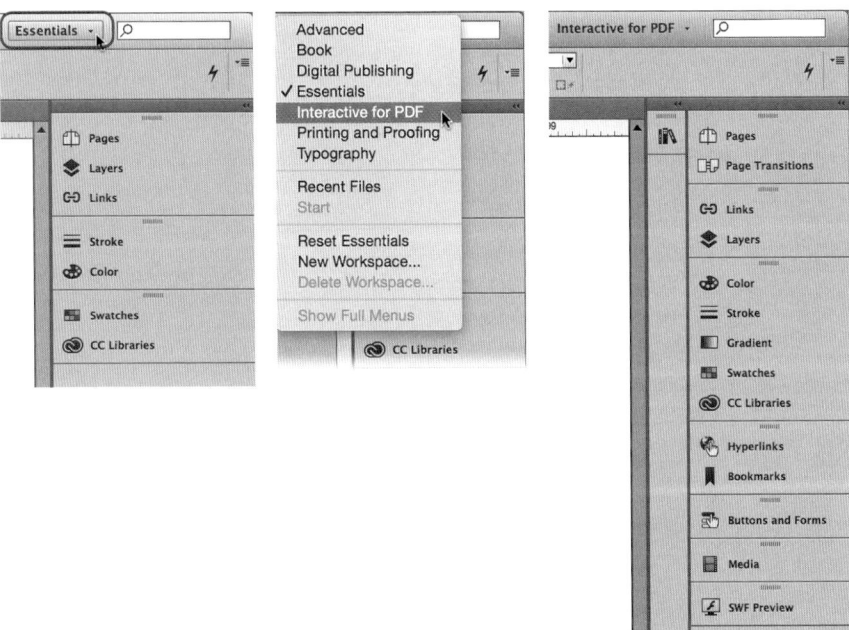

The InDesign default workspaces (**Figure 1.40**) include:

- **Essentials:** The default panel set: Pages, Layers, Links, Stroke, Color, Swatches, and CC Libraries panels.
- **Advanced:** This workspace includes the panels from Essentials plus Gradient, Effects, Object Styles, Paragraph Styles, and Character Styles panels. In Advanced, the Color panel does not display.
- **Book:** Adds panels such as Cross-References, Conditional Text, Index, and Bookmarks.

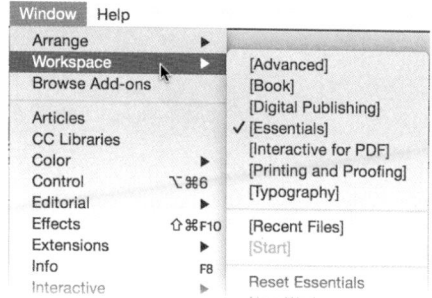

Figure 1.40 The InDesign default workspaces

- **Digital Publishing:** Adds panels for Animation, Timing, Media, Object States, and much more.

- **Interactive for PDF:** Adds the panels that support the creation of interactive PDF files, such as Page Transitions, Buttons And Forms, and Media.

- **Printing and Proofing:** Adds panels that help you check documents prior to delivery for commercial printing, and includes panels such as Separations Preview, Trap Presets, and Preflight.

- **Typography:** With a big focus on working with text, this workspace adds panels such as Glyphs, Story, Paragraph, Paragraph Styles, Character, and Character Styles.

NOTE

InDesign CC (2015.2) adds a Recent Files workspace that gives you quick and easy access to files you've worked on recently, by adding the Recent Files panel.

Using Shortcuts

★ *ACA Objective 3.3*

▶ *Video 1.9*

Throughout the upcoming chapters you'll find handy tips that often include keyboard shortcuts. By pressing the shortcut keys on the keyboard, you can skip navigation to a menu, submenu, or panel, and often apply commands faster. There are even global shortcuts that work across a lot of different applications that you might already be familiar with, such as:

- **Cut:** Ctrl+X (Windows) or Command+X (Mac OS).

- **Copy:** Ctrl+C (Windows) or Command+C (Mac OS).

- **Paste:** Ctrl+V (Windows) or Command+V (Mac OS).

- **Print:** Ctrl+P (Windows) or Command+P (Mac OS).

Many menu commands (**Figure 1.41**) display their shortcut, and the Tools panel shows you the shortcut for accessing each tool when you position the pointer over it.

Figure 1.41 Keyboard shortcuts for menu commands for Mac OS (left) and Windows (right)

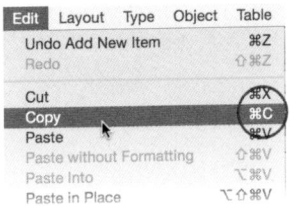
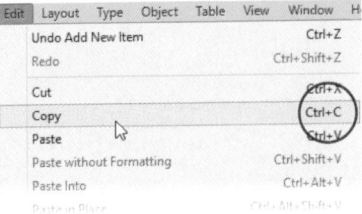

Figure 1.42 Drawing shapes with Shift+Alt (Windows) or Shift+Option (Mac OS) held down

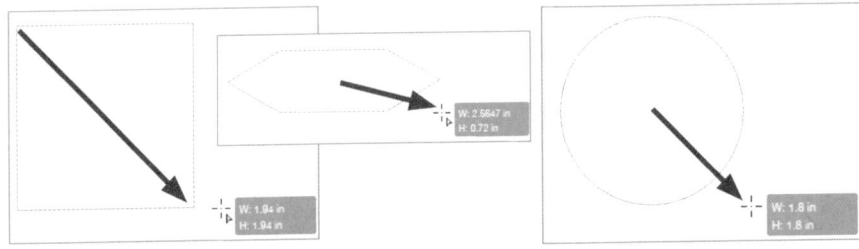

The Shift key and the Alt key (Windows) or Option key (Mac OS) have their own superpowers (**Figure 1.42**). For example:

- Press Shift to constrain movement to horizontal, vertical, or 45° angles.
- Press Shift when drawing a shape with a rectangle or ellipse tool to create squares or circles.

Use Alt (Windows) or Option (Mac OS) to:

- Copy when dragging selected object.
- Draw shapes from the center outwards.

Combining the keys, Shift+Alt (Windows) or Shift+Option (Mac OS), you can:

- Copy and constrain movement to a horizontal or vertical direction when dragging a selected object.
- Draw circles or squares from the center outwards.

Menu commands that have a keyboard shortcut display the shortcut next to the command name. For example, next to Object > Lock you see Ctrl+L (Windows) or Command+L (Mac OS). Many menu commands, particularly commands in panel menus, do not have shortcuts, however. When you lack a shortcut for a feature you might use often, it becomes tedious. Let's say you need to use the Interactive > Convert To Check Box command from the Object menu multiple times when designing a form. Luckily, you can create your own keyboard shortcut for any command that doesn't have one.

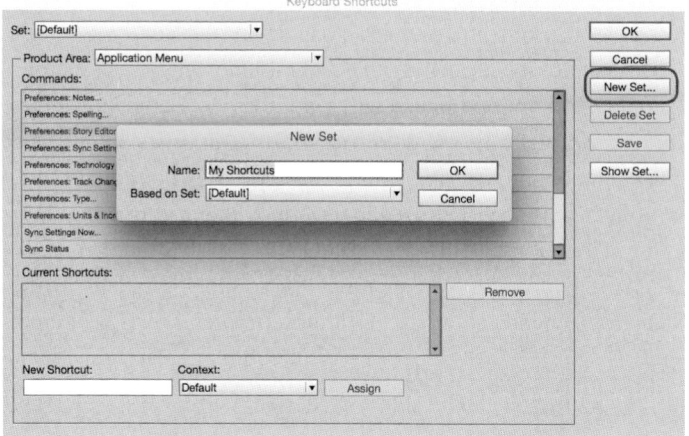

Figure 1.43 Creating your own keyboard shortcuts set

Before adding new shortcuts, you must first create a new keyboard shortcuts set (**Figure 1.43**):

1　Choose Edit > Keyboard Shortcuts.

2　Click New Set.

3　Enter the Name in the New Set dialog box.

4　Leave Based On Set set to [Default]. This ensures that all of the InDesign default shortcuts are part of your set.

5　Click OK; the newly added set is now the active set.

6　Click OK once more to close the Keyboard Shortcuts dialog box.

To add custom keyboard shortcuts (**Figure 1.44**):

1　Choose Edit > Keyboard Shortcuts.

2　Check that new shortcuts set you added previously is the active set.

3　Select a Product Area.

4　Click the Command name.

5　Click in the New Shortcut box.

6　Press the new shortcut keys on the keyboard.

7　Click Assign; this will list the new shortcut under Current Shortcuts.

8　Click OK.

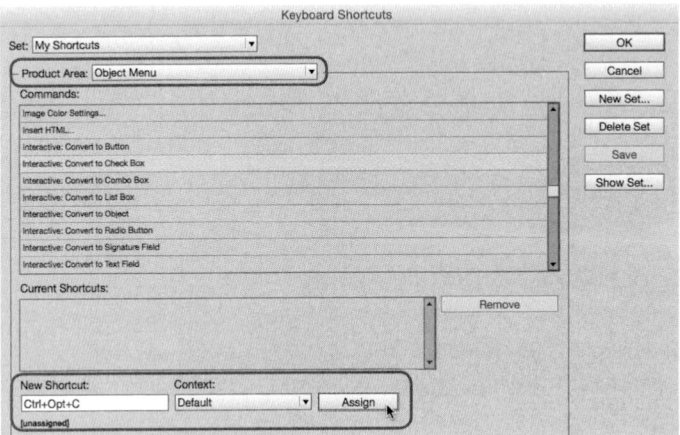

Figure 1.44 Adding a custom keyboard shortcut for the Convert To Checkbox command

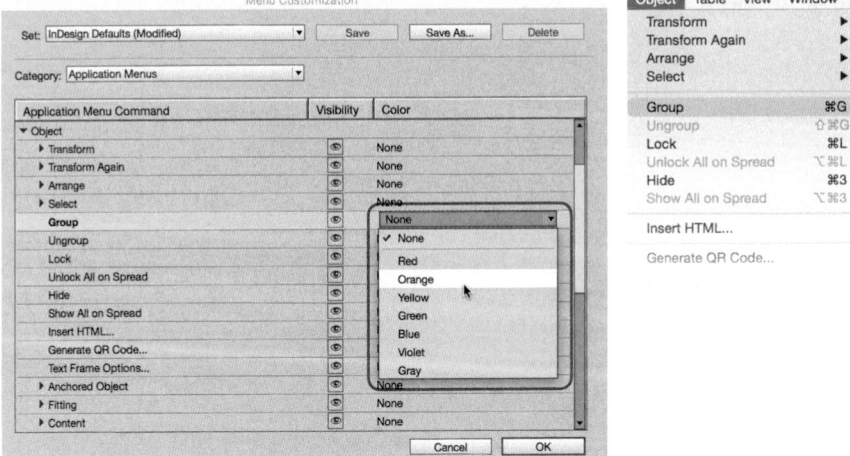

Figure 1.45 Customizing the way menus look in InDesign

Aside from customizing keyboard shortcuts, you can also customize the display of menus (**Figure 1.45**). Menus can be hidden or be highlighted with a color.

To edit menus:

1 Choose Edit > Menus.

2 Select a category from the Category menu in the Menu Customization dialog box.

3 Click the disclosure triangle to the left of an Application Menu Command.

4 Click the visibility icon to hide a menu.

5 Click a color name and select a color from the menu.

6 Click OK.

Creating Your Own Workspace

★ *ACA Objective 3.3*

▶ *Video 1.6*

Now that you know all about menu, shortcuts, and panel customization, you're all set to create your own workspace. Find those panels you love working with the most, group them as preferred, and create your own reusable workspace (**Figure 1.46**).

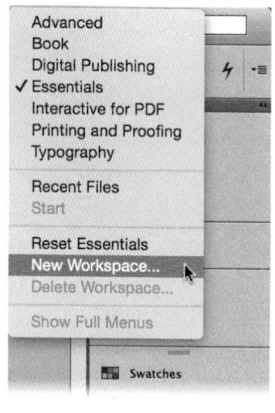
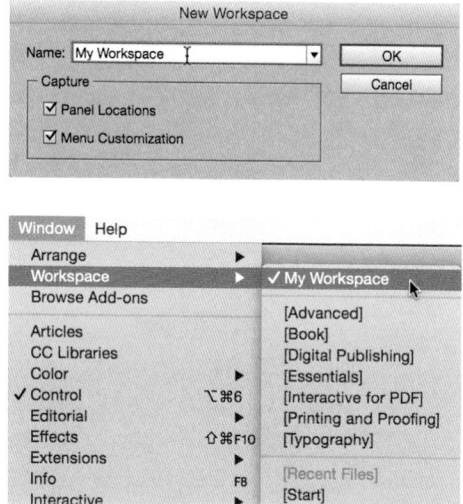

Figure 1.46 Creating your own custom workspace with all of your favorite panels and menu settings

To save a workspace:

1 Show and organize panels as preferred.

2 Choose New Workspace from the workspace switcher or Window > Workspace menu.

3 Enter the Name of your workspace in the New Workspace dialog box, and select the Panel Locations and Menu Customization options.

   Panel Locations ensure that the position of the panels on your screen is captured as part of the workspace. Menu Customization preserves any changes you might have made to menu colors or visibility.

4 Click OK to save your workspace.

The newly added workspace becomes the active workspace.

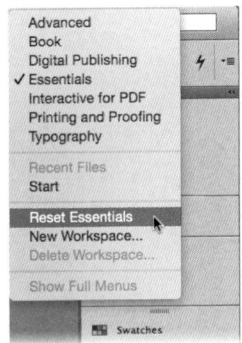

InDesign is very clever, and it knows you are working in a particular workspace, but it also sees that you move things around during the day. The Paragraph Styles panel might be pulled out of the docked panels and be floating, or maybe you increased the depth of the Pages panel. When you quit InDesign and relaunch it, InDesign does not clean up your workspace for you. As far as InDesign knows, you might have left that Paragraph Styles panel as a floating panel on purpose.

When it comes to cleaning up your workspaces, a simple reset will tidy things up for you (**Figure 1.47**).

Figure 1.47 Clean up the current workspace by resetting it.

To reset a workspace:

- Choose Reset Workspace from the workspace switcher or Window > Workspace menu.

★ *ACA Objective 4.1*

▶ *Video 1.9*

Before You Begin

At the start of each print or digital media design project, you'll consider what the intent of the document you're designing is going to be. For example: Are you creating an interactive eBook, an advertisement that is printed in a magazine, or a design to be viewed on a tablet device, such as an iPad?

Answering this question helps you choose the right page size, work with the correct units of measurement, such as pixels or inches, as well as choose the correct color mode for graphics.

As you create a new document (File > New > Document), you set the intent of the document at the top of the New Document dialog box (**Figure 1.48**). The next chapter covers the New Document dialog box in more detail, so for now just consider the basic differences between the settings.

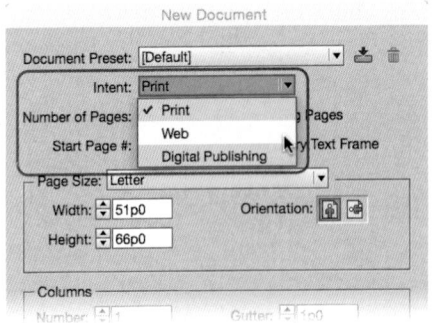

Figure 1.48 The Intent menu in New Document dialog box

Print

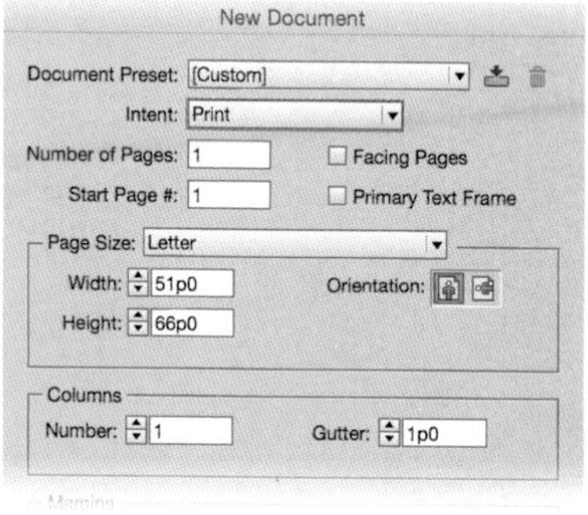

Choose the Print document intent when you plan to publish for commercial print, digital printing, or desktop printing. When you select this intent, InDesign applies the following settings in the document you create:

- The Swatches panel defaults to CMYK color.

- The Transparency Blend Space is set to Document CMYK (Edit > Transparency Blend Space). You'll learn more about transparency in a later chapter.

- The Page Size menu includes standard printed page sizes, such as Letter, and the default units of measurement is set to picas (p) (**Figure 1.49**).

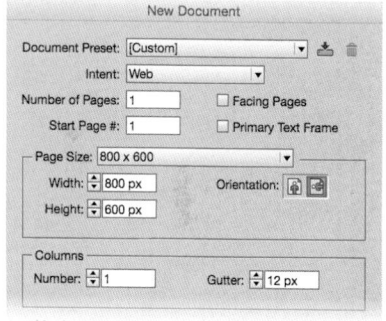

Figure 1.49 The New Document dialog box with the intent set to Print

Web

Web intent is useful when designing documents for online viewing. This could be an interactive PDF designed for viewing on an intranet or an eBook for an eReader. When you select this intent, InDesign makes the following changes:

- The Swatches panel defaults to RGB color.

- The Transparency Blend Space is set to Document RGB (Edit > Transparency Blend Space).

- The Page Size menu displays standard computer screen sizes, such as 800x600px, 1024x768px, with measurements set to pixels (px) (**Figure 1.50**).

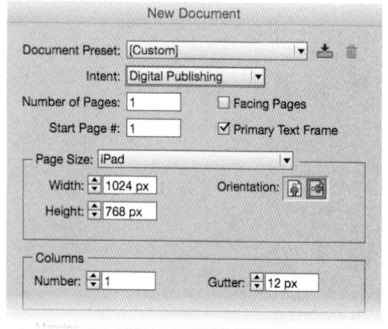

Figure 1.50 The New Document dialog box with the intent set to Web

Digital Publishing

When designing for mobile or tablet devices, choose the Digital Publishing intent as a starting point in the New Document dialog box (File > New > Document). InDesign changes your document settings as follows:

- The Swatches panel defaults to RGB color.

- The Transparency Blend Space is set to Document RGB (Edit > Transparency Blend Space).

- The Page Size menu options include standard mobile device sizes, such as iPhone, iPad, Kindle, and Android, with measurement units in pixels (px) (**Figure 1.51**).

Figure 1.51 The New Document dialog box with the intent set to Digital Publishing

CHAPTER OBJECTIVES

Chapter Learning Objectives

- Create a new project and identify the correct document setup settings to use for different publishing projects.

- Add ruler guides to a document.

- Create shapes through drawing and combine common shapes such as ellipses, rectangles, polygons, and lines.

- Understand the use of layers.

- Add and resize images.

- Add and format text.

- Identify different ways to colorize artwork.

- Identify the right PDF settings for different publications and uses.

Chapter ACA Objectives

For full descriptions of objectives, download the printable chart from your account on *peachpit.com*. See pages xi–xii.

DOMAIN 2.0
UNDERSTANDING PRINT AND DIGITAL MEDIA PUBLICATIONS
2.1, 2.2, 2.3, 2.4, 2.5

DOMAIN 3.0
UNDERSTANDING ADOBE INDESIGN CC
3.1, 3.2, 3.3, 3.4, 3.6, 3.8

DOMAIN 4.0
CREATING PRINT AND DIGITAL MEDIA PUBLICATIONS USING ADOBE INDESIGN
4.1, 4.2, 4.4

DOMAIN 5.0
PUBLISH, EXPORT, AND ARCHIVE PAGE LAYOUTS USING ADOBE INDESIGN
5.1

CHAPTER 2

Designing an Event Poster

In this first hands-on project, you'll design an event poster that is going to be printed commercially. As part of this project, you'll learn how to create a new document in InDesign, add various visual elements, images, and text, as well as apply color to objects.

You'll also learn how to submit your design as a Portable Document Format (PDF) proof to your client for review and as a press-ready PDF to your printer for production.

Starting the Project

As you start working in graphic design, you will likely create many different InDesign documents. You may need to design documents for print, such as a poster, report, or newsletter. Or perhaps you'll be working on a magazine that contains interactive slideshows or videos that is destined to be viewed on tablets or mobile devices. Or, maybe you need to design eBooks that will be read in an interactive form. You can create all these designs with InDesign, but you'll start with a printed event poster in this chapter (**Figure 2.1**).

Figure 2.1 Finished poster design

Creating a New Document

★ ACA Objective 2.1

★ ACA Objective 4.1

When creating a new document, first ask yourself: What is the intent of my document? Where will it be published? On which platform? As discussed at the end of the previous chapter, InDesign gives you the choice of three document intents:

- Print
- Web
- Digital Publishing

NOTE

This chapter supports the project created in video lesson 2. Go to the Project 2 page in the book's Web Edition to watch the entire lesson from beginning to end.

For an event poster that will be posted in shop windows or on notice boards, the intent is print. Even if the same poster is posted as a Portable Document Format (PDF) or graphic on a website later on, print is the intent to start with. Choosing Print means you intend to mix colors used in designs with Cyan, Magenta, Yellow, and Black (CMYK) inks, which is different than mixing with Red, Green, and Blue (RGB). Consider the following question: What two colors would you use to mix orange? If you needed to pick from CMYK, what two colors would that be? Now try answering that same question mixing RGB colors.

Starting your document with print intent does not mean you cannot use RGB in the design at all. A combined RGB/CMYK workflow is a common practice. For instance, you could specify swatch colors in CMYK, and use photos originating from digital cameras, which capture in RGB. Placing these photos without converting them to CMYK first means you retain their maximum tonal range for the web version of the design. Meanwhile, the RGB photos can be converted to CMYK as part of the file export to PDF for delivery to your printer.

When setting up a new InDesign document for print, be sure to ask yourself some key questions before you jump into the program:

- What will the finished page size for the print publication be?
- Will any design elements, such as background graphics and photos, run up to the edges of the page?

▶ Video 2.1

- Which area of the page will be the image area (that is, the area that contains most of the content, such as text and images)?

▶ Video 2.2

- Will the pages of multipage documents be bound? Smaller newsletters might use saddle-stitch binding, which binds folded sheets by putting staples through the spine.

With these answers in mind, you're ready to create a new document for your project in InDesign. For a single-page poster design destined for print, the new document setup is relatively simple:

1   Choose File > New > Document (**Figure 2.2**).

2   Select Preview so you can see how the changes affect the document setup.

3   Select Print from the Intent menu.

4   Select Tabloid from the Page Size menu and click the Portrait icon for Orientation. You can also enter custom Width and Height measurements here.

5   Deselect Facing Pages.

    Posters or flyers are designed as standalone pages. In contrast, publications such as books or magazines use facing pages. Facing pages are placed on either side of the spine or fold. Creating a new document with Facing Pages selected displays the left and right pages of the document side by side, with the spine in the middle (**Figure 2.3**).

6   Next, set the Columns and Margins settings for your document: Enter the margin settings and number of columns as well as the gutter amounts.

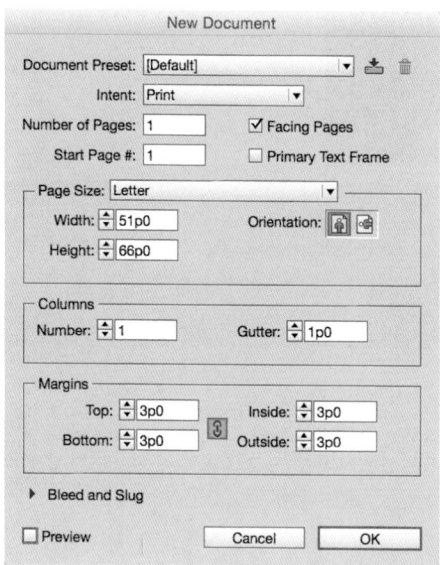

Figure 2.2 New Document dialog box

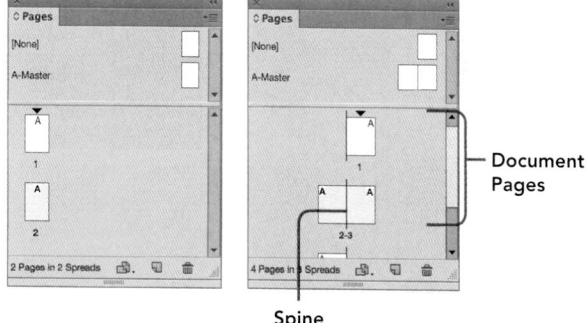

Figure 2.3 Pages panel display without facing pages (left) and with facing pages (right)

COLUMNS AND MARGINS

Column and margin settings add helpful nonprinting guides to your document, making it easier for you to consistently position design elements. Aligning them with top, right, bottom, and left margin guides or column guides creates balance and harmony in your design (**Figure 2.4**).

Margins define the image area on the page. The image area is the rectangular area on the page marked by the margin guides; it holds most of the content, such as text and images. When setting margins, keep in mind that headers and footers often fall outside this image area. Headers and footers are positioned in the top and bottom margin area between the page edge and the margin guides. The image area, once defined by the margins, can be divided into columns. The gutter value sets the spacing between the columns.

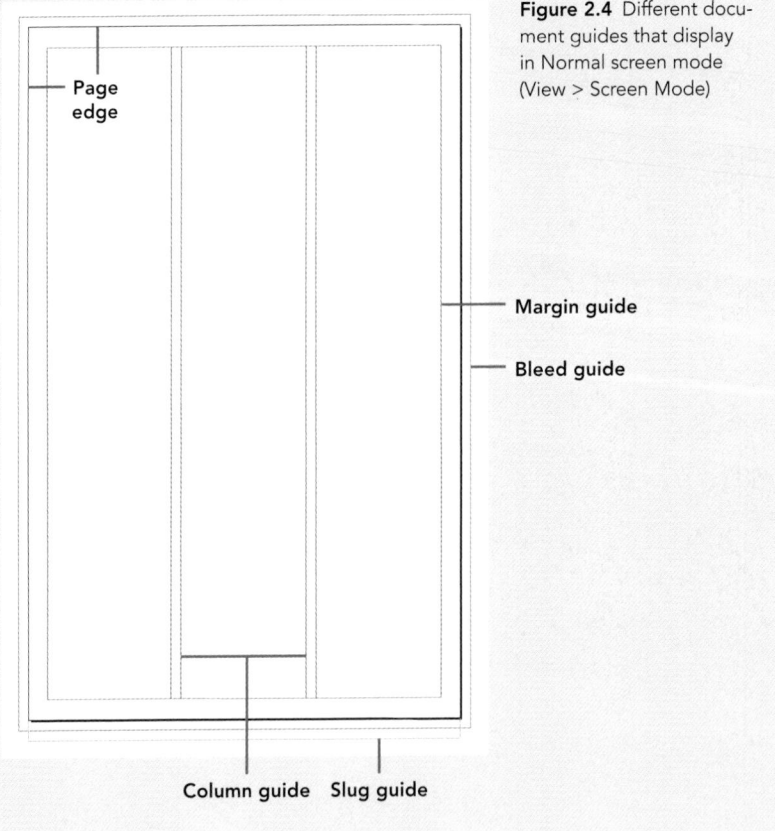

Figure 2.4 Different document guides that display in Normal screen mode (View > Screen Mode)

Page edge

Margin guide

Bleed guide

Column guide   Slug guide

7   To specify bleed and slug values, click the disclosure triangle to the left of Bleed And Slug (**Figure 2.5**).

8   Enter the bleed or slug amounts.

The *bleed* is an area outside the perimeter of the printable page. When content must print to the edge of a page, extending the artwork into the bleed area avoids slight variations that show white (or paper-colored) edges when pages are trimmed to their finished size. A bleed of 1/8 of an inch (0.125 in) on all sides before a publication is trimmed is generally sufficient. For a poster or postcard design, you need to set the bleed for all four sides.

The *slug* area falls outside the bleed area and is used for information such as print instructions or project sign-off instructions.

9   Click OK to close the New Document dialog box, and start working on your design.

As you start working through the event poster project, consider viewing the finished poster design side by side with your working document, so you can check your progress and compare results.

NOTE

Depending on the type of print publication, bleed values vary. A business card might require a smaller bleed than a saddle-stitched magazine or a bound book. Always consult with your printer regarding the bleed amount required for a print project.

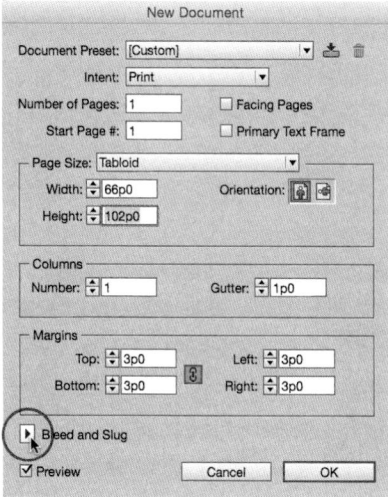
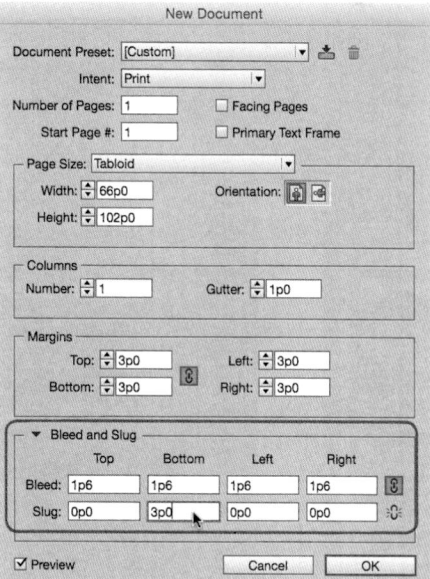

Figure 2.5 The New Document dialog box setup for creating a poster with bleed and slug areas

Figure 2.6 Displaying two open documents side-by-side using 2-Up

To view two open documents side by side, do one of the following:

- Select 2-Up from the Arrange Documents menu in the Application bar (**Figure 2.6**).

- Choose Window > Arrange > Tile.

To bring all the document tabs back into one window, do one of the following:

- Select Consolidate All from the Arrange Documents menu in the Application bar.

- Choose Window > Arrange > Consolidate All Windows.

Using Ruler and Smart Guides

★ *ACA Objective 3.4*

Creating a new document automatically adds a number of nonprinting guides for margins, columns, bleed, and slug to your page. Along with these guides, you can also add ruler guides to help position the elements of the poster.

DISPLAYING RULER GUIDES

Ruler guides are guides you add manually to further assist with the alignment of objects on your page. To add ruler guides, first ensure that the rulers are visible at the top and left of the document window.

To show or hide rulers, do one of the following:

- Choose View > Rulers.
- Press Ctrl+R (Windows) or Command+R (Mac OS).
- Select Rulers from the View Options menu in the Application bar.

ADDING AND MOVING RULER GUIDES

To add individual ruler guides (**Figure 2.7**):

1 Drag a guide from the ruler to the page.

2 Drag a guide from the ruler to the pasteboard area to create a guide across the page spread.

Ruler guides are cyan (kind of an aqua color) by default.

To reposition an existing ruler guide:

1 Using the Selection tool (![arrow]), click to select the guide.

2 Drag the guide to its preferred position. When the guide is selected, you can also enter horizontal (Y) or vertical (X) position values in the Control panel (**Figure 2.8**).

SHORTCUT

You can also drag a guide across the pasteboard area by Ctrl-dragging (Windows) or Command-dragging (Mac OS) from the ruler. Pressing the Shift key when dragging a guide from the ruler snaps the guide to even ruler increments.

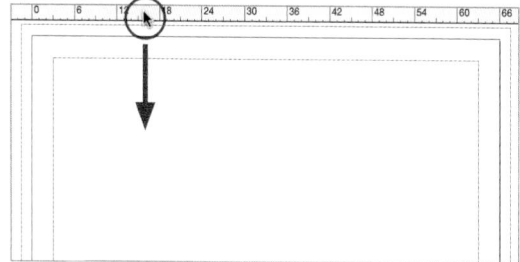
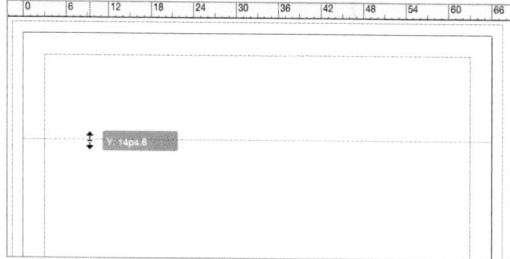

Figure 2.7 Dragging a horizontal ruler guide from the ruler onto the page

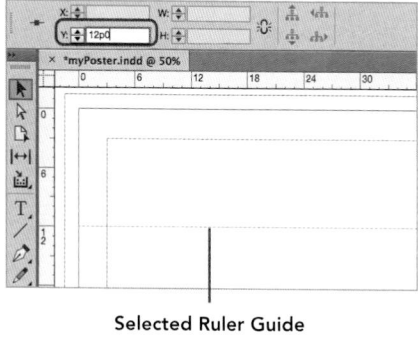
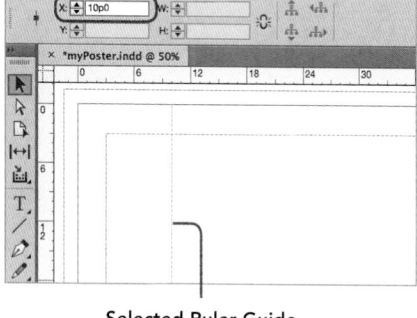

Selected Ruler Guide

Selected Ruler Guide

Figure 2.8 Horizontal and vertical ruler guides that are selected, so that the exact position can be set in the Control panel

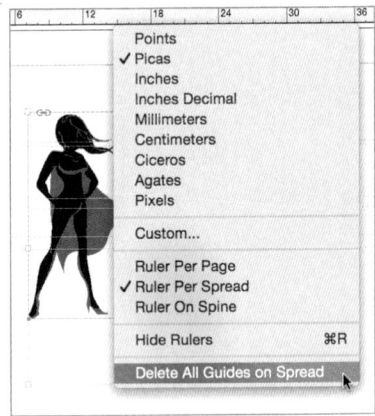

Figure 2.9 Using the context menu to delete all of the guides on a spread

LOCKING AND DELETING RULER GUIDES

To lock or unlock guides:

- Choose View > Grids & Guides > Lock Guides.

To delete a single ruler guide:

1 Using the Selection tool, click to select the guide.

2 Press Delete or Backspace.

To delete all of the ruler guides across a spread (**Figure 2.9**):

1 Right-click (Windows) or Control-click (Mac OS) in the vertical or horizontal ruler.

2 Select Delete All Guides On Spread from the context menu, or choose View > Grids & Guides > Delete All Guides On Spread.

CREATING EVENLY SPACED RULER GUIDES

When you need to create ruler guides that are equally distributed across a page, the "drag guide from ruler" technique becomes tedious. You would need to know the exact page width and use a calculator to figure out where to place the guides. Thankfully, the Create Guides (**Figure 2.10**) command lets you distribute guides across a page or between margins.

Figure 2.10 Using Create Guides to add three ruler guides that are equally distributed across the page

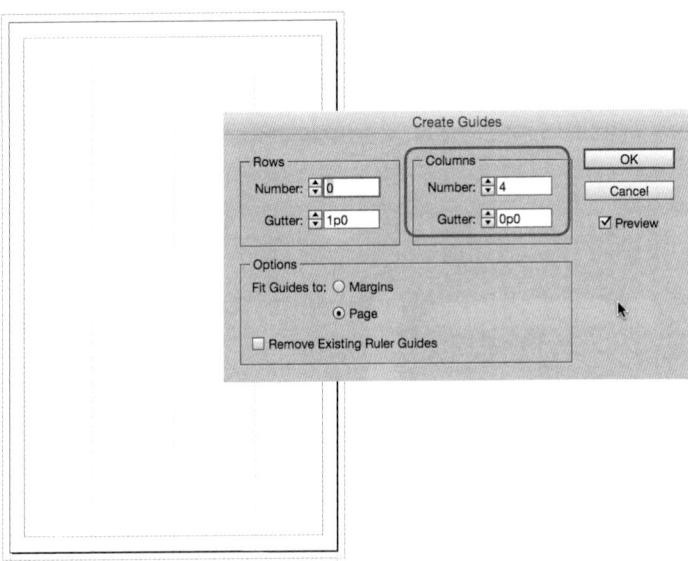

To create equally distributed guides:

1 Choose Layout > Create Guides.

2 Select Preview to see the changes as you make them.

3 Set the number of rows or columns, and gutter amounts.

4 Under Options, select Margins to distribute the guides between the margins, or Page to distribute the guides across the page width or depth.

5 To clear any previously added ruler guides, select Remove Existing Ruler Guides.

6 Click OK.

SNAPPING TO GUIDES

By default, InDesign has View > Snap To Guides enabled. As you start to add or edit design elements, you will notice small tool pointer changes as an object snaps to a guide:

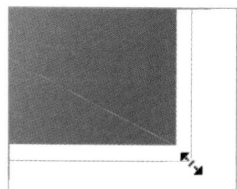

- When you move an object with the Selection tool, the move pointer (▶) changes to a hollow pointer (▷) once the object snaps to a guide.

- When you resize a frame or shape by dragging one of its bounding box handles, the double arrow appears hollow to indicate that releasing the mouse results in the frame edge snapping to a guide (**Figure 2.11**).

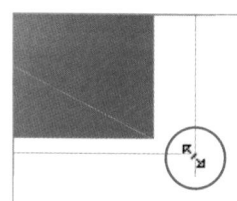

USING SMART GUIDES

While ruler guides are great for aligning design elements, sometimes seeing too many on the page at once can make working on a design a little chaotic. This is where smart guides come to the rescue: These guides automatically appear as you drag or resize objects, then disappear when you finish.

Figure 2.11 The tool pointer changes as the background rectangle is sized to show that the rectangle's edge snaps to the margin guide.

To start using smart guides, first ensure you can see them. To view smart guides:

1 Set the Screen Mode to Normal.

2 Choose View > Guides & Grids > Smart Guides, or select Smart Guides from the View Options menu in the Application bar.

> **NOTE** *If Smart Guides do not display, choose Edit > Preferences (Windows) or InDesign CC > Preferences (Mac OS), and then select Guides & Pasteboard. Make sure all of the Smart Guide Options are selected.*

- Green guides appear when an object aligns with the center or edges of other objects that are visible in the document window (**Figure 2.12**).
- Green arrows display when objects are equal distances apart.
- When you resize an object, green arrows indicate that the object has the same width or height as another nearby object (**Figure 2.13**).
- Pink guides appear when an object aligns to the page center.

Top aligned

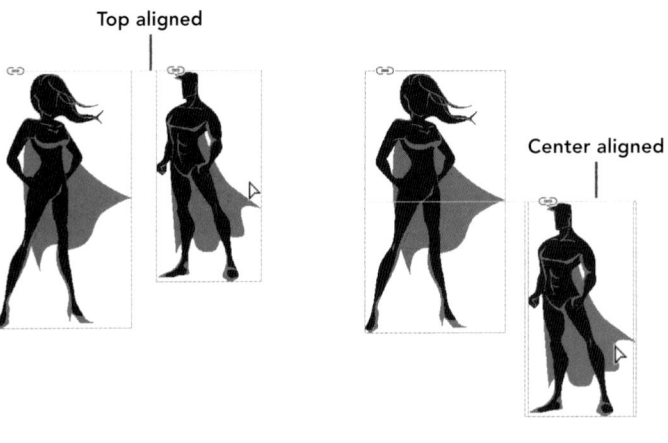

Center aligned

Figure 2.12 A green smart guide appears when the superhero image at right is moved upward and aligns with the top of the girl hero image to the left. Another green smart guide appears as the top of the superhero image aligns with the center of the female superhero image on the left.

Figure 2.13 The middle superhero figure (left) is moved horizontally until the image is an equal distance from the heroes on its left and right. A new shape is added (right) that is the same dimension as the superhero.

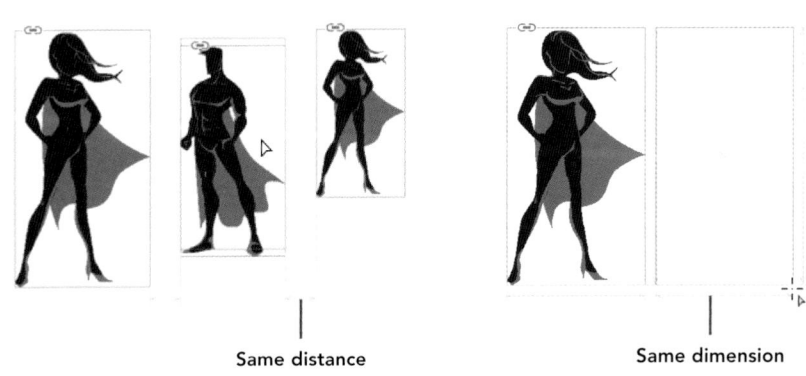

Same distance

Same dimension

★ *ACA Objective 3.3*

▶ *Video 2.5*

Preferences

As you start to work with InDesign, you'll likely encounter behaviors or settings you'd like to tweak. The Preferences dialog box contains preference settings for 20 categories, and each category offers numerous adjustable options. That is a lot of settings that can be changed!

MODIFYING PREFERENCES

A preference you might consider changing is the units and measurements. An English (North American) install of InDesign uses picas as the default units of measurement. Picas are an old typographical unit of measurement. One **pica** is approximately 1/6 inch, and consists of 12 **points**. To learn more about old typographical units such as picas, ciceros, and agates, search the Internet.

To change the measurement units to inches (**Figure 2.14**):

1 Choose Edit > Preferences (Windows) or InDesign CC > Preferences (Mac OS).

2 Select Units & Increments in the scroll list at left.

3 Change the Horizontal and Vertical Ruler Units from Picas to Inches, and click OK.

WARNING

To avoid unpredictable behavior of tools and features in InDesign, only modify preference settings when you have a very specific reason for doing so.

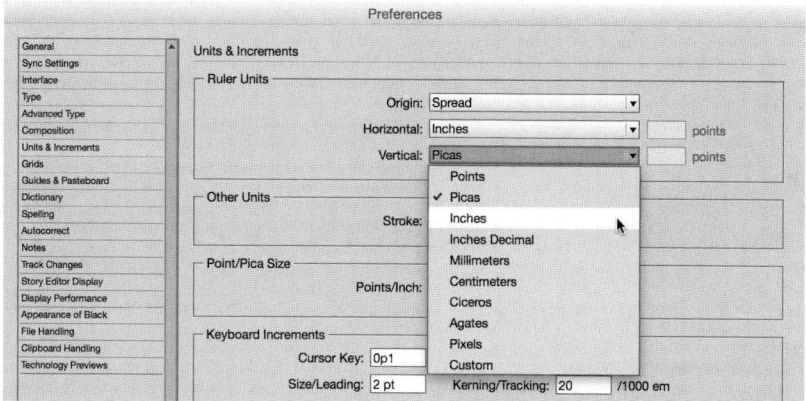

Figure 2.14 Changing the default ruler units from picas (p) to inches (in)

TIP

If you change a document-specific preference setting without having any InDesign documents open, the setting becomes a preference for all new documents you create.

REVERTING TO DEFAULT PREFERENCES

If you ever want to return to InDesign's default preferences, you can delete the InDesign Preferences files (**Figure 2.15**):

1 Hold down the Shift+Ctrl+Alt (Windows) keys or the Shift+Ctrl+Option+Command (Mac OS) keys as you start up InDesign.

2 When the Startup Alert dialog box appears, click Yes.

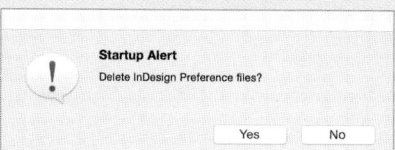

Figure 2.15 Deleting InDesign's preferences files using a keyboard shortcut on startup

Organizing Design Elements in Layers

Layers are like transparent pieces of paper that are placed on top of each other. Each can have their own design elements added to them. Layers are great for organizing related design elements and controlling the stacking order of objects. Layers are document based. Using layers, you can more easily isolate the design elements you are working on without accidentally changing other nonrelated objects. For example, when working on a magazine, you might work with separate layers for text, images, and background textures or colors.

CHANGING STACKING ORDER WITHIN A LAYER

When working with layers, you use the Layers panel. Every document has a default layer named Layer 1. Until you create more layers, everything you add to the page goes on Layer 1. When you add design elements, the last added element always appears above the previously added element. This order is referred to as the stacking order.

There are two ways to change the stacking order of objects in a layer.

First, you can change the order by using the various Object > Arrange commands:

1 Using the Selection tool, click the object.

2 Choose Object > Arrange and select one of the arrange options.

   Bring To Front: Moves the selected object to the top of the stack

   Bring Forward: Moves the selected object upward in the stack, one position at a time.

   Send Backward: Moves the selected object downward in the stack, one position at a time.

   Send To Back: Moves the selected object to the bottom of the stack.

Another way to change the stacking order is by using the Layers panel:

1 Choose Window > Layers to show the Layers panel.

2 Click the disclosure triangle to the left of the layer name. All the objects within the layer are revealed.

3 Select the object on the page. When an object is selected, a colored dot appears to the right of the object in the Layers panel.

4 In the Layers panel, drag the object to a different position in the stack. Release the mouse button when a thicker line appears at the insertion point (**Figure 2.16**). You can also drag the colored dot to move the selected object to another layer or to change the object's stacking order.

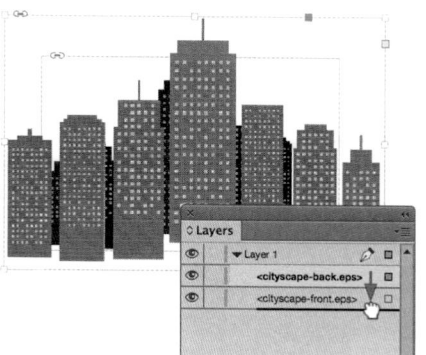
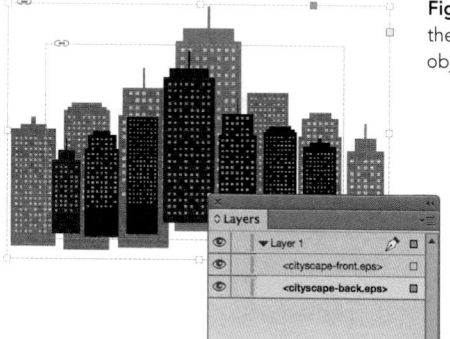

Figure 2.16 Changing the stacking order of objects in a layer

CREATING AND NAMING LAYERS

To organize design elements in layers, start by creating new layers and renaming existing layers. Giving layers meaningful names clarifies the purpose of the layer.

To create a new layer (**Figure 2.17**):

1 Select New Layer from the Layers panel menu.

2 Enter a meaningful Name.

3 Notice all the other options, such as Color and Print Layer. As you get more familiar with layers, you may find a need for these.

4 Click OK.

Alternately, you can create a new layer this way:

- Click the Create New Layer button at the bottom of the Layers panel.

  A new layer appears, automatically named Layer 1, Layer 2, etc.

No matter which method you choose, InDesign adds the new layer above the currently active layer.

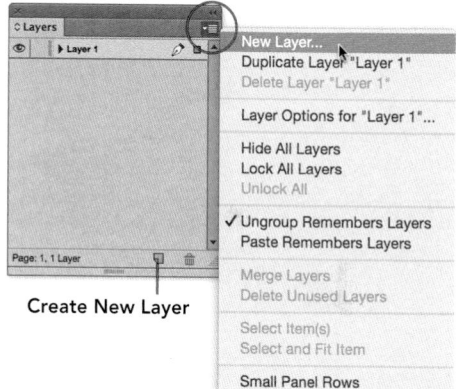

Create New Layer

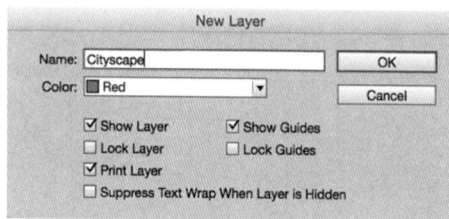

Figure 2.17 Adding a new layer above the selected layer

SHORTCUT *You can add a new layer below an active layer, press Ctrl (Windows) or Command (Mac OS) while you select New Layer Below from the Layers panel menu. To add a new layer above all other layers, press Shift+Ctrl (Windows) or Shift+Command (Mac OS) while you select New Top Layer from the Layers panel menu.*

TIP *Alt-click (Windows) or Option-click (Mac OS) the New Layer button to display the New Layer dialog box and Name the layer.*

To rename a layer (**Figure 2.18**), you have the choice of three methods:

A   Select a layer in the Layers panel and click the layer name. Enter a new name and press Enter (Windows) or Return (Mac OS).

B   Select a layer, then select Layer Options For [name of your layer] from the Layers panel menu. Enter the Name in the Layer Options dialog box. Click OK.

C   Double-click the layer name. Enter the Name in the Layer Options dialog box and click OK.

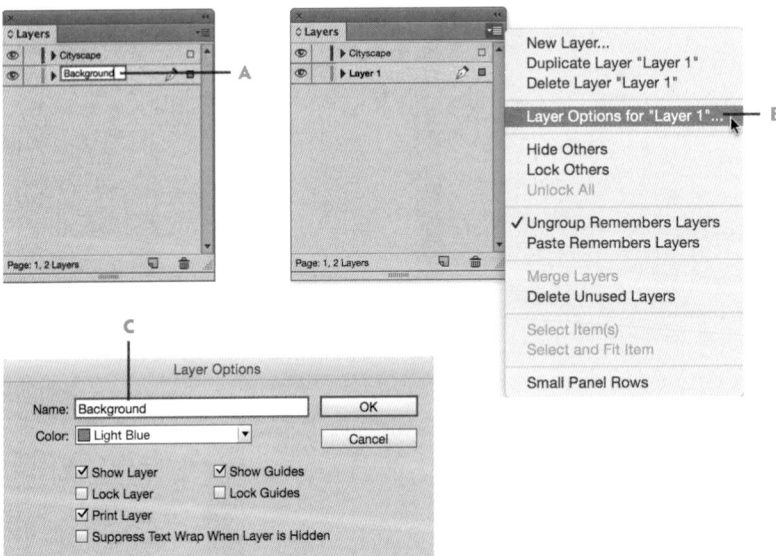

Figure 2.18 Renaming a layer

SHOWING AND HIDING LAYERS

The ability to hide layers enables you to focus on specific content—for example, edit text or fine-tune a drawing. You simply hide all the layers you are not currently working on. A small eye icon (👁) displays to the left of a visible layer's name.

To toggle layer visibility (**Figure 2.19**):

■   Click the Show/Hide box to the far left of the layer name in the Layers panel. All objects on the layer will show or be hidden.

To hide all layers except the active layer:

■   Alt-click (Windows) or Option-click (Mac OS) the Show/Hide box to the left of the layer you want to isolate.

Figure 2.19 Hiding a layer automatically hides all the objects on that layer

LOCKING LAYERS

If you prefer to see the content of all layers, but don't want to accidentally move objects around as you work on your design, consider locking the layers rather than hiding them. A locked layer displays a small padlock icon (🔒) next to its name. When a layer is locked, you'll see a warning dialog box (**Figure 2.20**) when trying to add content to the layer.

To lock a layer and all of its objects (**Figure 2.21**):

- Click the Lock/Unlock box to the left of the layer name in the Layers panel.

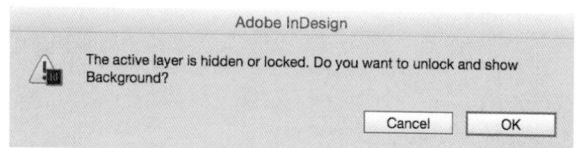

Figure 2.20 The warning dialog box that appears when you try to edit a locked or hidden layer

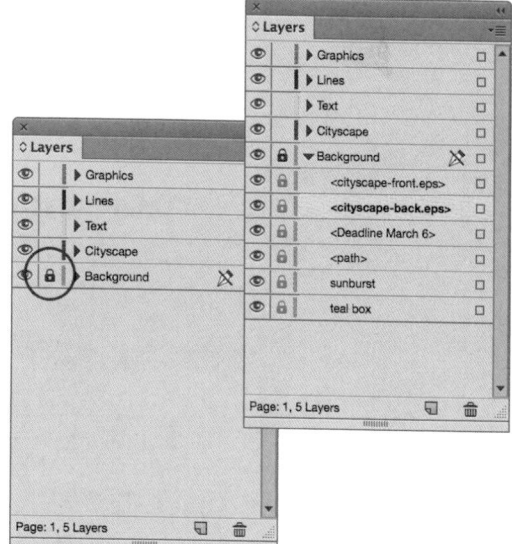

Figure 2.21 Locking a layer automatically locks all the page items.

Instead of locking a layer, you can also lock or unlock individual objects, or groups:

1 Click the disclosure triangle to the left of the layer name in the Layers panel. This displays the sublayers so you can see the objects and groups; a small padlock icon appears to the left of any locked groups or objects.

2 Click a lock icon to unlock an object or group. To lock an object or group, click in the box immediately to the right of the Visibility icon.

TIP *You can also lock selected objects by choosing Object > Lock. If you lock and unlock objects frequently, it's worth remembering the keyboard shortcut to toggle it on and off: Ctrl+L (Windows) or Command+L (Mac OS).*

CHANGING LAYER ORDER

As you add layers to a document, and add objects to those layers, you might find that the stacking order of the layers themselves needs reordering.

To move a layer and its objects to another position in the layer stack (**Figure 2.22**):

1 Select the layer in the Layers panel.

2 Drag it upward or downward until a line appears at the insertion point.

Figure 2.22 Moving the Graphics layer to the top of the layer stack reveals the hero graphics.

DESIGNING LAYERS FOR OBJECTS

Once you have created and named layers in your document, you can add new design elements to the designated layer. When you select a layer, it becomes the active drawing layer (✐) in InDesign:

- New objects such as text frames or graphic frames are automatically added to the active layer.

- Selecting an object to edit, such as a text frame, automatically selects its layer.

At times, you might forget to select the correct layer when adding new design elements to a page. You can always move objects to a different layer.

To move an object to a different layer (**Figure 2.23**):

1 Select the object.

A colored dot to the right of the layer name indicates the selected item.

2 Drag the dot to another layer.

Or, you can move objects between layers using this method:

1 Click the disclosure triangle to the left of the Layer name.

2 Select the objects within the layer.

3 Drag to another layer.

DELETING A LAYER

There might be times you created more layers than you need, for example multiple layers with images, where one layer would suffice. Or there might be a number of unused layers in the document.

Merging layers lets you delete layers and move any content to a target layer in a single step.

To merge layers:

1 Select the target layer.

2 Ctrl-click (Windows) or Command-click (Mac OS) the other layers.

3 Select Merge Layers from the Layers panel menu.

Only the target layer remains, and any content from other layers is moved to the target layer. Alternatively, you can choose to remove individual layers.

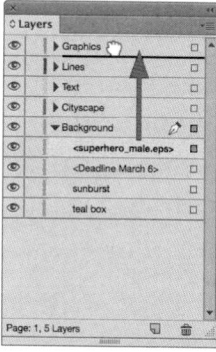

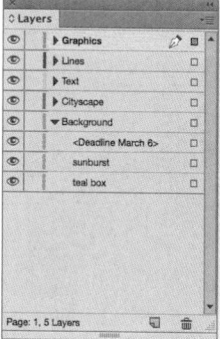

Figure 2.23 Moving an object from one layer to another

To delete a layer (**Figure 2.24**):

1   Select the layer in the Layers panel.

2   Choose Layer "[layer name]" from the Layers panel menu, or click the Delete Selected Layers button at the bottom of the Layers panel.

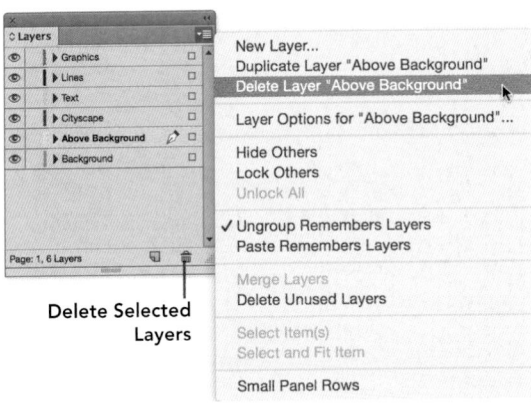

Delete Selected Layers

Figure 2.24 Deleting a selected layer

Adding Design Elements

With the new document created, guides added, and layers created, you are ready to start designing the poster. To do this, you will add colored shapes, lines, images, and text to create a beautiful composition.

Adding Shapes and Lines

★ *ACA Objective 2.2*

★ *ACA Objective 3.2*

InDesign documents consist of two primary page elements—shapes and lines—along with text and graphics in frames. Lines can be straight or curved, and they are used to join, organize, divide, direct, or construct other objects in your design. Geometric shapes, such as squares, circles, and triangles, are often used to visually combine related objects or to provide a hierarchy in the design.

The shape tools (**Figure 2.25**) and the Line tool (/) enable you to add visual elements to designs.

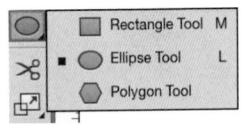

Figure 2.25 Rectangle, Ellipse, and Polygon tools

CREATING SHAPES

In the previous chapter, you learned about creating shapes with the shape tools. As a reminder:

- To add a shape, select the Rectangle, Ellipse, or Polygon tool in the Tools panel. Drag across the page until the shape is created to the preferred size (**Figure 2.26**).

- You can also click anywhere on the page to create a shape based on specific settings entered in the shape's options dialog box (**Figure 2.27**).

- At any stage, you can adjust the size of the shape by selecting it and editing its width (W) and height (H) settings in the Control panel. You can also drag out one of the bounding box handles of a selected shape (**Figure 2.28**).

By default, shapes created with the Rectangle tool (▢), Ellipse tool (◯), or Polygon tool (◯) have a fill color of [None] and a 1 pt black stroke. The color [None] is empty or see-through, and the shapes that are created are unassigned frames (as opposed to text frames or graphic frames).

Note that you cannot click the Selection tool inside a shape with a fill of [None] to select it. You need to click on the frame's edge. Think of it as trying to pick up an empty cup by sticking your fingers inside the cup. That does not really work. However, when you pick up the cup by its edge, you can lift it without any problems.

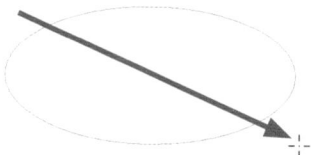

Figure 2.26 Drawing an ellipse with the Ellipse tool

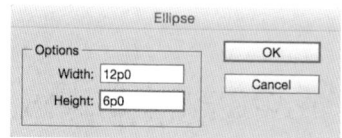

Figure 2.27 Ellipse options dialog box

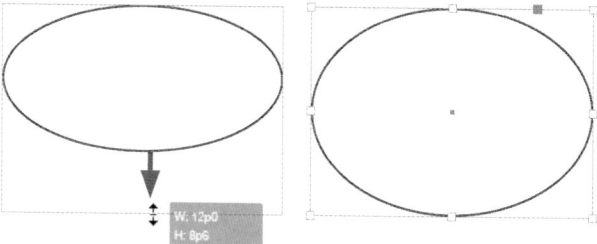

Figure 2.28 Dragging the center-bottom handle to change the height of the ellipse

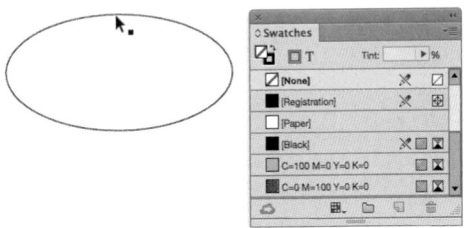

Figure 2.29 Selecting an ellipse with a fill color of [None] with the Selection tool

To select an unassigned frame with a fill color set to [None] (**Figure 2.29**):

1 Select the Selection tool.

2 Move the tool over the edge of the shape. The tool pointer changes from an arrow to an arrow with a dot to indicate that you can select the object.

3 Select the shape by clicking once. You can now resize, move, or delete the shape.

So, why do we see this selection issue for shapes created with the Rectangle, Ellipse, or Polygon tools? These tools create unassigned frames. Like those empty cups, you can't pick them up by clicking in their middle.

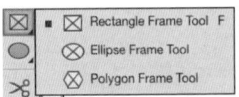

Figure 2.30 Rectangle, Ellipse, and Polygon Frame tools

The frame tools (**Figure 2.30**), on the other hand, create graphic frames to hold images. You can recognize a graphic frame by the X that displays inside it (when the Screen Mode is set to Normal). Graphic frames with a fill color set to [None] can be selected from their fill area. You can think of them as cups filled with a sticky sugar. When you grab the sticky contents, the cup comes too.

That leaves the question: Why would you want to use one tool over another, when both seemingly create similar shapes, albeit with a difference in behavior when the fill color is set to [None]. An obvious answer might be that you create a graphic frame because you want to import a graphic into it. However, the answer is not that simple: You actually can place a graphic into either type of frame.

Here's why you create unassigned frames for shapes: Let's assume you want to show a relationship between some design elements on the page, such as some text and graphics. Adding a line around the related items combines them visually. You create a rectangular shape with the fill color set to [None] and a stroke (**Figure 2.31**). When using an unassigned frame, you can easily select the objects that fall within the rectangular area. But when you use a graphic frame instead, you'll need to click through the stack of objects to get to the objects below the frame.

Figure 2.31 A border created with the Rectangle tool (unassigned frame) at left, and Rectangle Frame tool (graphic frame) at right

SHORTCUT *To select objects in a stack with the Selection tool, Ctrl-click (Windows) or Command-click (Mac OS) to click through the stack of objects.*

CREATING STRAIGHT LINES

The line tool is used to create straight lines. To draw a line (**Figure 2.32**):

1 Select the Line tool.

2 Drag in any direction to create a line of preferred length.

3 With the line still selected, use the options on the Control or the Swatches and Stroke panels to change the width and color of the line.

> **TIP** *To draw an orthogonal line (horizontal or vertical), press Shift as you drag to create the line. The Shift key can also be used to draw lines at 45-degree increments.*

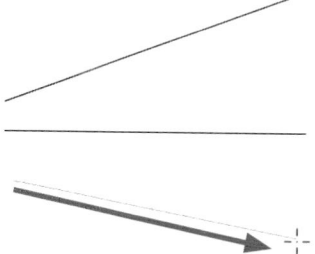

Figure 2.32 Various lines created with the Line tool, by dragging in different directions

Creating Combined Shapes

★ *ACA Objective 3.2*

▶ *Video 2.9*

The Pathfinder panel and command in InDesign lets you combine two or more shapes to create new shapes.

▶ *Video 2.10*

To create a new shape using the Pathfinder panel:

1 Choose Window > Object & Layout > Pathfinder to show the Pathfinder panel.

2 Using the Selection tool, Shift-click multiple objects to combine them. You can also drag a marquee around the objects you want to select.

3 Click the preferred pathfinder button on the Pathfinder panel. Alternatively, you can choose Object > Pathfinder and select one of the Pathfinder options.

   ▪ **Add:** Unites two shapes into a new form (**Figure 2.33**).

   ▪ **Subtract:** Knocks the topmost object out of the back object, with the resulting shape adopting the color of the backmost object (**Figure 2.34**).

   ▪ **Intersect:** Retains only the area where two objects overlap, with the resulting shape taking on the color of the topmost object (**Figure 2.35**).

   ▪ **Exclude Overlap:** Knocks out the areas where two objects overlap, with the resulting shape taking on the color of the topmost object (**Figure 2.36**).

   ▪ **Minus Back:** Knocks the backmost object out of the front objects, with the resulting shape adopting the color of topmost object (**Figure 2.37**).

In the following chapters, you will learn how to edit shapes and how to create free-form and natural shapes.

Figure 2.33 Creating a new shape by adding shapes

Before

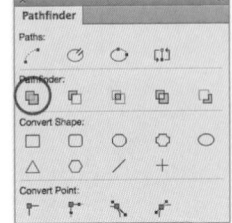

After

Figure 2.34 Creating a new shape by subtracting shapes

Before

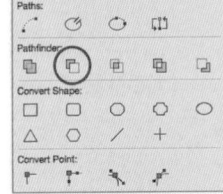

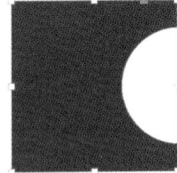

After

Figure 2.35 Creating a new shape by retaining overlapping areas

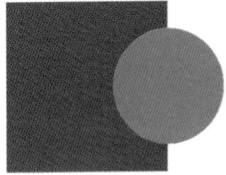

Before

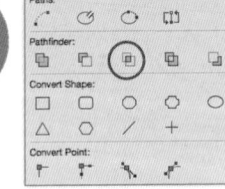

After

Figure 2.36 Creating a new shape by excluding overlapping areas

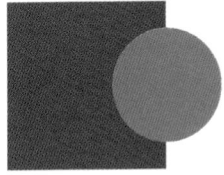

Before

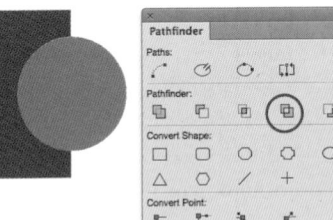

After

Figure 2.37 Creating a new shape by removing the back shape from the front shapes

Before

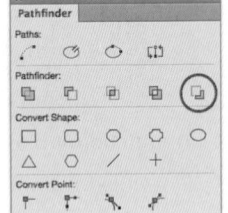

After

Adding Color

Color is possibly the most powerful visual element you can use in your designs. It attracts attention, adds meaning, and evokes emotion in designs. For example, red is an eye-catching color that could also represent danger, and green often means safe. Think of traffic light colors: red means stop, yellow means caution, green means go. Blue, on the other hand, is a cooler color that reflects calmness. In contrast, pink is more reflective of love and kindness.

As an exercise, jot down some colors that spring to mind. Now, hop online and search for "psychology of colors." Look for information about the colors you wrote down. Extend the search to discover more about the role color plays in marketing and branding.

★ ACA Objective 2.4

★ ACA Objective 3.6

▶ Video 2.5

▶ Video 2.14

COLOR THEORY BASICS

RGB color—which stands for red, green, and blue—is composed of the primary colors of light. Any device that captures or displays colors with light works with RGB color. When designing jobs exclusively for screens, such as digital publishing, eBooks, and websites, you would work with the Web or Digital Publishing document intent and mix colors using RGB.

CMYK color—which stands for cyan, magenta, yellow, and black (K)—is composed of the subtractive primary colors used in print, such as commercial presses and office printers. When designing jobs for print, use CMYK color combinations to build up your ink colors.

Process colors are made up of multiple color components. For instance, a CMYK process orange color might be 100% yellow and 50% magenta (**Figure 2.38**). An RGB process color for yellow might use 255 red and 255 green. In print terminology, **process** colors always refer to the mixing of CMYK colors.

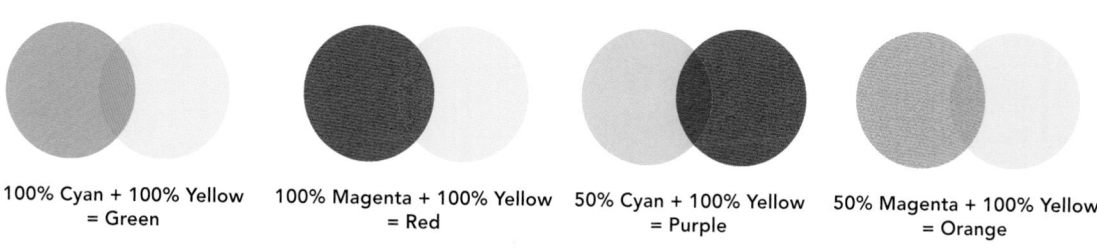

| 100% Cyan + 100% Yellow = Green | 100% Magenta + 100% Yellow = Red | 50% Cyan + 100% Yellow = Purple | 50% Magenta + 100% Yellow = Orange |

Figure 2.38 Examples of CMYK color mixing

Spot colors, in contrast to process colors, are premixed inks created specifically for print. The Pantone Color Matching System (PMS), for example, is used to define spot colors. Spot colors are used for jobs that require:

- Less than four colors.
- Accurate logo and branding colors.
- Colors that can't be achieved in process color-printing, such as a metallic or varnish.

You'll learn more about spot versus process colors in Video Project 4 and later chapters.

CREATING A NAMED COLOR WITH THE SWATCHES PANEL

In Chapter 1, you were introduced to applying stroke and fill colors to selected objects using the Control panel or Swatches panel. With the Swatches panel, you name the colors you create and they can be applied to page elements, included in styles (such as character styles and object styles). Additionally, if you edit a swatch, anywhere that it is applied reflects the color change; this enables you to quickly make global changes across a document. The Swatches panel makes it easy to create and use tints (shades) of color as well.

To create a new CMYK color swatch (**Figure 2.39**):

1 Choose Window > Color > Swatches to show the Swatches panel.
2 Choose New Color Swatch from the Swatches panel menu. Alternatively, Alt-click (Windows) or Option-click (Mac OS) the New Swatch button at the bottom of the Swatches panel.
3 In the New Color Swatch dialog box, make sure Process is selected from the Color Type menu.
4 Select CMYK from the Color Mode menu. Specify the Cyan, Magenta, Yellow, and Black values as desired.
5 Deselect Name With Color Value, and enter the new color's name in the Swatch Name field.
6 Deselect Add to CC Library to add the color only to the active document, and click OK.

You can now apply the swatch to the stroke or fill of selected objects and text. Use the Swatches panel or Control panel for quick access to swatches.

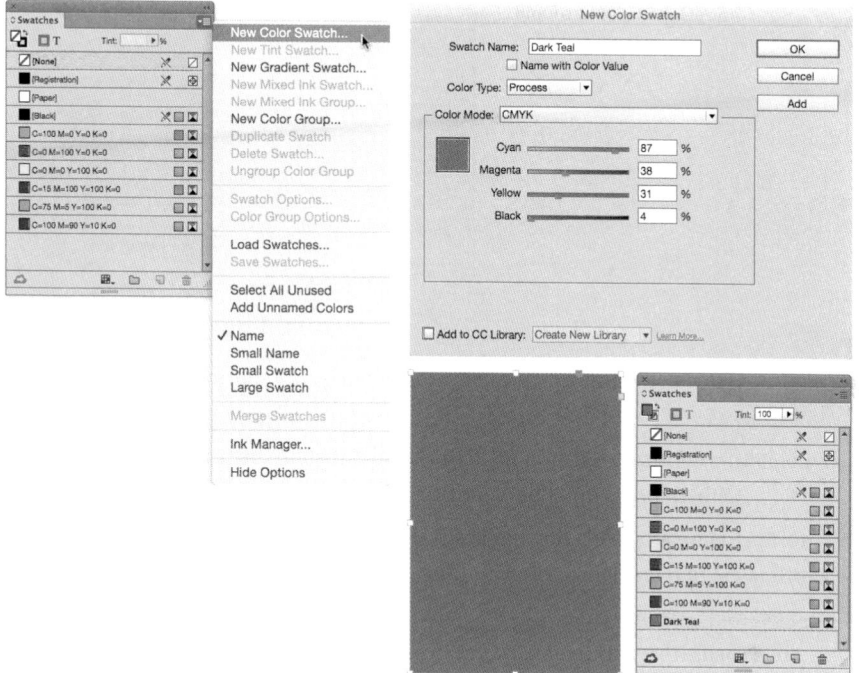

Figure 2.39 Adding a new color swatch to the Swatches panel

APPLYING COLOR WITH THE COLOR PANEL

The Color panel allows you to mix and apply colors as you design. These colors are not named, and are therefore difficult to use consistently throughout a layout. Fortunately, you can add them to the Swatches panel.

Fill box

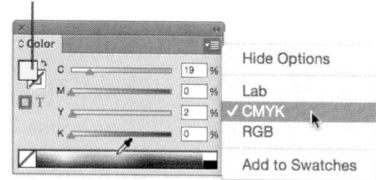

To apply a stroke or fill color using the Color panel (**Figure 2.40**):

1   Choose Window > Color > Color to show the Color panel.

2   Using the Selection tool, click an object to apply a color. (You can also select text with the Type tool.)

3   Click the Stroke or Fill box in the Color panel or Tools panel.

4   From the Color panel menu, select CMYK when working on a document with print intent. Select RGB when working on documents for web or digital publishing.

5   Click anywhere in the color ramp to select a color, or use the sliders to adjust the color values.

Figure 2.40 Using the Color panel to set a fill color

6   To add the color as a reusable color to the Swatches panel, choose Add To Swatches from the Color panel menu.

APPLYING COLOR WITH THE COLOR PICKER

The Color Picker lets you mix colors based on any color mode by entering color values.

To add a CMYK swatch using the Color Picker (**Figure 2.41**):

1   Double-click the Fill box (or Stroke box) in the Color panel or Tools panel.

2   Enter the Cyan, Magenta, Yellow, and Black values.

3   Click Add CMYK Swatch.

APPLYING COLOR TO A LINE

To change the appearance of a line (**Figure 2.42**):

1   Using the Selection tool, click the line.

2   In the Swatches panel, click the Stroke box and then click a color swatch.

3   In the Stroke panel, adjust the thickness of the line by entering a new Width value or clicking the arrows next to the field.

4   In the Stroke panel, select a different option from the Type menu to create a wavy, dotted, or dashed line.

TIP   *Remember that the Tools panel provides quick access to the Stroke/ Fill box. In addition, the Control panel offers many options for formatting the selected object. As you get comfortable with InDesign, you will discover which options best suit your work style.*

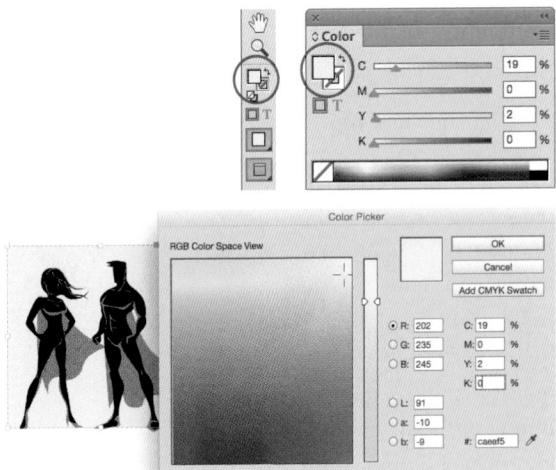

Figure 2.41 Mixing colors with the Color Picker

Stroke box

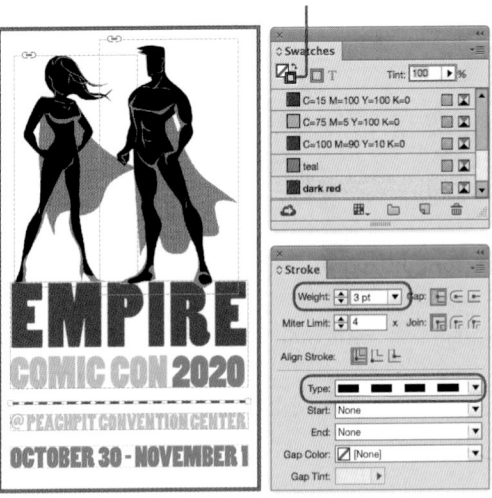

Figure 2.42 Adding a dashed horizontal line to break up the focal points for the text

REMOVING A STROKE OR FILL COLOR

To remove a stroke or fill color from an object:

1 Select the object.

2 Click the Stroke or Fill Box.

3 Click [None] in the Swatches panel.

You'll learn about more techniques and tools for capturing, creating, and applying colors in the next chapter.

Gradients

Gradients are blends between different colors or shades of color. A teal to white gradient would display a gradual blend that starts with a teal color at one end and gradually fades toward white at the other end. Gradients can break up the use of single tint colors and tones in a design, or be used to create interesting backdrops behind page designs or boxed content. You can apply two types of gradients to an object's fill or stroke: linear and radial (**Figure 2.43**).

To create a blend between two colors, use the Gradient panel (Window > Color > Gradient), which contains a **gradient ramp** that shows a preview of the color blend. Each starting point for a color is marked by a **color stop** at the bottom of the gradient ramp. Between two color stops, the colors blend from the first to the second stop. You can add any number of colors to a gradient by adding more color stops. A movable midpoint controls where the two colors blend, with a 50% portion of each color.

TIP

To quickly remove a stroke or fill color from a selected object, press / on the keyboard.

★ ACA Objective 3.6

▶ Video 2.6

TIP

If you plan to use gradients frequently, consider changing your workspace to Advanced. This will add the Gradient panel to the docked panels onscreen.

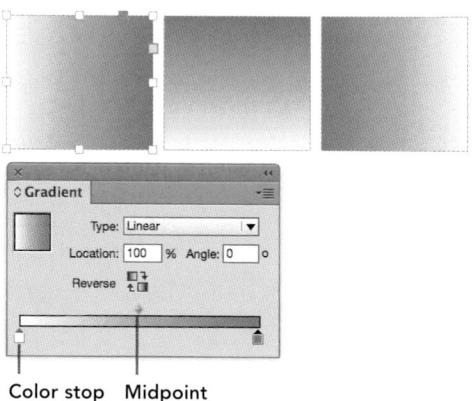

Color stop   Midpoint

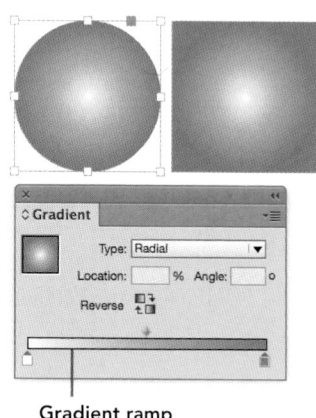

Gradient ramp

Figure 2.43 Examples of linear and radial gradient fills

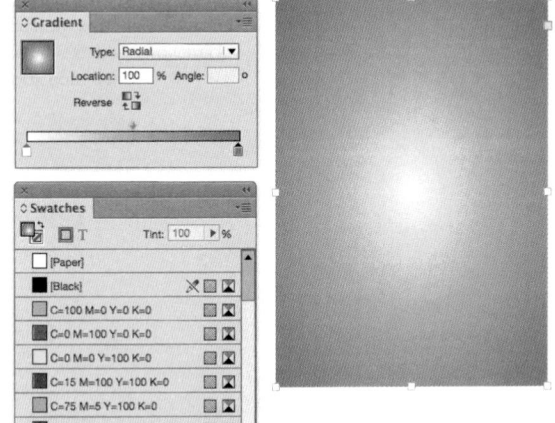

Figure 2.44 Applying a gradient fill color

To apply a gradient fill with the Gradient panel (**Figure 2.44**):

1 Choose Window > Color > Gradient to show the Gradient panel. Make sure that you can also see the Swatches panel.

2 Select an object.

3 Click the Gradient Swatch in the Gradient panel.

4 Select a color stop on the gradient ramp, then Alt-click (Windows) or Option-click (Mac OS) a swatch color in the Swatches panel. Alternately, you can drag and drop a swatch color onto the color stop.

5 Drag the gradient thumbnail in the top left of the Gradient panel into the Swatches panel to add a reusable Gradient Swatch.

Adding Images and Graphics

★ ACA Objective 2.5

★ ACA Objective 3.1

★ ACA Objective 4.4

Although you can complete a significant part of your design work in InDesign, images and graphics are generally created separately and supplied to you as individual files.

Pixel-based images, such as photos or photo compositions, are captured with a digital camera, scanned, or compiled in photo-editing programs, such as Adobe Photoshop. Vector-based graphics, such as a drawings, cartoons, logos, or technical drawings, are created in drawing programs, such as Adobe Illustrator. The shapes and lines that make up vector-based graphics are drawn mathematically, resulting in graphics that you can scale to different sizes without loss of quality. This means that vector-based graphics are resolution independent. In contrast, the quality of pixel-based images depends on their size and image resolution, measured in pixels per inch (ppi).

InDesign supports the import of native Photoshop and Illustrator files, as well as a range of other image and graphics file formats.

UNDERSTANDING IMAGE FILE FORMATS

For pixel-based images (**Figure 2.45**), commonly supported file formats are:

- **Adobe Photoshop native files (PSD):** PSD files may contain transparency, layers, and layer comps (snapshots of layer visibility, appearance, and position). Top-level layers and layer comps can be enabled or disabled within InDesign.

- **Tagged Image File Format (TIFF):** TIFF files can be compressed and may contain layers and transparency.

- **Joint Photographic Experts Group files (JPEG):** A compressed file format that significantly reduces file sizes. The format does not support transparency, layers, or spot color, and should be used with caution, as high compression rates could result in significant loss of quality. JPEG format is more commonly used for web images and digital publishing images.

For vector graphics (**Figure 2.46**) the more common formats are:

- **Adobe Illustrator native files (AI):** AI files retain transparency and layers. Top-level layers can be enabled or disabled within InDesign after import. During import, any available Illustrator artboard can be selected for import. Illustrator files appear as Adobe PDF Format in InDesign's Links panel.

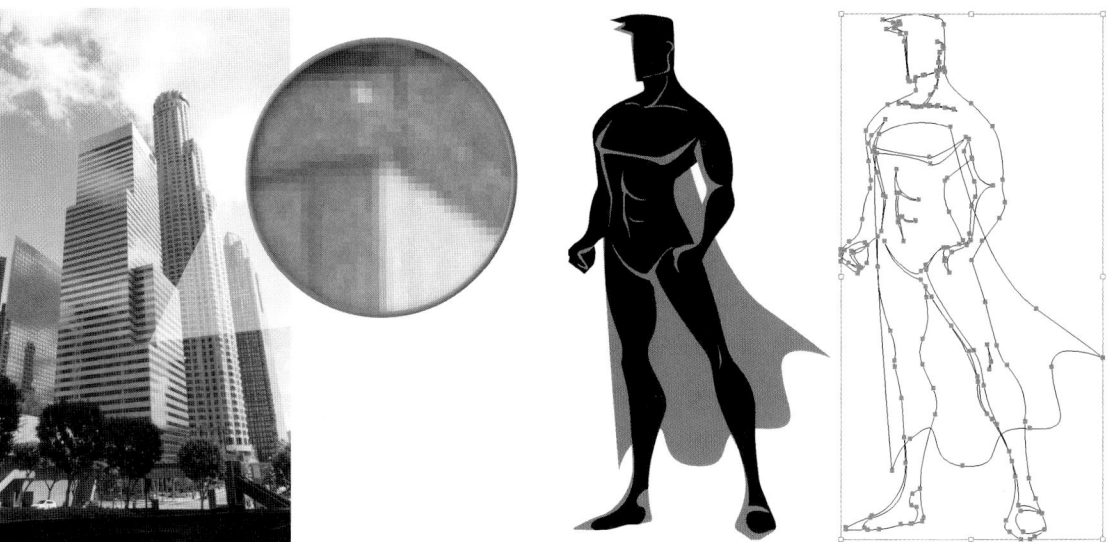

Figure 2.45 When you zoom into a section of this cityscape image, the pixels are revealed.

Figure 2.46 The superhero is an example of a vector graphic.

- **Encapsulated PostScript (EPS):** An older file format that does not support transparency and is gradually being phased out. You will see this format used in the signage industry and with some older pagination systems newspapers use to place ads. Vector-based illustrations are fully opaque within the vector shape, but can be see-through outside the area defined by the vector shapes.

- **Portable Document Format (PDF):** A document format that is platform independent and can be viewed with the Adobe Acrobat Reader. PDF files embed images and graphics as well as fonts. The format is supported as an import format in InDesign. However, it is more commonly used to export finished art from InDesign for delivery to a printer or to provide a compatible version of the document for general viewing.

TRANSPARENCY

Transparency is created when visual elements are no longer opaque. Changing the opacity level from 100% (opaque) to 50%, for example, creates transparency. Elements below transparent objects become visible. Additionally, effects applied to objects, such as drop shadows, create transparency. We'll cover transparency and effects in more detail in Chapter 3.

These file formats work well for print publishing, and can also be used for digital publishing. With the exception of JPEG, the file formats discussed here are not supported in web design. Common file formats used when designing for web are JPEG, PNG, and GIF. When using non-web supported formats in InDesign projects for images or graphics, such as AI or PSD, InDesign converts these file formats to JPG, PNG, or GIF as appropriate.

PLACING AN IMAGE INTO AN EMPTY FRAME

To place an image into an empty frame (**Figure 2.47**):

1 Choose Edit > Deselect All before placing content into InDesign.

2 Choose File > Place.

3 Navigate to a graphic or image file on your system and select it.

4 Deselect Show Import Options.

5 Click Open.

6 Position the pointer over the empty frame and click.

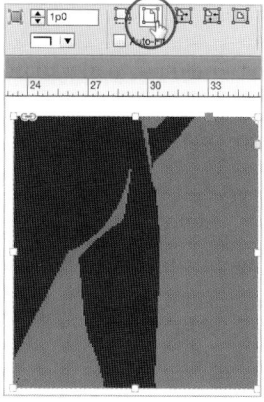

Figure 2.47 Placing an image into a placeholder frame and sizing it

7 To resize the image in the frame, choose Object > Fitting and select one of the Proportional fitting options:

■ **Fill Frame Proportionately:** Sizes the graphic to fill the entire frame; some parts may be cropped at the edge of the frame. This is useful for placing photos.

■ **Fit Content Proportionately:** Sizes the graphic to fit entirely in the frame; this is useful for placing logos, illustrations, and graphs.

▶ Video 2.8

▶ Video 2.13

PLACING AND SIZING IMAGES

To place and size image or graphic as you are placing it (**Figure 2.48**):

1 Choose Edit > Deselect All before placing content into InDesign.

2 Choose File > Place.

3 Navigate to the graphic or image file and select it.

4 Deselect Show Import Options.

5 Click Open. This "loads" the image on the pointer.

6 Drag with the loaded pointer to size and add the image to the page at the same time.

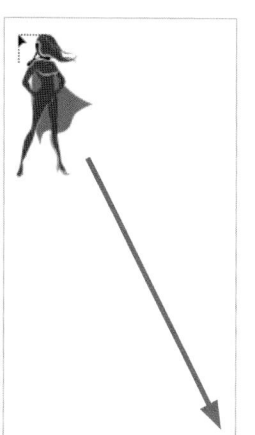

Figure 2.48 Drag with the loaded pointer to add the image to the page.

> **SHORTCUT** *If you click on the page with a loaded pointer instead of dragging, you place the image at that location at 100% size.*

Link badge

Status

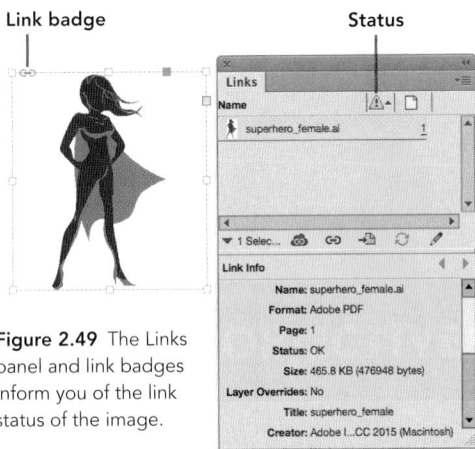

Figure 2.49 The Links panel and link badges inform you of the link status of the image.

MANAGING LINKS TO IMAGES

InDesign maintains a link to the original location of the placed image files. It does not embed the images; rather, it gives you a preview of the image for positional and sizing purposes. As you print or export your document, InDesign will locate the original image files and embed them into the exported format.

The Links panel (Window > Links) manages all the links in your InDesign documents, and will flag any missing or modified links (**Figure 2.49**). For example, if you retouch a photo after placing it in InDesign, you will need to update the link for the retouched version to display on the page.

Whenever you open a document that contains missing or modified links, a warning dialog appears that enables you to update modified links or relink missing links.

To quickly see link status in Normal screen mode, choose View > Extras > Show Link Badge. The link status appears to the top left corner of any placed images.

A modified link is flagged by a yellow warning triangle (⚠), which indicates that the image had been edited since it was placed in InDesign. Updating modified links refreshes their preview in the document.

To fix a modified link (**Figure 2.50**), do one of the following:

- Click the Link Badge on the image.
- Click the Update Link button at the bottom of the Links panel.
- Choose Update Link from the Links panel menu.

A missing link is flagged with a red octagon, like a stop sign (🛑) (**Figure 2.51**). Missing links appear when image files cannot be found in their original location. Moving an image to a different folder can cause a missing link, as can renaming an image.

To fix a missing link, do one of the following:

- Click the Link Badge on the image.
- Click the Relink button or Relink From CC Libraries at the bottom of the Links panel.
- Choose Relink or Relink From CC Libraries from the Links panel menu.

Navigate to the image on your system or locate it in the CC Library.

NOTE

To minimize issues with linked images or graphics, consider placing all of the images and graphics used in your design in a folder called Links and keeping that folder as a subfolder of the project folder on your system.

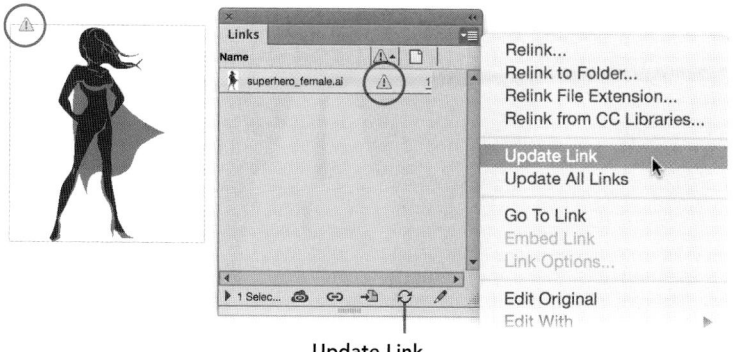

Update Link

Figure 2.50 Updating a modified link

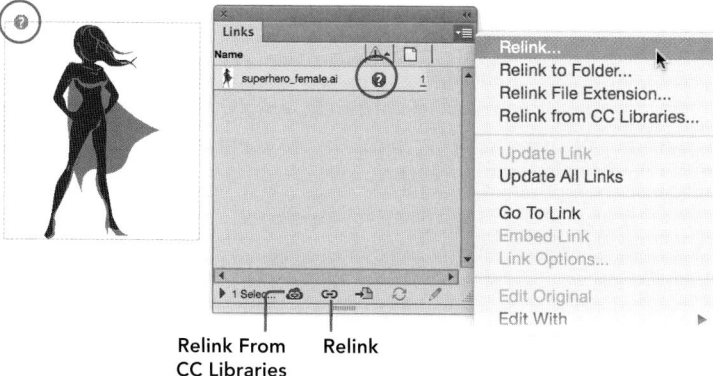

Relink From **Relink**
CC Libraries

Figure 2.51 Fixing a missing link

CROPPING AND RESIZING IMAGES

A placed image or graphic in InDesign appears as content inside a graphic frame. Cropping images allows you to hide parts of an image that you don't want to include in your design. You can crop an image by dragging the bounding box handles on the graphic frame. If you pause a second before you start dragging the handles, you'll see the area of the image (content) that doesn't fall within the graphic frame appear ghosted outside the frame area. For example, in **Figure 2.52**, cropping away the red building at left centers the focus of the image more on the skyscraper.

To crop an image (Figure 2.52):

1 Using the Selection tool, click the image.

2 Select one of the bounding box handles and drag inward.

Figure 2.52 Hiding parts of the image by cropping

Figure 2.53 Changing the image position within its frame using the Content Grabber

Figure 2.54 Changing the size of an image while maintaining the graphic frame size

To reposition an image within its graphic frame (**Figure 2.53**):

1 Using the Selection tool, click the Content Grabber in the center of the image.

2 Drag the image within the frame to the desired position.

TIP

You can also select an image and choose Object > Transform > Scale to enter a specific scale amount.

To resize an image within its graphic frame (**Figure 2.54**):

1 Using the Selection tool, click the Content Grabber in the center of the image. The image (content) is now selected within the frame.

2 Press Shift-drag a bounding box handle to constrain the image's proportions.

To scale an image and its graphic frame simultaneously:

1 Using the Selection tool, select an edge of the graphic frame. Be sure the Content Grabber (donut shape) is not displaying in the middle of the image as it moves the image within the frame.

2 Ctrl-drag (Windows) or Command-drag (Mac OS) one of the corner bounding box handles on the image. Add the Shift key as well to maintain the proportions of the image as you drag.

Adding and Formatting Text

★ ACA Objective 3.2

★ ACA Objective 3.8

★ ACA Objective 4.2

Fonts and typography make up an important part of graphic design. For example, using different fonts and sizes to distinguish headings from the body copy (the main part of the text) helps organize information. Text formatting not only provides visual hierarchy, but can also communicate a specific message through font choice, size variations, color, alignment, and more. In the previous chapter, you learned a little about the Type tool (T) and adding text frames to your designs. Now it's time to dig a little deeper into formatting text.

Your computer and InDesign come with a series of preinstalled fonts. To make your designs unique so they stand out, you'll often be on the lookout for new fonts. One of the first places to look for new fonts to add to your designs is Adobe Typekit, which integrates with InDesign. As part of your Creative Cloud membership, you have access to fonts that can be used across Desktop and Mobile applications, such as Adobe InDesign and Adobe Comp CC. Typekit fonts are available for use in web and desktop designs.

To use Typekit fonts in your designs (**Figure 2.55**):

1   Choose Type > Add Fonts From Typekit. You can also choose Add Fonts From Typekit from the font menu in the Control panel or Character panel.

   The Typekit web page opens in your default browser.

2   Enter your own preview text, then choose fonts based on classification (for example Sans Serif or Serif), as well as specific properties for Weight, Width, Height, Contrast, and a number of other settings. Typekit displays a list of fonts that meet the selected criteria.

3   When you find a font you want to use in your designs, move the pointer over the font and click Use Fonts.

4   In the Use This Family dialog box that appears, select which font styles you want to use, then click Sync Selected Fonts.

5   Once the fonts are synced, return to InDesign and you'll be able to use the font in your design.

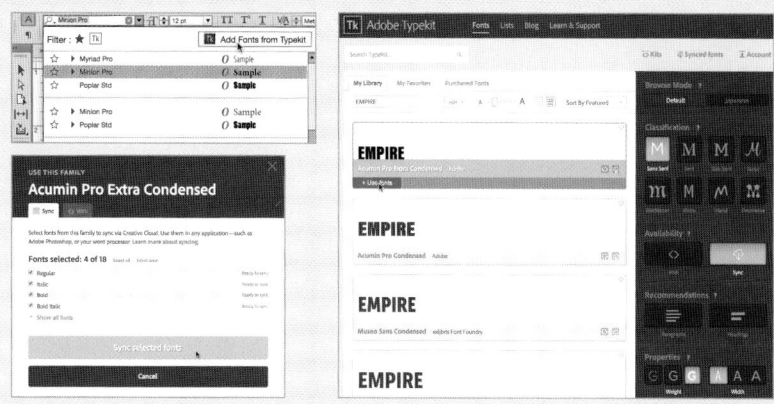

Figure 2.55 Using Typekit fonts in your designs

▶ Video 2.14

▶ Video 2.15

▶ Video 2.16

When editing or adding text, changing your workspace to the Typography workspace can help. This workspace gives you quick access to a multitude of typography-related panels, such as Character, Paragraph, Glyphs, and much more. These panels offer many text formatting options.

You can set text formatting at two separate levels: paragraph and character. To adjust formatting at the character level, first select the text with the Type tool, then make the formatting changes. When adjusting paragraph-level formatting, it is sufficient to have the text insertion point set anywhere within a paragraph.

What's the difference between the levels?

Paragraph formatting includes the horizontal alignment (left, center, right, justified) of the text, as well as spacing before or after paragraphs. **Alignment** controls how the text is positioned horizontally within the text frame.

Character formatting includes the font choice, font style (bold, italic), size, and leading. **Leading** or line spacing is the distance between lines of text within a paragraph. InDesign by default applies an automatic leading setting that is 120% of the font size. For instance, a 10-point font would be set to 12-point leading.

To adjust chararacter formatting (**Figure 2.56**):

- Click the Character Formatting Controls button (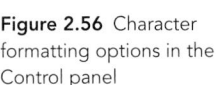) in the Control panel, or choose Type > Character to show the Character panel.

To learn more about character formatting controls, position the mouse over each icon in the Control panel; a tool tip reveals what the control does.

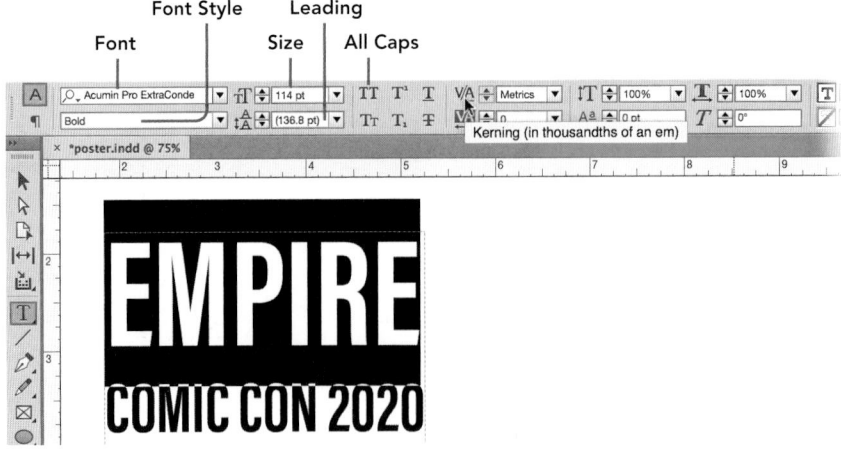

Figure 2.56 Character formatting options in the Control panel

To change the color of text:

1 Select the text.

2 Click the Fill box in the Tools, Swatches, or Control panel.

3 Select a color from the Swatches panel or Control panel.

To adjust paragraph formatting (**Figure 2.57**):

■ Click the Paragraph Formatting Controls button (¶) in the Control panel, or choose Type > Paragraph to show the Paragraph panel.

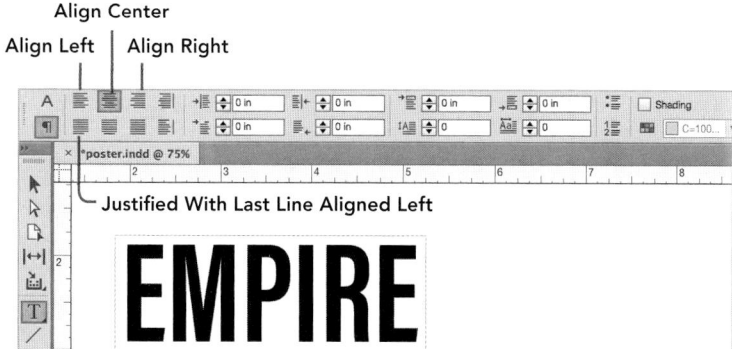

Figure 2.57 Paragraph formatting controls in the Control panel

UNDERSTANDING LEADING

The fact that leading (line spacing) is a character attribute by default can be a bit confusing. Shouldn't leading apply to all of the text in a paragraph? When you set a fixed leading value, the leading amount is locked in and doesn't change when you increase or decrease the font size of the text. You must select all the text in a paragraph, including the paragraph return ¶, before changing the value (**Figure 2.58**). If you select only a few lines within a paragraph, the leading applies only to those few lines.

TIP

To see the paragraph return ¶ characters, choose Type > Show Hidden Characters (with the Screen Mode set to Normal). All hidden (nonprint-ing) characters, such as spaces and tabs, display in the text.

Figure 2.58 A paragraph with different font sizes and a fixed leading value of 18 pt

continues on next page

continued from previous page

Some designers prefer that fixed leading values always apply to the entire paragraph. You can change the default leading behavior of InDesign:

1 Choose Edit > Preferences (Windows) or InDesign CC > Preferences (Mac OS).

2 Select Type from the scrolling list at left.

3 Under Type Options, select Apply Leading To Entire Paragraphs.

4 Click OK.

You can now simply click in a paragraph to select it when you apply a fixed leading value.

In addition to using a fixed leading value, you can use auto leading. With auto leading, InDesign automatically applies line spacing according to a percentage of the font sizes in use (120% by default). Auto leading values display in parentheses in the Leading field. Few designers use auto leading because it can lead to inconsistent spacing—for example, if you increase the size of a few words in a paragraph for emphasis, the leading will vary (**Figure 2.59**).

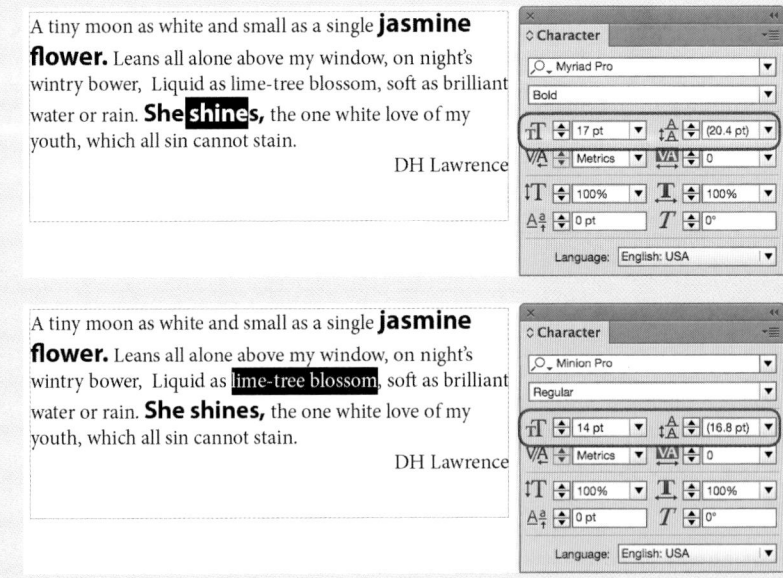

Figure 2.59 With auto leading, different font sizes in a single paragraph result in different leading values across the different lines in the paragraph.

Submitting Your Poster

★ *ACA Objective 5.1*

▶ *Video 2.17*

It is common practice for designers to send design proofs to their clients. In the early stages of project work, you would provide your client with a detailed project description, an overview of pricing, as well as a list of the various **deliverables** that you will provide. Early on in a project, deliverables might be sketches, rough layouts, or design proposals that show the client your ideas and progress. These early deliverables give your client an opportunity to provide suggestions, refinements, and other feedback. Near the end of a project, you typically provide proofs of your finished work so the client can sign off, or approve, the project. A proof sign-off takes you to the last deliverable: the finished delivery format. In the case of the event poster design, that would be the physical printed copies of the poster.

Submitting Proofs to Clients

Proofs are generally submitted to clients in Portable Document Format (PDF) form via email. As a file format, PDF enables people to share, view, and print documents independently from any software or computer system. With PDF, clients can review an exact representation of a design without having InDesign, the document's fonts, and the image files. PDFs can even contain form elements, 3D objects, movies, sound, and other interactive elements (Chapter 4 covers interactive PDFs in more detail).

When submitting a proof to a client via an email (**Figure 2.60**):

1 Choose File > Adobe PDF Presets > Smallest File Size.

2 Enter a specific Name for the PDF in the File Name (Windows), or Save As (Mac OS) field.

Figure 2.60 Adobe PDF Presets (File menu)

3 Navigate to the location where you want to save the PDF file.

4 Click Save. The Export Adobe PDF dialog box appears.

5 Click General in the scroll list at left.

6 Under Options, select View PDF After Exporting. Leave all other settings at the defaults.

7 Click Export.

8 If a warning dialog box indicates a change in the destination color space, click OK. Smallest File Size PDFs are converted to RGB from CMYK, which makes them a bit smaller; this is fine for proofing purposes.

The new PDF will open in Acrobat (either the free Adobe Acrobat Reader or any Adobe Acrobat Pro version you have installed). Ensure that the PDF is as expected, and then send it off to your client for review. Your client can print the PDF or review it onscreen in the free Adobe Acrobat Reader, add comments and other annotations to the PDF, and submit these back to you.

Some clients will want to "backproof" changes and see a new PDF for each round of changes you make. Others may say something like, "Make these changes and send it to the printer." Save all these proofs and communication as a record of client instructions if any problems arise down the line. Do not accept verbal sign-offs.

Submitting a PDF to the Printer

Once your client signs off on the last proof for your poster design, you are ready to submit the poster to the printer. You can submit print designs in two ways: as a print-ready PDF or as a packaged InDesign file. PDFs are all-in-one files that contain the pages, fonts, illustrations, and graphics used. When submitting a packaged InDesign file, you collect all design components (InDesign file, fonts, and graphics) into a single folder. Chapter 3 will cover packaging in depth, so for now let's focus on PDFs.

PDFs can be exported with different quality settings, and the PDF presets that ship with InDesign provide a great starting point. No matter which preset you choose, each will embed fonts and images and capture your design perfectly.

The following PDF Export Presets are available:

- **High Quality Print:** Retains transparency, leaves the document colors unchanged. Used for printing to desktop printers or proofing devices.
- **Press Quality:** Retains transparency, embeds all fonts, converts colors to CMYK (but retains spot colors), retains high-resolution images. Used for submitting jobs to commercial printers.

- **Smallest File Size:** Retains transparency, converts all colors to sRGB, an RGB color space that captures the common RGB colors that can be displayed across a range of different devices, such as computer screens, or scanners, compresses and downsamples images to lower resolution. Used for web- or email-ready PDFs.

PDF/X is an International Standards Organization (ISO) standard for the exchange of documents within the graphics and printing industry. A number of PDF Export presets meet ISO standard requirements.

- **PDF/X-1a:2001:** Flattens transparency, embeds all fonts, supports only CMYK and spot color, converts RGB color to CMYK, retains high-resolution images. Used to submit designs to commercial printers.

- **PDF/X-3:2002:** Flattens transparency, embeds all fonts, retains color (CMYK, spot, and RGB), embeds color profiles, retains high-resolution images. Used for combined CMYK/RGB print workflows (for example, when photos are placed in RGB and color swatches are defined as CMYK color).

- **PDF/X-4:2008:** Retains transparency, embeds all fonts, supports color models (CMYK, spot, and RGB), embeds color profiles, retains high-resolution images. Used for combined CMYK/RGB print workflows that don't require transparency flattening.

To learn more about the various PDF/X standards, enter "PDF/X and print industry" in your favorite search engine. You will find great in-depth articles out there.

When submitting a press-ready PDF to your printer, always consult with the printer regarding the preferred export settings. In some cases, they may provide a PDF preset file for you to import.

To submit a press-ready PDF to your printer (**Figure 2.61**):

1 Choose File > Export.

2 Enter a specific Name for the PDF in the File Name (Windows), or Save As (Mac OS) field.

3 Navigate to the location where you want to save the PDF file.

4 Select Adobe PDF (Print) from the Save As Type (Windows) or Format (Mac OS) menu.

5 Click Save. The Export Adobe PDF dialog box appears.

6 Select [Press Quality] from the Adobe PDF Preset menu.

7 Click Marks And Bleeds in the scroll list at left.

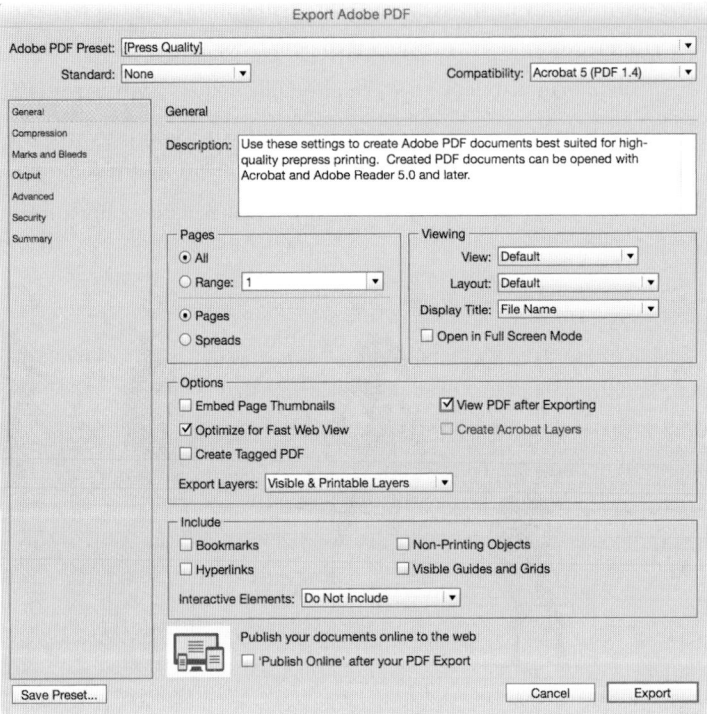

Figure 2.61 Exporting a finished event poster as a press-ready PDF with crop marks and bleed included

8 Under Marks, select Crop Marks, Registration Marks, and Page Information.

9 If your document contains bleeds, select Use Document Bleed Settings.

10 If your document includes a slug area and you want to add any print instructions, select Include Slug Area.

11 Click Export.

You are now ready to submit the press-ready PDF to the printer. The next time you see it, the poster will be in its finished printed format. Congratulations!

CHAPTER OBJECTIVES

Chapter Learning Objectives

- Distinguish between paragraph and character formatting controls.
- Identify the different uses of the Selection and Direct Selection tools.
- Demonstrate knowledge of common checks in preflight.
- Package a design for delivery to a print or service provider.
- Create an alternate layout for your design.

Chapter ACA Objectives

For full descriptions of objectives, download the printable chart from your account on *peachpit.com*. See pages xi–xii.

DOMAIN 2.0
UNDERSTANDING PRINT AND DIGITAL MEDIA PUBLICATIONS
2.2

DOMAIN 3.0
UNDERSTANDING ADOBE INDESIGN CC
3.1, 3.2, 3.4, 3.5, 3.6, 3.8

DOMAIN 4.0
CREATING PRINT AND DIGITAL MEDIA PUBLICATIONS USING ADOBE INDESIGN
4.1, 4.2, 4.3, 4.4

DOMAIN 5.0
PUBLISH, EXPORT, AND ARCHIVE PAGE LAYOUTS USING ADOBE INDESIGN
5.1

CHAPTER 3

A Colorful Magazine Cover Design

The project for this chapter is a magazine cover design. You'll learn new techniques for applying and creating colors and gradients, as well as work with creative effects. Plus, you will be introduced to new text-formatting options, and amazing transparency effects that can make your designs pop (**Figure 3.1**).

Before submitting files to the printer, you always need to perform a pre-flight check that flags any errors in the InDesign document. This chapter will walk you through that process and teach you how to fix the most commonly encountered errors. Finally, you'll use InDesign's alternate layouts to repurpose your cover design for web or digital publishing.

Figure 3.1 Finished cover design

Starting a Magazine Cover Design

★ ACA Objective 2.2

★ ACA Objective 3.1

NOTE

This chapter supports the project created in video lesson 3. Go to the Project 3 page in the book's Web Edition to watch the entire lesson from beginning to end.

As you've seen in previous projects, each design project starts with some questions that require answering. What questions would you ask and answer when designing a magazine cover?

To begin, you might ask:

- Is this cover design going to be used for a print edition of the magazine? Or will it be used for a digital version published as an app with the Adobe Digital Publishing Solution (DPS)?

- What is the finished size of the magazine going to be? Does the InDesign document require bleed?

Answering these questions allows you to determine the page size for the document you are creating, and set the intent (Print, Web, or Digital Publishing).

After creating the new document, you generally follow a few common steps when designing a cover:

▶ Video 3.1

▶ Video 3.2

▶ Video 3.7

- Add a series of layers so you can more easily manage the content on the page, such as a Headline layer for the **masthead**, which is the title of the magazine, and a layer for all the text (**Figure 3.2**).

- Use the Layout > Create Guides command to add a grid of ruler guides that breaks up the cover page into a grid of six rows and three columns (**Figure 3.3**). Creating a design grid that works in thirds enables you to design using the rule of thirds. Positioning design elements, such as the masthead or the hero image, so that they align with the intersecting lines of the grid helps you create a balanced page composition.

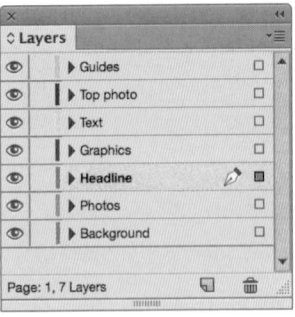

Figure 3.2 Layers added for the magazine cover design

- If you are designing a cover for a publication that needs to adhere to corporate branding guidelines, such as a cover for a company's annual report, you will need information about the company's **corporate colors** and fonts, as they are part of its corporate identity. Add these colors to the Swatches panel and make sure the fonts are available on your system.

Capturing Color and Creating Color Themes

In Chapter 2, you learned how to add and use color swatches. Creating new colors swatches by mixing Cyan, Magenta, Yellow, and Black tints is fun, but InDesign offers other options for adding colors. You can work with colors that appear in the images in your designs and capture colors using your phone. Plus, InDesign can offer great color combination suggestions, including colors that complement each other. This section will help you learn about these features.

Figure 3.3 Ruler guides on the magazine cover design created with the Layout > Create Guides command

Picking Up Colors from a Document

★ *ACA Objective 3.2*

Adding color to your designs is exciting. Within InDesign, you can use the Eyedropper tool ( ) and the Color Theme tool ( ) to pick up color from within a document. In addition, Adobe offers a companion app for phone and tablet devices (iOS, Android) that enable you to capture color and color themes with the camera on the device, and then use these colors in your designs.

EYEDROPPER TOOL

The Eyedropper tool lets you pick up such attributes as stroke, fill, character, paragraph, or object settings from design elements on a page by clicking on them with the tool. Attributes you pick up are loaded into the Eyedropper tool ( ), and you can then apply them to other objects in the document or even in another open document.

★ *ACA Objective 3.1*

To pick up a color from an image and apply it to another object as a fill color (**Figure 3.4**):

1. Select the Eyedropper tool, position it over an area in the image from which you want to pick up the color, and click.

2. Select the Fill box in the Tools panel or Swatches panel.

3. With the loaded Eyedropper tool, click on the object to fill. The object takes on the fill color.

To control which of the attributes picked up by the Eyedropper tool are applied to another object, you can adjust the settings for the tool. For example, to retain the yellow stroke on the starburst in the previous example and apply only the fill, you can adjust the tool settings so that any picked-up stroke attributes are ignored and only the color and tint for the fill are applied (**Figure 3.5**).

Figure 3.4 Applying the purple color from the background image to the starburst

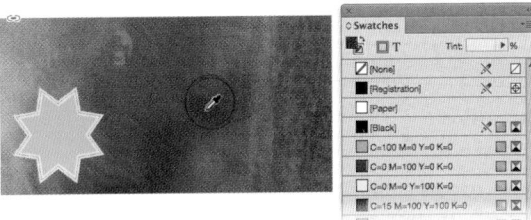

 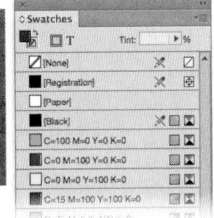 

Figure 3.5 The Eyedropper Options dialog box, with some of the fill settings unchecked

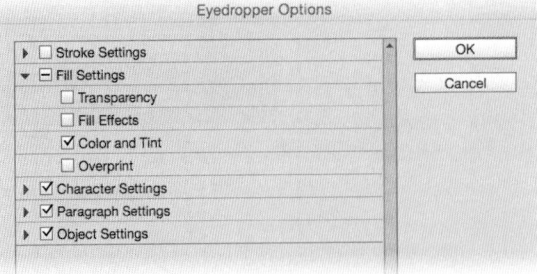

To adjust the Eyedropper tool options:

1   Double-click the Eyedropper tool in the Tools panel.

2   In the Eyedropper Options dialog box, select and deselect the settings for attributes you want to apply or ignore.

As you soak up a color from the image, the active Stroke or Fill box changes to this color. (Remember, the Stroke/Fill box is available on the Tools panel, Control panel, Swatches panel, and Color panel. Use whichever you find most convenient.)

To create a new color swatch in the Swatches panel from the active stroke or fill color (**Figure 3.6**):

1   Choose New Color Swatch from the Swatches panel menu.

2   In the New Color Swatch dialog box, uncheck Name With Color Value and uncheck Add To CC Library.

3   Enter the Swatch Name, then click OK.

 Video 3.3

 Video 3.4

> **SHORTCUT** *To clear the contents of the Eyedropper tool and pick up attributes from another object, Alt-click (Windows) or Option-click (Mac OS) on another object.*

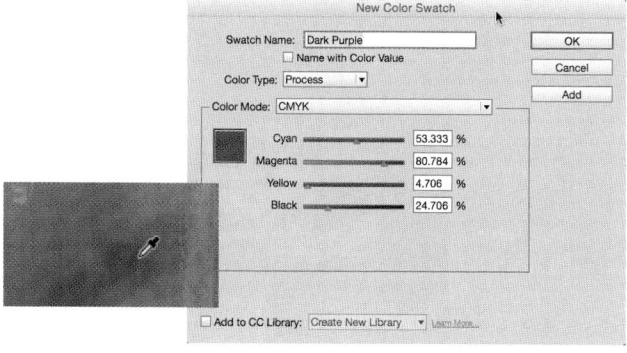
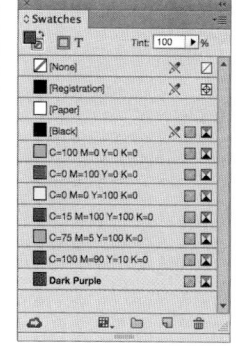

Figure 3.6 Applying the purple color from the background image to the starburst

COLOR THEME TOOL

The Color Theme tool not only lets you pick up individual colors from your design, it also builds color themes. This allows you to quickly add a number of colors that work well together to your Swatches panel.

★ *ACA Objective 2.2*

★ *ACA Objective 3.1*

Color themes capture a maximum of five different color swatches. The swatches are based on a theme choice, such as Colorful, Bright, Dark, Deep, or Muted, or a color rule. Color rules use the color wheel when selecting color. For example, the complementary color rule selects colors that are found on the opposite ends of the color wheel, and a monochromatic color rule captures colors based on a single color, creating different shades or tints of that color (**Figure 3.7**).

To create a color theme based on the colors in a section of a page (**Figure 3.8**):

1 Select the Color Theme tool.

2 Drag a marquee around the desired area on the page.

3 From the Theme Options menu in the Color Theme Options panel, select a theme choice. Note that the number of options available depends on the selected color range.

4 With the theme selected, you can opt to add the colors to the Swatches panel. To do so, click the Add Theme To Swatches button.

5 To add a color theme to a Library in your CC Libraries panel, click the Add Theme To Current Library button. (We will cover Libraries in more detail in Chapter 6.)

TIP

To add only a single color from the theme to the Swatches panel, Alt-click (Windows) or Option-click (Mac OS) the swatch in the theme.

Figure 3.7 Complementary (left) and monochromatic (right) colors selected on the color wheel in Adobe Color

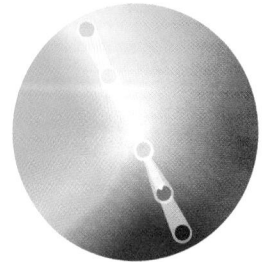

Figure 3.8 Creating a new color theme from a selected area in a design

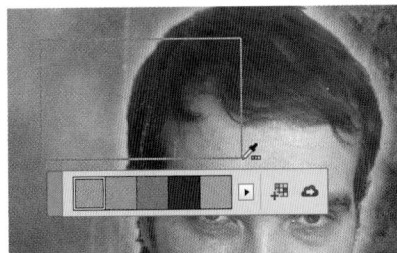

Add Theme To Current CC Library

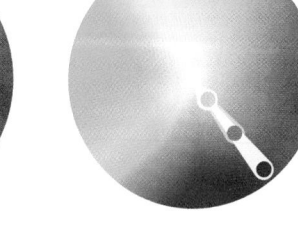

Add Theme To Swatches

To create a color theme based on color rules (**Figure 3.9**):

1 With the Color Theme tool, shift-click an image or object on the page.

2 The Theme Options menu in the Color Theme Options panel lists color rules, using the color you clicked as the base color. Select a theme choice.

3 Click Add Theme To Swatches, or click the Add Theme To Current CC Library icon.

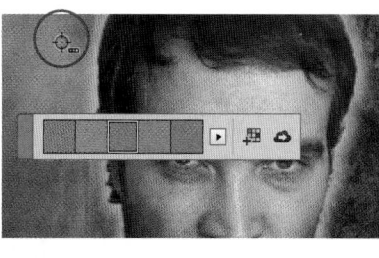
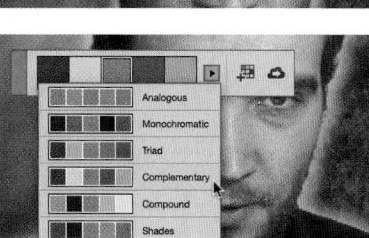
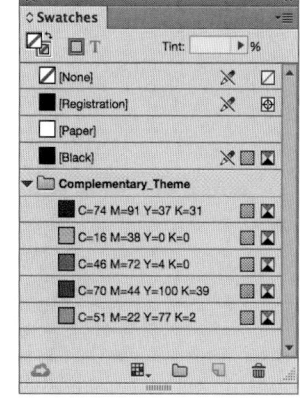

Figure 3.9 Creating a color theme based on color rules by Shift-clicking a base color

The Color Theme tool by default converts the colors it picks up to those that match the document intent. This means that for Print documents, the colors automatically convert to CMYK, and for Web and Digital Publishing documents the colors convert to RGB.

To change the Color Theme options:

1 Double-click the Color Theme tool.

2 In the Color Theme Options dialog box, select the preferred options, then click OK.

   You can select the Ignore Opacity And Other Applied Effects While Picking Colors option to ensure that colors created by changing opacity levels or applying effects, such as an outer glow are ignored. Instead, the original object colors are picked up. For example, if a dark green object has its opacity set to 50%, the tool would pick up the dark green color, rather than a lighter shade of that color created by lowering the opacity.

SHORTCUT

To clear the contents of the Color Theme tool and pick up attributes from another object, Alt-click (Windows) or Option-click (Mac OS) another object.

To force the Color Theme tool to convert colors to either RGB or CMYK, regardless of the document intent, you can change the When Applying Colors setting to either Convert To CMYK, or Convert To CMYK, from the default Convert As Per Document Intent setting.

Adobe Color

★ *ACA Objective 2.2*

★ *ACA Objective 3.6*

In the previous examples, you picked up color from within your design project. Adobe Color is a color capture technology that allows you to capture colors anywhere and share color themes you create with your workgroup and the public. Similarly, you can access publicly shared color themes by others, and add these as swatch colors to the Swatches panel.

ADOBE CAPTURE CC

Adobe Capture CC is a live capture app that can capture and create shapes, brushes, colors, as well as looks. *Looks* capture color and light values that can be applied to video projects. With the app installed and open on your phone or tablet, click Colors to start a color capture. Colors lets you use photos you take while out in the field to create different color themes. Additionally, you can use photos from your camera roll or Creative Cloud to create new themes (**Figure 3.10**).

Figure 3.10 The Adobe Capture CC app is capturing colors from an Oleander image.

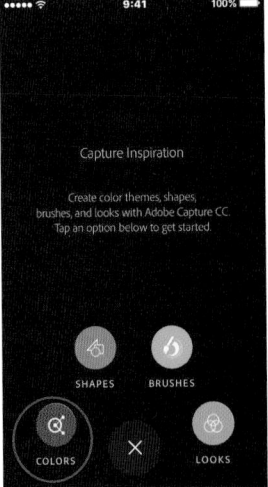  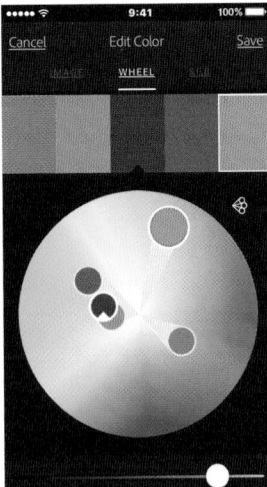

The five-swatch color themes you capture can be edited within the app and added to a Creative Cloud Library. If you sign in to the app with the same credentials as the Creative Cloud desktop app, you can sync the color theme through Adobe CreativeSync and access it in various apps and applications across all your devices.

In InDesign you can see the themes in the allocated library in the CC Libraries panel (**Figure 3.11**):

- Choose Window > CC Libraries, then select the appropriate library from the menu at the top of the panel.

Figure 3.11 The Oleander color theme appears in the Design Project library in the CC Libraries panel.

Themes you create appear in the Adobe Color Themes panel (**Figure 3.12**):

- Choose Window > Color > Adobe Color Themes, then click My Themes.

Adobe Color CC is also available online via *color.adobe.com*. With the online application, you can upload a photo and capture colors from the image or create a brand new theme using a color rule, such as complementary, that is applied to a base color (**Figure 3.13**).

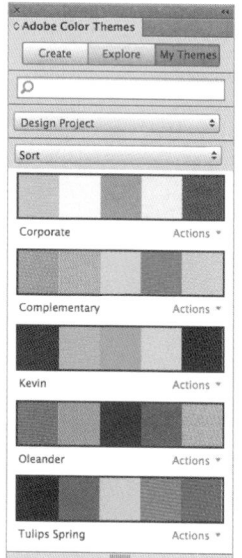

Figure 3.12 The Oleander color theme appears in the Adobe Color Themes panel.

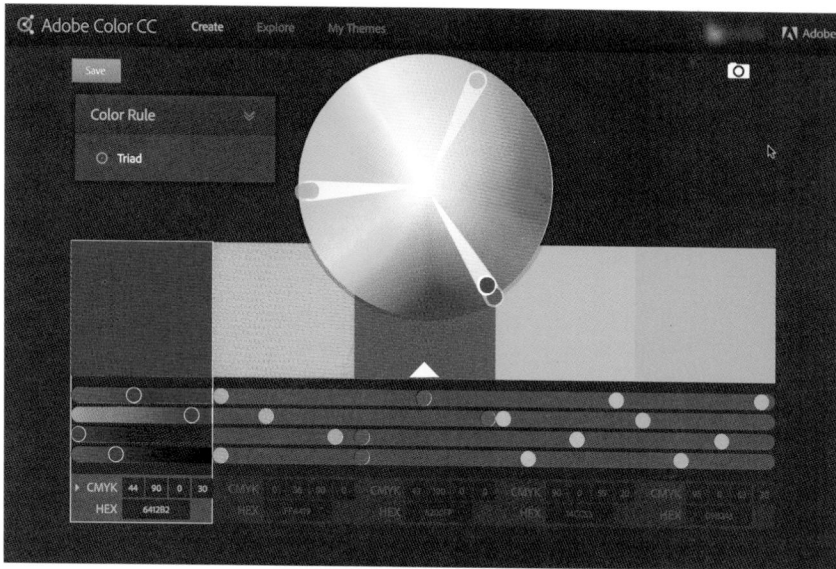

Figure 3.13 Capturing color themes with the online version of Adobe Color CC

ADOBE COLOR THEMES PANEL

★ *ACA Objective 3.6*

The Adobe Color Themes panel (Window > Color > Adobe Color Themes) ties all the color capture abilities together. It gives you access to all the themes you create, lets you explore popular themes and search for themes, and create your own themes (**Figure 3.14**).

Figure 3.14 Adobe Color Themes panel

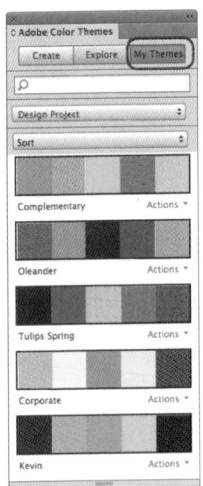 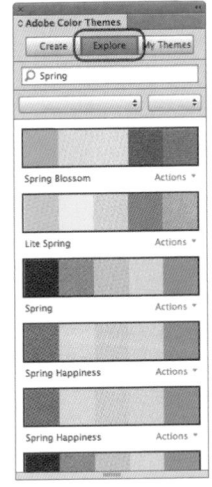 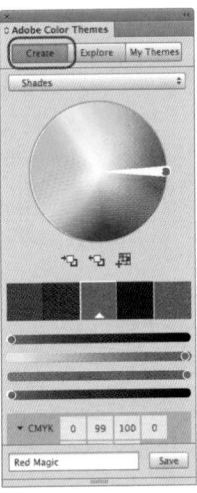

▶ *Video 3.3*

▶ *Video 3.4*

In the cover project, you will use the Adobe Color Themes panel to create a complementary color theme based on the purple color you added to the Swatches panel earlier.

To create a complementary color theme based on a swatch color (**Figure 3.15**):

1 Click Create at the top of the Adobe Color Themes panel.

2 Select a color swatch to serve as the base color for the theme in the Swatches panel.

3 Click the middle of the five theme swatches, and then click the Set Selected Swatch From Active Color icon to load the base color.

4 From the Color Rule menu, select Complementary.

5 Make adjustments to any of the five color swatches as needed.

6 Click the Add To Swatches icon.

7 Enter the name of the theme at the bottom of the panel, and click Add To Swatches to add a new color group for the theme to the Swatches panel. Clicking Save will prompt you to select one of the libraries in the CC Libraries panel and add the theme to a library.

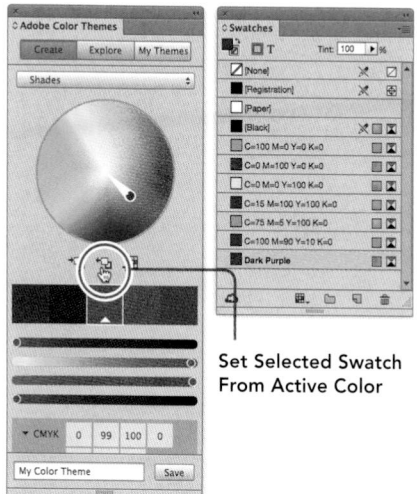

Set Selected Swatch From Active Color

Add To Swatches

Figure 3.15 Creating a color theme with the Adobe Color Themes panel, based on the Dark Purple swatch color

More Swatches Panel Actions

By now you've become familiar with using the Swatches panel, you've learned how to apply swatch colors to strokes and fills, as well as to source colors from design elements on your page, and to create new color swatches. In this section, you'll learn to organize color swatches in color groups, merge similar-looking swatches to a single swatch color, share swatches between applications and projects, and more.

⭐ *ACA Objective 3.6*

⭐ *ACA Objective 4.4*

WORKING WITH COLOR GROUPS

Adding color themes to the Swatches panel from the Color Theme Options panel or Adobe Color Themes panel automatically places the swatch colors in a color group.

You can create new color groups manually at any stage, rename them, delete colors, duplicate colors, or merge colors.

To create a new color group from selected swatches (**Figure 3.16**):

1 Ctrl-click (Windows) or Command-click (Mac OS) the swatches to select them.

2 Choose New Color Group from the Swatches panel menu.

3 Enter a name for the color group, and click OK.

TIP

You can also Alt-click (Windows) or Option-click (Mac OS) the New Color Group button at the bottom of the Swatches panel to quickly create a color group.

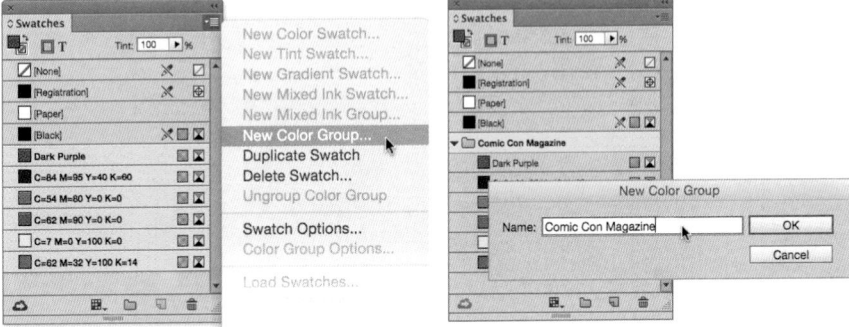

Figure 3.16 Creating a new color group from selected swatches

MERGING COLOR SWATCHES

Merging swatches is useful when you find that you have created a series of very similar-looking swatches and might have even applied them to different elements in your design. Instead of deleting colors one by one and replacing them with the preferred color, merging allows you to delete multiple swatches and replace them with another swatch in a single step. Any design elements, objects, text, or images to which the color was applied are updated to the merged color. For example, you might consider merging a number of similar-looking purple swatches, applied to various elements in a project, into a single (merged) color.

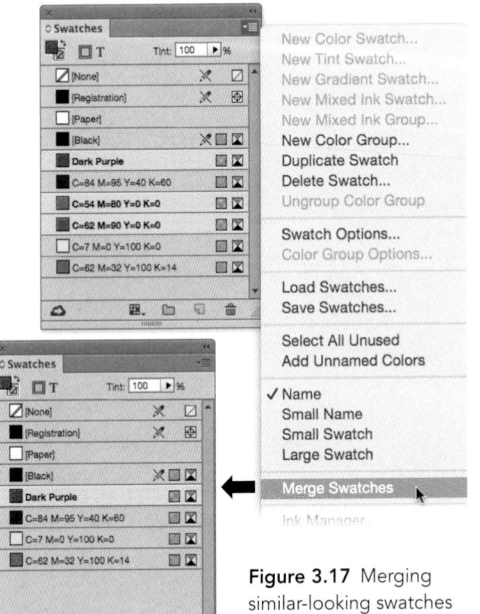

To merge swatches (**Figure 3.17**):

1 In the Swatches panel, start by selecting the swatch you would like to use as the replacement color.

2 Ctrl-click (Windows) or Command-click (Mac OS) the swatches you want to merge.

3 Select Merge Swatches from the Swatches panel menu.

DUPLICATING COLOR SWATCHES

Opposite to merging swatches, at times you might want to create more variations of a particular color.

To duplicate a color swatch (**Figure 3.18**):

1 Select a color swatch in Swatches panel.

2 Select Duplicate Swatch from the Swatches panel menu. A copy of the swatch is added to the Swatches panel.

Figure 3.17 Merging similar-looking swatches into a single Dark Purple swatch

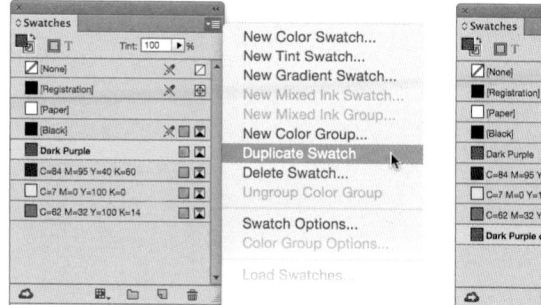
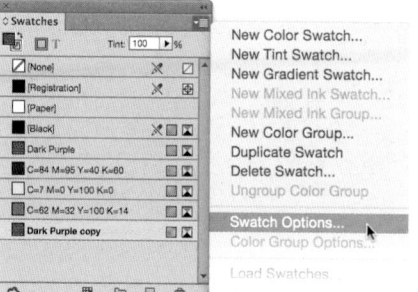

Figure 3.18 Duplicating a swatch and editing the duplicated swatch

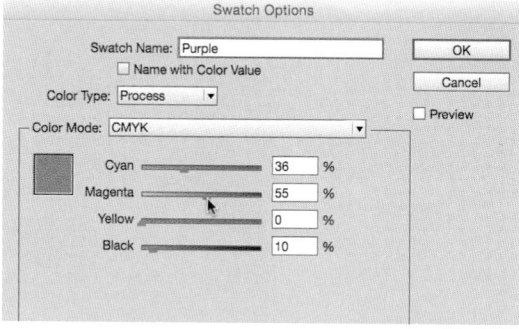
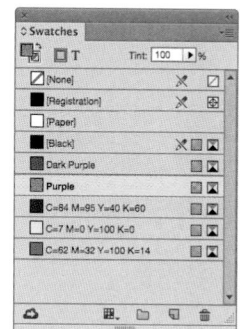

3   To modify the copied swatch, select it and choose Swatch Options from the Swatches panel menu. You can also double-click the swatch.

4   In the Swatch Options dialog box, enter the new name for the swatch and adjust the CMYK settings. Click OK.

CREATING TINT SWATCHES

You can apply a tint of a swatch color to an object's stroke or fill at any time by adjusting the Tint slider in the Swatches panel. However, when you apply the same tint percentage repeatedly, adding a tint swatch to the panel eases the task of having to remember the exact percentage with each application.

To add a tint swatch to the Swatches panel (**Figure 3.19**):

1   Select a color swatch in Swatches panel.

2   Select New Tint Swatch from the Swatches panel menu.

3   Set the Tint value, and click OK.

TIP

Tint swatches are also useful when creating gradients that blend tints of a swatch color. You must first create tint swatches for the various tint percentages you want to blend, before you can apply them to a gradient's color stops.

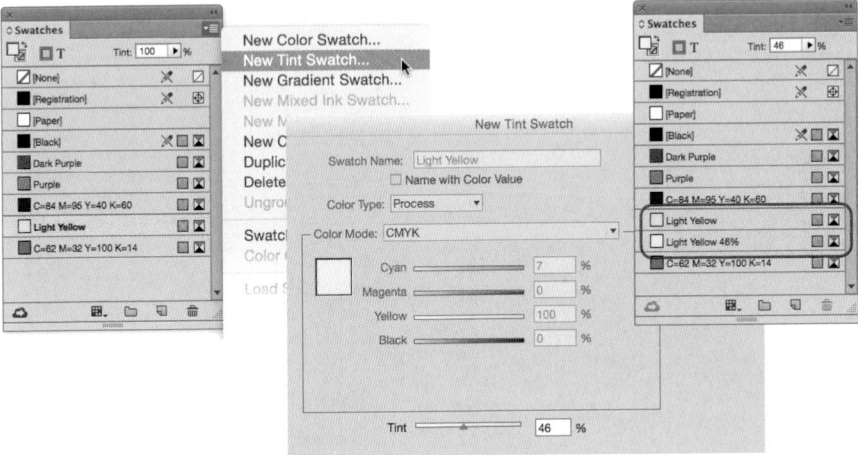

Figure 3.19 Creating a reusable tint swatch

SHARING COLOR SWATCHES

To share selected color swatches from an InDesign document across different Adobe applications, such as Photoshop and Illustrator, or with other InDesign users, you can create an Adobe Swatch Exchange file (ASE) or add the swatch colors to CC Libraries.

To save a selection of swatches from the Swatches panel (**Figure 3.20**):

1   Ctrl-click (Windows) or Command-click (Mac OS) the swatches you want to export in the Swatches panel.

2   Choose Save Swatches from the Swatches panel menu. A warning dialog box appears, informing you that certain swatches, such as gradient and tint swatches, will not be visible when the ASE file is opened in other applications.

3   Enter a file name in the File Name (Windows), or Save As (Mac OS) field, and navigate to the folder where you want to save the ASE file.

4   Click Save.

You can load swatches from another InDesign document or from an ASE file.

To load swatches into the Swatches panel (**Figure 3.21**):

1   Select Load Swatches from the Swatches panel menu.

2   Navigate to another InDesign document, or an ASE file, and select it.

3   Click Open.

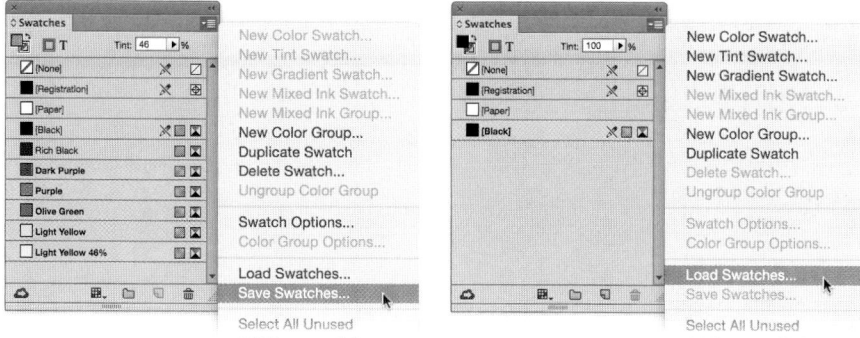

Figure 3.20 Saving selected swatches for use in other documents or applications

Figure 3.21 Loading swatches from another InDesign document or ASE file into the Swatches panel

CC Libraries are available across different desktop applications, such as Adobe Photoshop and Illustrator, as well as in Adobe mobile apps. Adding swatches to a CC Library makes them accessible in other applications, and makes them available to other users. We will cover libraries in more detail in Chapter 6.

To share swatches using CC Libraries (**Figure 3.22**):

1   In the CC Libraries panel (Window > CC Libraries) select a library for storing the swatches.

2   Ctrl-click (Windows) or Command-click (Mac OS) the swatches you want to add to the library in the Swatches panel.

3   Click the Add Selected Swatches To My Current CC Library button.

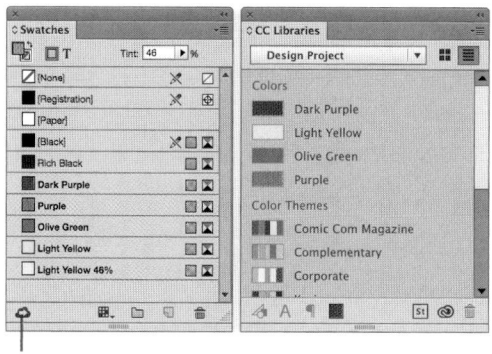

Figure 3.22 Saving swatches in a library

Add Selected Swatch(es)
To My Current CC Library

Fine-Tuning Text Formatting and Text Frame Options

Text has been part of every project you have worked on so far, and we gradually introduced you to some of the common character and paragraph-level formatting features in earlier chapters. Can you remember for which of the two formatting levels you only need to set the insertion point somewhere in the text for the formatting to apply, but don't need to select all the text?

▶ Video 3.5

▶ Video 3.9

▶ Video 3.11

That's right. For paragraph-level formatting, it is sufficient to have the text insertion point set anywhere within a paragraph.

By now you've learned to:

- Choose a font, including adding Typekit fonts.

    The masthead font for the magazine cover is Cooper Black. If you don't have this font on your system, try using Typekit to find a serif font that is very heavy in weight and quite wide.

- Increase or decrease the font size.

    What unit of measurement is used for font sizes?

- Change the leading, or line spacing, of text.

    What is the default auto leading percentage InDesign uses?

- Set text alignments.

    What are some of the horizontal text alignments you can apply to text?

Setting the Leading Amount

★ ACA Objective 3.2

★ ACA Objective 3.8

TIP

As a rule of thumb for body copy, such as paragraphs in a magazine article, use a leading amount that is approximately 2 points larger than the font size used.

For headings or cover lines, which vary in font size depending on their level of importance, you will often adjust the font size as you design. With the leading set to a fixed size, adjusting the font size means that you will continuously need to change the leading, especially when the text runs over a few lines.

For such headings and cover lines, consider applying auto leading and adjusting the automatic setting to a much smaller amount than the default 120%. For headings that run over multiple lines or that are set in larger font sizes, this default amount generally provides too much space. Lowering the auto leading percentage allows you to easily increase or decrease the font size without having to adjust the leading amount separately each time you change the font size. Proportionally, the line spacing goes up or down as you increase or decrease the font size. **Figure 3.23** compares the cover line text with leading set to 120% (left) and 94% (right).

To adjust the auto leading percentage (**Figure 3.24**):

1 Select the heading or cover line text with the Type tool (T).

2 To open the Justification dialog box that lets you modify the leading percentage, Alt-click (Windows) or Option-click (Mac OS) the Leading icon in the Control panel (Character Formatting Controls).

3 Enter the Auto Leading amount, and select Preview to see the changes. Click OK.

TIP

You can also select Justification from the Control panel or Paragraph panel menu to open the Justification dialog box and adjust the auto leading percentage.

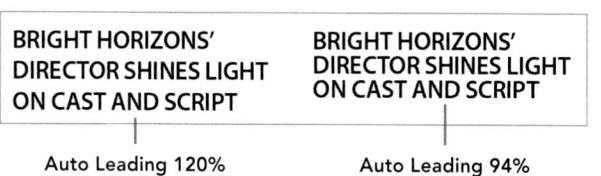

BRIGHT HORIZONS' DIRECTOR SHINES LIGHT ON CAST AND SCRIPT

Auto Leading 120%

BRIGHT HORIZONS' DIRECTOR SHINES LIGHT ON CAST AND SCRIPT

Auto Leading 94%

Figure 3.23 The same text with different auto leading percentages applied

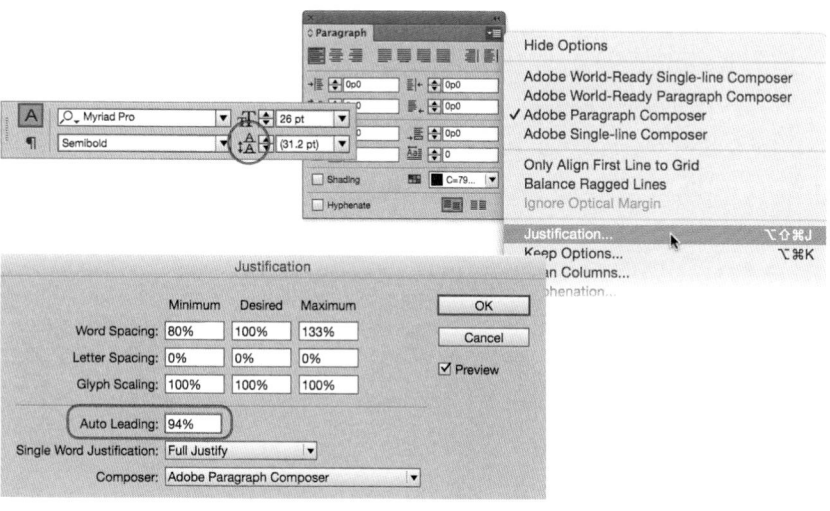

Figure 3.24 Adjusting the auto leading percentage for a cover line

Kerning and Tracking

Kerning and tracking control the amount of space applied between letters. **Kerning** increases or decreases the amount of space between two characters, and is used to fix proportional spacing issues seen in larger font sizes as well as capitalized text. **Tracking**, like kerning, adjusts the spacing between letters; however, it applies to

★ *ACA Objective 3.2*

★ *ACA Objective 3.8*

two or more selected characters and applies a uniform amount of spacing between each letter pair within the selection.

- Manual kerning helps designers fix subtle spacing issues by adding or reducing space between letter pairs. Especially in headings, titles, and larger font sizes, you will benefit from mastering manual kerning adjustments.

- Tracking is more often used to change the typographical appearance of text. It works well with uppercase text. For example, a person's name on a business card set in small caps, with positive tracking, will make the name stand out. A headline set in all caps will look less compacted with an increase in tracking.

WORKING WITH KERNING

There's a trick you can apply when you are fixing kerning issues. Cover up part of the text, so that you only see three letters at a time. As you look at the two letter pairs, determine whether certain letters need to be closer together or farther apart. As you move from left to right across the letters in your words, continue to fix the kerning in the letter pair on the right. Proper kerning is a true balancing act (**Figure 3.25**).

InDesign's default kerning technique is **metric kerning**, which kerns letter pairs based on information it draws from the specifications of the font in use. Extremely bad kerning can be improved by changing from metric to optical kerning. With **optical kerning**, InDesign does its very best to ensure that more even kerning is applied between letter pairs. However, even with optical kerning, you will often find yourself manually kerning letter pairs, especially when using larger font sizes. The capitalized text masthead set with the bold and bulky serif typeface Cooper Black is a good example of text that requires additional manual kerning.

To change the kerning from metric to optical (**Figure 3.26**):

- Select the text. From the Kerning menu in the Control panel, select Optical. (You can also find the Kerning menu in the Character panel.)

To apply manual kerning (**Figure 3.27**):

1 Place the text insertion point between two characters.

2 Increase or decrease the kerning amount from the Control panel or Character panel.

NOTE

Words typed in capital letters are referred to as being set in **uppercase**. *The rest of the letters thus being* **lowercase**. *These words find their origin in printing. To discover the history behind them, enter "history of uppercase and lowercase" in your favorite search engine, and learn how typographers used to set type in the old days.*

Figure 3.25 Review the letter kerning in a word by focusing on three letters at a time.

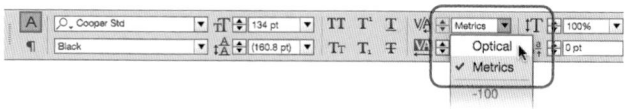

Figure 3.26 Optical kerning (bottom), does not fix all the kerning issues with COMIX, but does visually close the bigger gap between the letters C and O, and O and M for example.

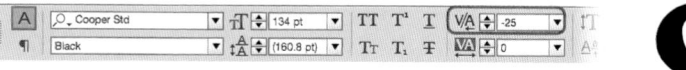

Figure 3.27 Adjusting kerning

WORKING WITH TRACKING

Tracking can be used for creative reasons, but it also has a practical purpose in bringing a **runt** (a single word that appears on the last line of a paragraph) back to the previous line. In general, you apply the same tracking value to entire paragraphs.

To change the tracking (**Figure 3.28**):

1 Select the text to which you want to apply tracking.

2 Increase or decrease the tracking amount from the Control panel or Character panel.

> **SHORTCUT** *Press Alt+Shift+ Left Arrow (Windows) or Option+Shift+Left Arrow (Mac OS) to decrease the kerning or tracking, or Press Alt+Shift+ Right Arrow (Windows) or Option+Shift+Right Arrow (Mac OS) to increase the kerning or tracking amount.*

TIP

Quadruple-clicking on paragraph text with the Type tool selects the entire paragraph. Triple-clicking selects a line within a paragraph, double-clicking a word.

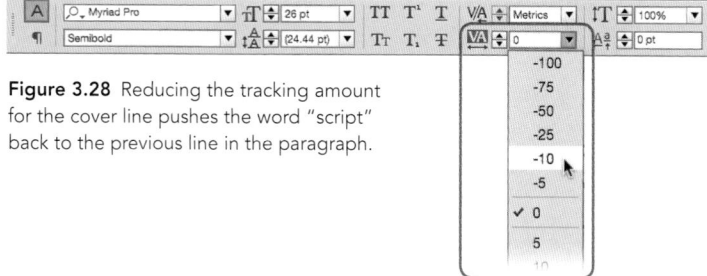

Figure 3.28 Reducing the tracking amount for the cover line pushes the word "script" back to the previous line in the paragraph.

Working with Text Frames

★ *ACA Objective 3.2*

★ *ACA Objective 4.2*

★ *ACA Objective 4.4*

Each bit of text you've added to the design projects thus far was added to the page by first creating a text frame, then inserting text into that frame. You've formatted the text within the frame using different paragraph and character formatting controls. In this section, you'll learn to do more with text frames, such as applying color to text or frame, moving the text away from the frame edge, and automatically adjusting the height of the frame as you add more text.

APPLYING A FILL COLOR

Most text in a design appears inside text frames, which may have a transparent ([None]), white, or colored background. Instead of creating a second frame and placing it behind the text frame containing the text, you can apply a fill color to the text frame itself.

To apply a color to the fill of the text frame (**Figure 3.29**):

1 Select the text frame.

2 Select the Fill box in the Control panel or the Swatches panel.

3 Select Formatting Affects Container.

4 Click the swatch color to apply it.

APPLYING A TEXT COLOR

To change the color of the text in a selected text frame (**Figure 3.30**):

1 Select the Fill box in the Tools panel or the Swatches panel.

2 Select Formatting Affects Text.

3 Click the swatch color to apply it.

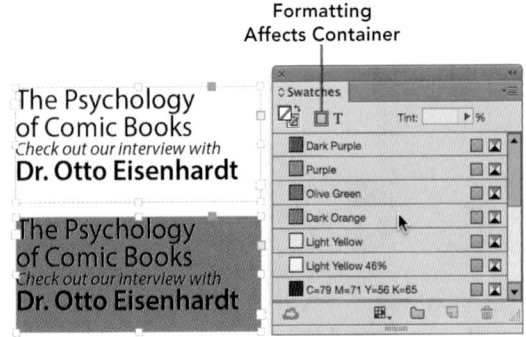

Figure 3.29 Applying a fill color to a text frame

Figure 3.30 Applying a fill color to the text by selecting the text frame

ADJUSTING SPACING WITHIN A TEXT FRAME

When you apply a fill color to a text frame, you may want to adjust how the text is positioned within that frame. The Text Frame Options dialog box provides settings that allow you to move the text away from the edge of the frame, vertically align it in the frame, and automatically adjust the height of the frame to prevent overset text from occurring.

To add a text inset to the text frame (**Figure 3.31**):

1   Select the text frame and choose Object > Text Frame Options.

2   Click the General tab.

3   Select Preview to see the changes as you make them.

4   Enter an Inset Spacing value.

With Make All Settings The Same () enabled, any Inset Spacing value you enter is automatically entered in the Top, Right, Bottom, and Left fields. To enter different values for the sides of the text frame, disable this setting (   ).

5   When you are satisfied with the insets, click OK.

As a result of setting inset spacing, text might become overset. Overset text occurs when not all text fits in the text frame; it is marked with a red plus sign at the lower-right corner of the text frame.

To fix overset text (**Figure 3.32**) by manually adjusting the text frame:

- Expand the height (or width) of the text frame by dragging one of the frame handles.

- Alternatively, double-click a frame handle.

TIP

To quickly adjust the height of an overset text frame, double-click the top-middle or bottom-middle handle of the text-frame bounding box.

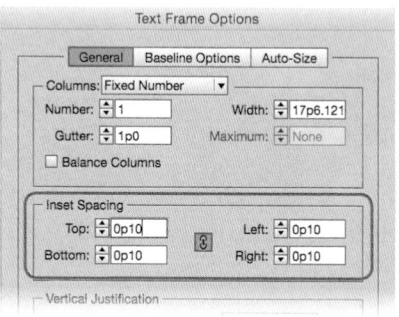

Figure 3.31 Moving the text away from the frame edge by increasing the inset spacing

Figure 3.32 Drag the bottom-center frame handle to resolve overset text.

You can also vertically align text within a frame using settings in the Text Frame Options dialog box.

To vertically center the text in a frame (**Figure 3.33**):

1. Select the text frame and choose Object > Text Frame Options.

2. Click the General tab.

3. Under Vertical Justification, set the Align setting to Center.

Another way to change the vertical alignment is to:

- Select the text frame with the Selection tool, and click the Align Center option in the Control panel.

Auto-Size is another useful feature in the Text Frame Options dialog box (**Figure 3.34**). It allows text frames to automatically grow in depth (or width) as more text is added to the frame or a text inset is applied. This eliminates the need for manual resizing of the text frame to avoid overset text.

To enable automatic adjustment of the height of a text frame:

1. Select the text frame and choose Object > Text Frame Options.

2. Click the Auto-Size tab.

3. Select Height Only from the Auto-Sizing menu, and click OK.

Figure 3.33 ▼ Vertically aligning the cover line text in its text frame

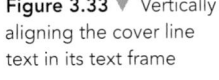

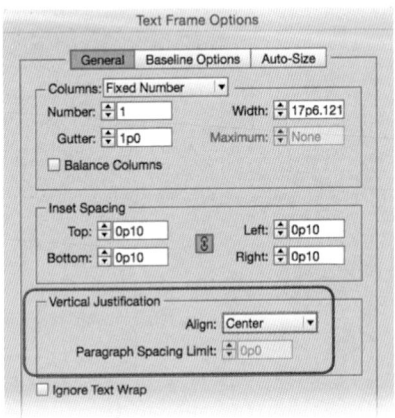

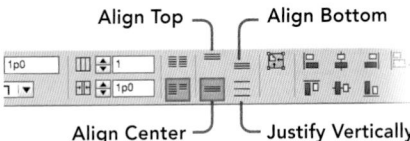

Figure 3.34 ▲ Automatically adjusting the height of a text frame with Auto-Size enabled

Editing Shapes

So far, the shapes and frames you have been adding as design elements to your poster and magazine cover—the graphic frames, the text frames, and the unassigned frames—are all vector shapes called paths.

Paths are shapes that are assembled from **anchor points** and line segments. Each **line segment** is joined by two anchor points. This is a bit like how you would build a fence: A single corner post is placed first; a panel is then attached to the corner post and held in place with a second post at the opposite end and so on. When the line segments are curved, the anchor points contain a **direction line** that controls the curvature of the path (**Figure 3.35**).

▶ Video 3.12

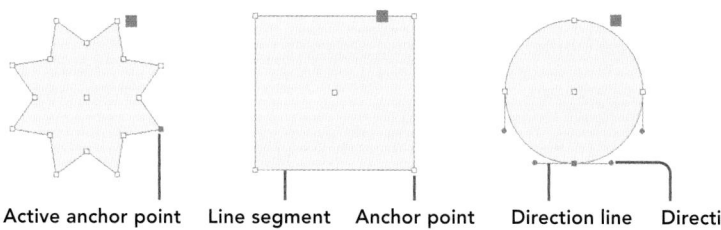

Active anchor point   Line segment   Anchor point   Direction line   Direction point

Figure 3.35 Different-shaped paths with their building blocks exposed

Selection Tool Revisited

★ *ACA Objective 3.2*
★ *ACA Objective 3.5*

Thus far, we have selected design elements with the Selection tool (▶), and discovered that the Selection tool is a genuine multipurpose tool that lets you select objects and then move, resize, and rotate them. When working with images, the Selection tool is used for cropping and positioning images with their graphic frames.

You can also use the Selection tool to select multiple objects (by Shift-clicking the objects or dragging a marquee around them) or to select grouped objects. Grouped objects behave as if they are a single object when selected with the Selection tool.

To group multiple objects (**Figure 3.36**):

1 Select two or more objects. If you accidentally select objects you don't want in the group, you can Shift-click to remove them from the selection.

2 Choose Object > Group.

A single dashed bounding box indicates that you have selected a group.

Figure 3.36 Two objects selected (left) and grouped (right)

If objects originate from different layers, grouping will move them to the layer of the top-most object you selected. When ungrouping objects, you can release them back to their original layer.

To ungroup objects and release them back to their original layer:

1   Select the group.

2   Select Ungroup Remembers Layers from the Layers panel menu.

3   Choose Object > Ungroup.

Direct Selection Tool

★ *ACA Objective 3.2*

In contrast to the Selection tool, which selects entire objects, the Direct Selection tool (⬉) puts you in construction mode. Now, you can select and reposition anchor points, move line segments and adjoin anchor points, and change the curves on line segments by adjusting the direction lines.

Let's take a look at the starburst on the cover of the magazine, and then edit the shape we create with the Direct Selection tool.

Double-clicking the Polygon Frame or Polygon tool when a polygon frame is selected allows you to edit the polygon settings for the frame. You can even convert a nonpolygon or star-shaped frame into a polygon shape this way.

To create a star with the Polygon Frame tool (⊗):

1   Double-click the Polygon Frame tool, to show the Polygon Settings dialog box.

2   Enter the Number of Sides (number of points the star will have).

3   Enter the Star Inset percentage, and click OK.

4   With the Polygon Frame tool still selected, drag across the page to create the starburst.

5   You can adjust the size further by entering values in the Width and Height fields in the Control panel, or by dragging one of the frame handles.

You can also create a starburst with the Polygon tool (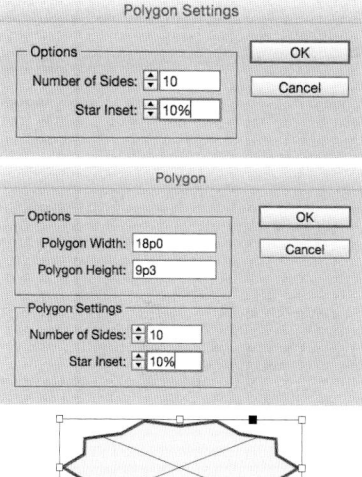) (**Figure 3.37**):

1 Select the Polygon tool.

2 Clicking anywhere on the page to display the Polygon dialog box.

3 Enter the Polygon Width and Polygon Height settings, as well as the Number of Sides and Star Inset amounts, and click OK.

To edit a star shape with the Direct Selection tool (**Figure 3.38**):

1 First, make sure nothing is selected (Edit > Deselect All).

2 Move the Direct Selection tool over the starburst; the anchor points become visible.

3 Click an anchor point to select it, and drag the point to a new position.

4 Repeat step 3 for other anchor points you want to reposition.

5 Click anywhere outside the starburst to deselect it, or choose Edit > Deselect All.

Similar to moving an anchor point, you can move line segments by clicking on a line and dragging it. You can also adjust the direction and length of direction lines by clicking an anchor point to display the direction line, then dragging the direction point (**Figure 3.39**).

Figure 3.37 Creating a starburst with the Polygon tool

TIP

When working with groups, the Direct Selection tool also allows you to select individual items within a group and edit them without the need to ungroup the group first.

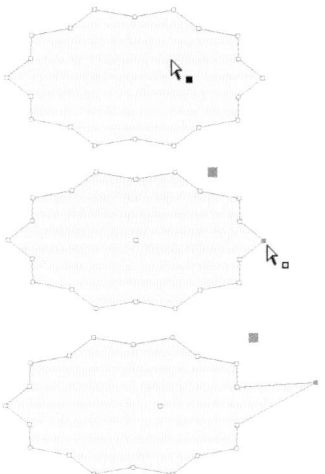

Figure 3.38 Changing a starburst shape by moving anchor points with the Direct Selection tool

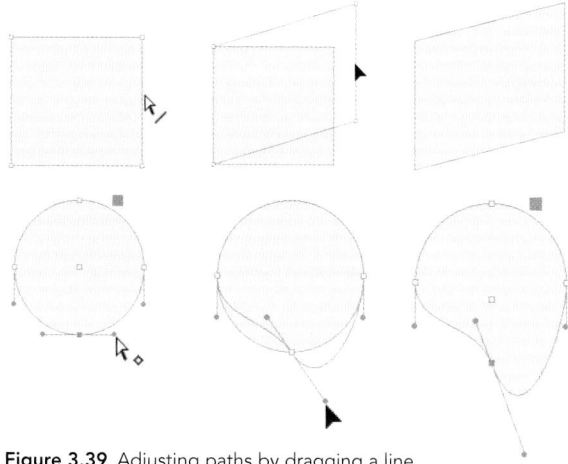

Figure 3.39 Adjusting paths by dragging a line segment or direction point

Adding Transparency and Effects

▶ Video 3.8

▶ Video 3.10

In InDesign, you can apply a wide range of transparency effects to design elements. You can apply effects to text or any object (text frame, graphic frame, and so on). The effects range from simply bringing the opacity level down on a filled object, so that objects below become (partially) visible, to applying creative effects such as drop shadows, embossing, or feathering. In addition, you can adjust the way in which overlapping colors interact with each other by changing their blending modes.

Transparency

★ ACA Objective 3.6

The easiest way to add transparency to your designs is to adjust the opacity levels of an object. Objects with **opacity** set to 100% are nontransparent. As you lower the opacity amount, the object becomes see-through, and anything below the object starts to show.

To change an object's opacity (**Figure 3.40**):

1 Select an Object with the Selection tool.

2 In the Control panel, drag the Opacity slider or enter an opacity amount.

Another way to change the opacity level:

1 Show the Effects panel (Window > Effects).

2 Drag the Opacity slider or enter an opacity amount.

Figure 3.40 Changing the opacity level of the yellow frame to 60% reveals the purple background image.

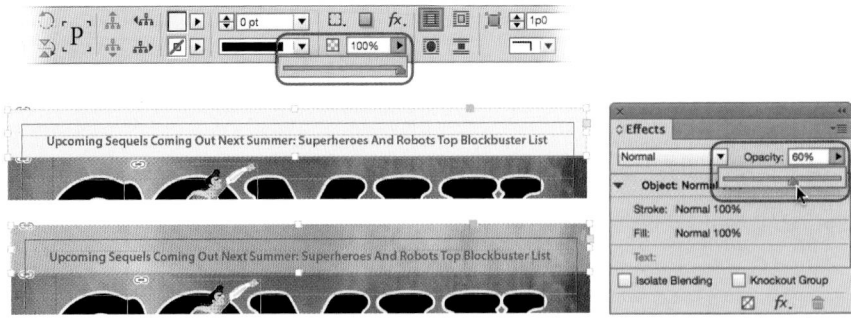

Blending Modes

A blending mode is another way to make overlapping objects and colors interact. As you work on your designs, experiment with different blending modes. They are fun, and you might discover some surprisingly stunning results. Take a look at some blending mode examples applied to the top photo in **Figure 3.41** and notice how the colors of the photo interact with the purple background.

★ ACA Objective 3.6

- *Multiply* takes the color of the object and fully mixes it with the colors below, making the overall appearance darker.

- *Screen* does the opposite of Multiply, making the colors appear lighter.

- *Overlay* tries to preserve dark and light colors while at the same time mixing the color with the colors underneath.

- *Lighten* blends darker colors into the background, almost making them disappear while retaining the lighter colors. How cool is this effect?

- *Luminosity* works well when you overlay a color image over a background that contains shades of one color. The image will take on a sepia tone appearance, using the underlying color to create the different shades and tones in the image. **Sepia tones** are similar to what you see in black-and-white photos. Instead of representing the different shades of gray in the picture with black tones, in this case the image appears in different shades of a reddish-brown color.

Figure 3.41 Some examples of blending modes applied to the photo of Stanley, the man on the cover

Normal **Multiply** **Screen** **Overlay** **Lighten** **Luminosity**

To apply a blending mode to an object (**Figure 3.42**):

1 Select the object.

2 In the Blending Mode menu in the Effects panel, change the mode from Normal to one of the available modes.

3 Alternatively, choose Object > Effects > Transparency, and select the Mode under Basic Blending. Select Preview to see the different modes in action.

Figure 3.42 Changing the blending mode for a selected object

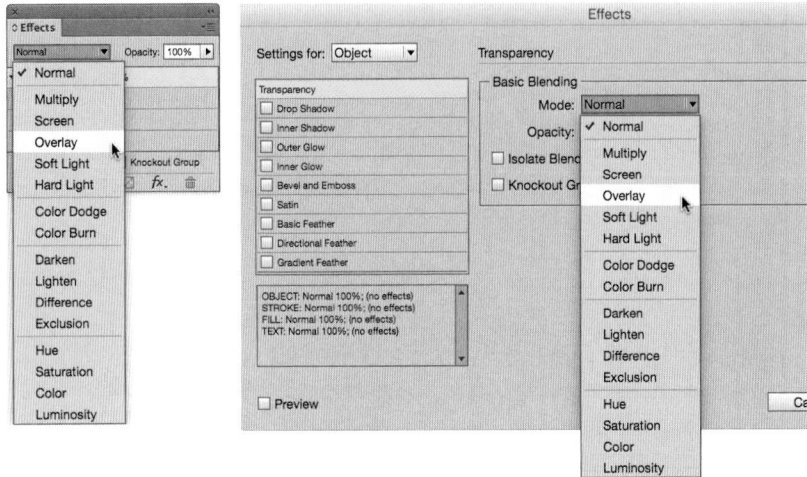

Effects

★ *ACA Objective 3.6*

★ *ACA Objective 4.4*

InDesign offers a series of super-cool effects you can apply to objects: drop shadows, outer glow, and so much more.

To apply an effect (**Figure 3.43**):

1 Show the Effects panel (Window > Effects).

2 Select a page element, such as an image.

3 At the bottom of the Effects panel, click the *fx* button to access the effects menu.

4 Select an effect to apply.

5 Modify settings in the Effects dialog box to fine-tune the effect.

6 Select another effect from the list at left, and fine-tune that effect.

7 Apply as many effects as you want, then click OK.

In the Effects panel, a small fx appears to the right of the component that has an effect applied to it. Double-clicking the *fx* icon lets you modify the effect.

You can also apply effects using options in the Control panel or by choosing Object > Effects (**Figure 3.44**).

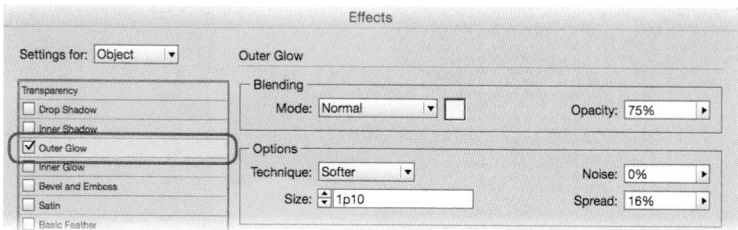

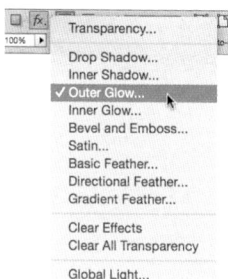

Figure 3.43 Applying an outer-glow effect to the image on the cover

When you select an object, the transparency effects apply to the object's frame as well as its contents. This might not be what you want. For example, what if you only want to apply the effect to the fill color of a text frame, and not to the text itself?

To apply a transparency effect, such as a blending mode, to a specific component (**Figure 3.45**):

1   Select the object.

2   In the Effects panel, click the component (such as Stroke or Fill) to apply the effect to. Alternatively, choose Object > Effects > Transparency, and select the component from the Settings For menu.

The components vary depending on the type of object selected. For a text frame, you would see Object, Fill, Stroke, or Text settings.

3   Apply the blending mode, opacity, or effect settings, and click OK.

Figure 3.44 Applying effects from the Control panel

> **NOTE**   *You cannot apply an effect to a selected range of characters in a text frame.*

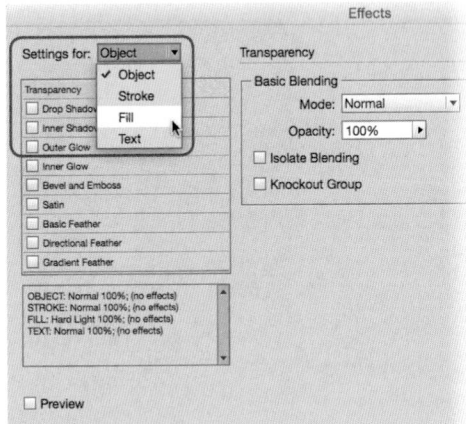

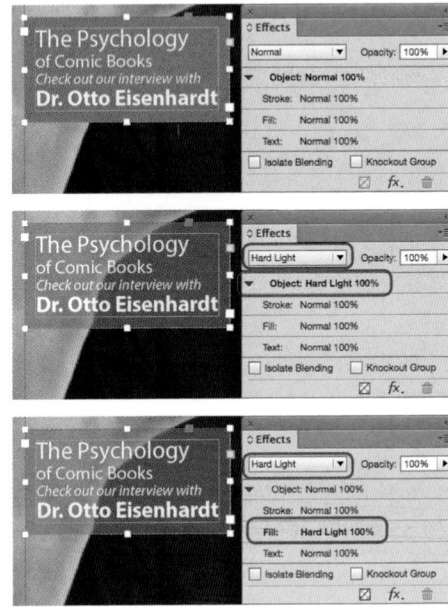

Figure 3.45 In this case, when you apply a blending mode to an object, the text color becomes a mixed white/yellow color. Applying the blending mode only to the fill retains the yellow text color.

Figure 3.46 Removing all effects and transparency settings from a selected object

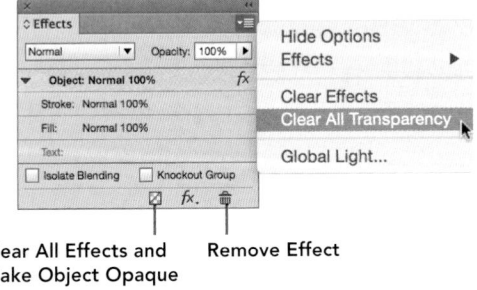

Clear All Effects and Make Object Opaque **Remove Effect**

TIP

The Effects panel menu and the Objects > Effects submenu both include the Clear commands.

At times, you might decide that the opacity change, blending mode, and/or effects applied to an element in a design just doesn't work as you envisioned. Luckily, there is a quick way to remove the applied settings (**Figure 3.46**).

- To remove all effects from the selected object, including blending mode and opacity changes, click the Clear All Effects And Make Object Opaque button at the bottom of the Effects panel.

- To remove only the applied effects and retain blending mode and opacity changes from the selected object, click the Remove Effect button at the bottom of the Effects panel.

To learn more about each of the different blending modes or effects, refer to the InDesign Help.

Preflight and Packaging
for Print Delivery

In the previous chapter, you learned how to convert your InDesign file to a press-ready PDF and submit this to your printer. As important as it is to create amazingly beautiful and eye-catching designs that wow your client, it is just as important to make sure that the finished InDesign documents you create meet the delivery requirements for its intended media.

▶ Video 3.14

Preflight

InDesign has a built-in Preflight feature that enables you to check your documents against delivery requirements as you work, as well as prior to handing the files to your printer or service provider for final processing. Ensuring your documents meet delivery requirements helps prevent costly changes. For example, let's say that after you send a project to the printer, you discover one of the text frames in your job is missing a line of text. The problem is that the line became overset while you made some last-minute changes. You could be saddled with extra costs for reprinting the corrected version.

★ ACA Objective 5.1

Preflight, which is enabled by default, would highlight this error. The feature flags any document errors in the status bar, so you can fix them in time to avoid extra costs and angry clients (**Figure 3.47**).

As another layer of safety, InDesign automatically checks a document for missing or modified links, as well as missing fonts, when you open the file. If issues exist, a warning dialog box appears (**Figure 3.48**).

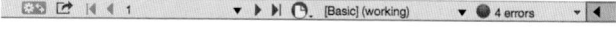

Figure 3.47 With Preflight enabled, the status bar lists any errors in the document.

HANDLING MISSING OR MODIFIED LINKS

When you click Update Links in the warning dialog box, any links that have been modified (such as graphics that were edited) will automatically update. For any missing links, you'll be prompted to find a graphic to relink to. If you click Don't Update Links, you can use the Links panel to manage any modified or missing links later.

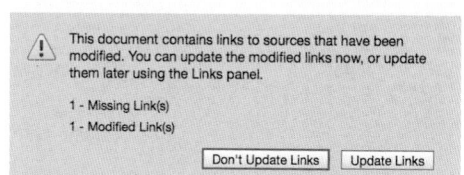

Figure 3.48 The missing and modified links warning that can display when opening an InDesign document

HANDLING MISSING FONTS

After the links warning, an additional missing fonts dialog box might appear (**Figure 3.49**). This dialog box lists any fonts used in the document's design that are not available on your system.

Missing fonts available through Adobe Typekit are easily added to your system:

1 Select Sync to the right of the font name.

2 Click Sync Fonts.

3 Click Close when all the fonts have been synchronized on your system.

For fonts that continue to be missing, it is preferred that you obtain the fonts and install them on your system. This ensures that the typographical choices in the design are preserved. However, if you are unable to obtain the fonts, the only alternative would be to replace the missing fonts with similar-looking fonts that you do have access to.

To replace missing fonts (**Figure 3.50**):

1 Click Find Fonts.

2 In the Find Font dialog box, select the missing font.

3 Select a replacement Font Family and Font Style under Replace With.

4 Select Redefine Style When Changing All to ensure that missing fonts referenced by paragraph styles and character styles are also updated.

5 Click Change All, and click Done when all font issues have been resolved.

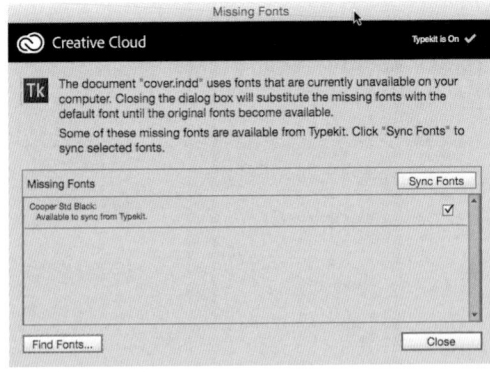

Figure 3.49 The Missing Fonts dialog box

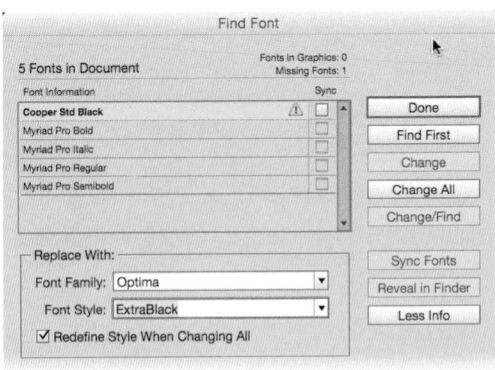

Figure 3.50 The Find Font dialog box; Cooper Std Black is being replaced with Optima ExtraBlack.

USING PREFLIGHT

Let's take a closer look at Preflight.

To enable or disable Preflight (**Figure 3.51**):

- Select Preflight Document from the Preflight menu in the status bar.

When you turn on Preflight, your document is automatically checked against a particular preflight profile. Any errors will be flagged in the status bar. A preflight profile contains all the criteria against which your document is compared. By default, InDesign uses the Basic profile, which checks for the following common issues:

- Missing or modified links.
- Missing fonts.
- Overset text.
- Hyperlinks to web addresses.
- Live captions.

NOTE

Live captions are automatically generated captions that use information (metadata) available in the image to populate the caption text. If the metadata for the image changes, the live caption will require updating.

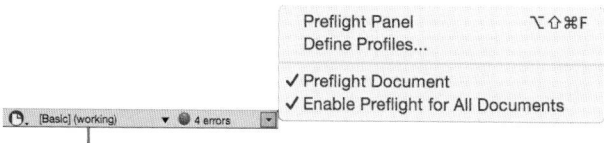

Preflight Profile

Figure 3.51 The status bar with Preflight enabled

The status bar will indicate if your document contains any errors. To find out more about those errors, the types of errors, where they occur in your document, and how to fix them (**Figure 3.52**):

1. First, open the Preflight panel. To do this, double-click an error listed in the status bar, choose Window > Output > Preflight, or select Preflight Panel from the menu in the status bar. The Preflight panel lists any errors in the document.

2. Click the disclosure triangle to the left of the error type, and continue to click the subsequent arrows to drill down until you see the exact error with a page reference link on the right.

3. To navigate to an object in your document that has a particular issue, click the page link to the right of the error.

4. To see information about the problem and suggestions on how to fix it, select the problem in the errors list and click the disclosure triangle to the left of Info.

Figure 3.52 The Preflight panel with errors listed (left) and all errors fixed (right)

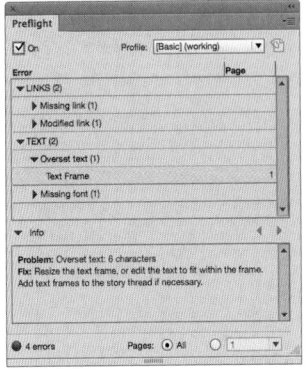 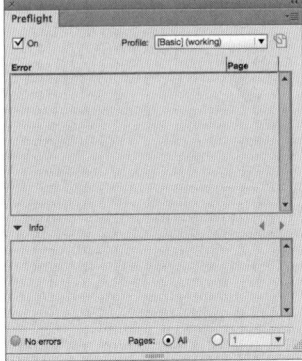

5   With the help of the Preflight panel, fix all the errors it has flagged.

As you fix errors, they are removed from the Preflight panel. Once all the errors are fixed the Preflight panel, the status bar will list No Errors.

Your printer or service provider might supply you with a preflight profile to check your documents against. This helps ensure that your documents meet their specific press and print requirements, such as a minimum resolution of 300 ppi (pixels per inch) for placed images or an exact bleed size.

To load a custom preflight profile and use it to check your document (**Figure 3.53**):

1   Choose Window > Output > Preflight.

2   Choose Define Profiles from Preflight panel menu.

3   In the Preflight Profiles dialog box, choose Load Profile from Preflight Profile menu.

4   Navigate to the IDPP (InDesign Preflight Profile) file, double-click it, and click OK to return to the Preflight panel.

5   Select the Profile, and close the Preflight panel.

Figure 3.53 Loading a custom preflight profile

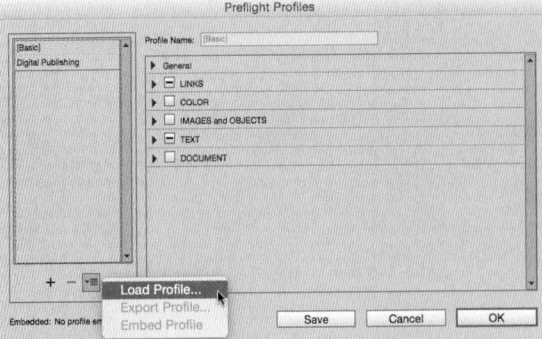 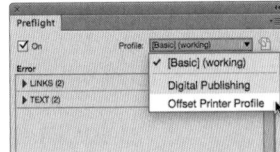

In Chapter 2, you learned that pixel-based images depend on resolution measured in pixels per inch (*ppi*) for their quality. Image-resolution requirements vary depending on the intent of your document. The resolution requirement for print media, for example, is higher than for web or digital media.

SELECTING RESOLUTION FOR PRINT MEDIA

To produce the various shades, tints, and gradients, commercial printers use a screening process. In web (newspaper) and offset printing, a unique plate is created for each of the primary CMYK colors and spot colors in your design. In addition, the different tints for each color are converted to larger and smaller dots, each spaced an equal distance apart within an invisible grid. A cluster of larger dots appears as a dark tint, and a group of smaller dots as a lighter shade of that color (**Figure 3.54**). When printers refer to the *screen* or *line frequency*, they refer to the grid distance within which the dots of ink are placed. Line frequency is referenced as *lines per inch* (*lpi*).

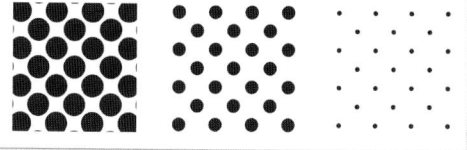

Figure 3.54 Printing different colors through screening. Printing larger and smaller dots to visualize tints for each print color

continues on next page

continued from previous page

For different types of paper, the line frequency will vary. For example, for newspaper printing, a lower line frequency is used, placing the dots farther apart so that, due to the ink absorbancy of the paper, the dots don't merge together. In a glossy magazine, those dots are much closer together.

The recommended image resolution (ppi) for a print job is generally two times the lpi value.

- Newspapers use a line frequency of 85–100 lpi, which means the image resolution would be 170–200 ppi.

- For magazines printed on coated paper, the line frequency would be 150–175 lpi, so the image resolution would need to be 300–350 ppi.

As an exercise, find a printing company near you and visit its website. Most printing companies will list their image resolution and other print specific requirements on their websites. As you start producing designs for print media, always consult with your printer about any specific output requirements it has.

SELECTING RESOLUTION FOR WEB AND DIGITAL MEDIA

For publications that are viewed onscreen, the norm is to focus on the screen width and height, ensuring that your images contain that amount of pixels (using 72 ppi as a base resolution). However, as more and more people today have high-resolution screens, 144 ppi images produce a crisper and more detailed view on those screens. For eBooks and digital publishing, 150 ppi is the recommended minimum resolution.

Keep in mind that the higher the image resolution is, the bigger the file size. So if file size is a contributing factor when producing a digital magazine or an eBook that is downloaded to a device, reducing the resolution could help. Be sure to maintain an acceptable quality, though.

Packaging Files for the Printer

★ *ACA Objective 5.1*

Packaging an InDesign document collects the InDesign file and related files into a single folder that you supply to the printer or service provider. Can you think of some of the files you would need to submit to a commercial printer? What are the things a printer would need to be able to print your InDesign file?

For someone to print your document, they would need to have (at least) the InDesign document itself, all of the linked graphics and images, as well as the fonts.

To package the InDesign document and related files (**Figure 3.55**):

1 Choose File > Package.

The Package dialog box provides a summary that lists any issues with your files. In other words, it performs its own little mini-preflight check.

2 To see any problems, click the categories on the left. Select Show Problems Only to see any issues listed.

The Fonts category and the Links and Images category provide you with buttons to fix issues. The Fonts tab contains a Find Font button for Typekit font synchronizing or font replacement. The Links and Images tab has an Update button to update modified links and a Repair All button that updates modified links and prompts you to relink any missing links.

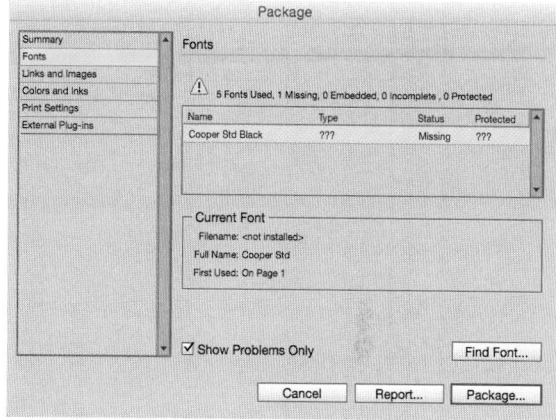

Figure 3.55 The Font category in Package dialog box indicates any missing fonts.

3 Click Package, and fill out the Printing Instructions dialog box.

4 Click Continue, and enter the name of the folder you want to save to, and navigate to the save location. Select all of the files to include (**Figure 3.56**).

Ensure that at least the Copy Fonts, Copy Linked Graphics, and Update Graphic Links In Package options are selected. A Links and Document fonts folder is added to the package folder, and the links in the packaged InDesign file will point to the new Links folder.

If your printer doesn't have the same copy of InDesign as you do, select Include IDML. IDML (InDesign Markup Language) provides backward compatibility with earlier versions of InDesign. An IDML document can be opened in InDesign CS4 or later. You can also include a press-ready PDF, select Include PDF (Print), and then select the PDF Preset.

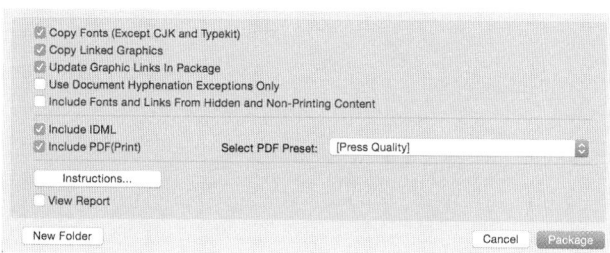

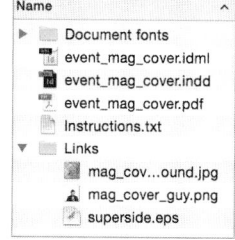

Figure 3.56 Package the InDesign document and related files so they are ready to hand off to your printer or service provider.

5   When you're finished with the specifications, click Package. If a warning about copying fonts appears, click OK.

The primary reason for using the Package command is to deliver a complete set of files to a printer or service provider. The Package command also provides you with a great way to archive your documents and designs. Whenever you get a repeat job or need to create a new edition of a document, it will be good to have all the components you need in one folder.

Creating Alternate Layouts

★ ACA Objective 3.1

★ ACA Objective 4.1

▶ Video 3.13

Alternate layouts, along with liquid page rules, let you create different layout versions of an original layout you created in InDesign. These features retain links to the parent layout, which means that text, design, and other changes made in the parent layout can automatically ripple through the alternate layouts (the child pages). Alternate layouts can work well in a number of scenarios:

- A single advertisement design might need to be delivered to different publications at varying sizes, always containing the same text and images.
- A print publication, such as a magazine, might need to be redesigned for digital publishing to an iPad or other tablet devices.
- Brochures for an international company with branches in the United States and Europe might need to be supplied in two different standard page sizes: US Letter as well as metric A4.

NOTE

You'll put liquid layouts to work when creating the recipe book in Project 5.

Alternate layouts can retain links to the original layout text, images, and formatting. When editing content in the original layout, the Links panel allows you to update the linked content in the alternate layouts.

When creating an alternate layout, liquid page rules control how objects on pages are resized or repositioned as new pages, with different orientation or page size, for the alternate layout are created. You can apply a single layout rule to all pages of the document, or apply different layout rules for different pages. This way, InDesign gives you the ability to apply the rules that work best for the various pages of your document.

To set different layout rules for different pages (**Figure 3.57**):

1   Show the Liquid Layout panel (Window > Interactive).

2   Select the Liquid Page Rule for the active page.

A number of different techniques can be used to build an alternate layout:

- **Scale:** Retains original layout, but scales it so that it fits on the new layout size.

- **Re-center:** Retains original layout size and centers this in the new layout size.

- **Guide-based:** Resizes objects within the layout based on their interaction with liquid guides.

- **Object-based:** Resizes objects relative to their position on the page. Objects may be anchored to particular page positions.

The Object-Based Liquid Page Rule allows you to determine, for each object on the page, how it is resized or positioned as a result of a page-size change. For example, the masthead can be kept at the top of the page, the purple background can be automatically resized to fit the new page size, and the cover lines can remain on the left side of the page.

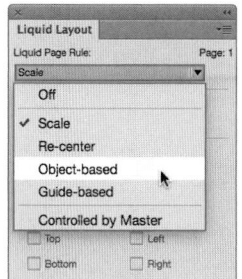

Figure 3.57 Selecting a liquid layout rule for an active page

To work with object-based liquid layout rules (**Figure 3.58**):

1 Show the Liquid Layout panel (Window > Interactive > Liquid Layout).

2 Select an object on the page with the Selection tool.

3 Change the Liquid Page Rule to Object-based in the Liquid Layout panel.

4 Set the Object Constraints.

5 Repeat this process for all the objects on the page.

> **TIP** *When repurposing a print layout to a page size for the web or digital publishing, consider changing the default units of measurement to pixels. Right-click (Windows) or Control-click (Mac OS) at the intersection of the horizontal and vertical rulers and choose pixels. This makes setting the new page size easier.*

Figure 3.58 Setting an Object-based page rule to the masthead of the magazine

To create an alternate layout (**Figure 3.59**):

1 Select Create Alternate Layout from the Pages panel menu, or choose Layout > Create Alternate Layout.

2 Name the new layout.

3 Set the Page Size and Orientation.

4 Set the following options:

- Select a rule from the Liquid Page Rule menu. For example, to apply the liquid layout rules you set for pages with the Liquid Layout panel, choose Preserve Existing.

- Select *Link Stories* to link text to the original layout text.

- Select *Copy Text Styles to New Style Group* to create a second set of styles for the new layout. This allows you to adjust font sizes across alternate layouts more easily. (We'll cover styles in detail in Chapter 5.)

Figure 3.59 An alternate layout for a landscape iPad design created using object-based liquid layout page rules with some final manual changes to complete the new layout

 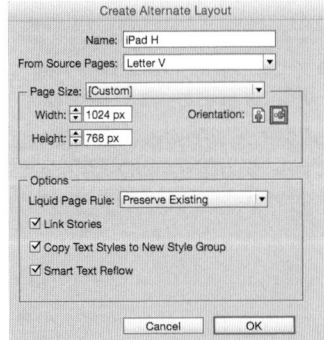 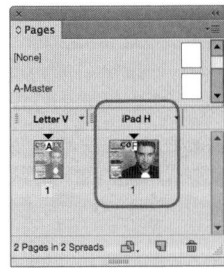

Parent layout (Letter V)

Alternate layout for landscape iPad design created with object-based rules

Some content manually repositioned and resized

- Select *Smart Text Reflow* to automatically increase/decrease the number of pages for the new layout. This is a setting more commonly used when reflowing book content.

5 Click OK to create the alternate layout. When completed, the new pages are added to the Pages panel.

The idea behind creating the alternate layout is to get the best possible result. You'll still need to resize and reposition some content, especially when moving from a portrait to a landscape layout, but it's definitely a lot less work than starting from scratch for each individual layout.

As you make edits to the parent layout, the Links panel will indicate some of the content in the alternate layouts as modified with the yellow warning triangle. With the document pages viewed in Normal screen mode and Link Badges enabled (View > Extras > Show Link Badge), the child objects also display a modified warning.

To update the child layouts (**Figure 3.60**):

- From the Links panel menu, select Update All Links.

With that you've completed your second project. You are well on your way to being a professional designer. Well done!

Figure 3.60 Make changes to the parent layout, so that you can easily update the alternate layouts.

CHAPTER OBJECTIVES

Chapter Learning Objectives

- Create a multicolumn layout.
- Add master items to master pages.
- Apply master pages to document pages.
- Work with spot colors.
- Use dummy text to create a design proposal.
- Thread stories across multiple pages.
- Wrap text around images.
- Add form elements.
- Create an interactive PDF form.

Chapter ACA Objectives

For full descriptions of objectives, download the printable chart from your account on *peachpit.com*. See pages xi–xii.

DOMAIN 2.0
UNDERSTANDING PRINT AND DIGITAL MEDIA PUBLICATIONS
2.1, 2.4

DOMAIN 3.0
UNDERSTANDING ADOBE INDESIGN CC
3.4, 3.6, 3.8

DOMAIN 4.0
CREATING PRINT AND DIGITAL MEDIA PUBLICATIONS USING ADOBE INDESIGN
4.1, 4.2, 4.3, 4.4, 4.6

DOMAIN 5.0
PUBLISH, EXPORT, AND ARCHIVE PAGE LAYOUTS USING ADOBE INDESIGN
5.1, 5.2

CHAPTER 4

Designing a Magazine Layout

In this design project, you will put together a basic layout to present to your customer. Specifically, you will provide design and text formatting ideas for the editor's note pages, a subscription form that will be included as a foldout in the print version of the magazine, and an interactive form readers can fill out in the PDF version of the magazine. As part of this project you will be introduced to the concept of master pages, try additional paragraph formatting controls, and learn how to wrap text around images. Finally, you will gain an understanding of the various form elements used in PDF form designs (**Figure 4.1**).

Figure 4.1 Finished newsletter design

Foldout

Mastering a Multicolumn and Multipage Layout

▶ Video 4.1

NOTE

This chapter supports the project created in video lesson 4. Go to the Project 4 page in the book's Web Edition to watch the entire lesson from beginning to end.

Similar to the previous project, this project's primary output medium will be print. The magazine content is made up of photos, headlines, body copy, background tints, line, and form elements. The magazine example in this project is folded to a finished portrait Letter size (8.5 in by 11 in). The magazine is designed with facing pages (left and right pages), and text appears in three columns. Additionally, its cover and some of its content design contains images and background color frames that extend to the edge of the page.

NOTE *The most commonly used magazine or newsletter size in the US is 8 3/8 in x 10 7/8 in.*

Given this briefing, what settings would you select in the New Document dialog box (File > New > Document)?

Here are some of the settings (**Figure 4.2**):

- **Intent:** Print. This sets the document's default color mode to CMYK.

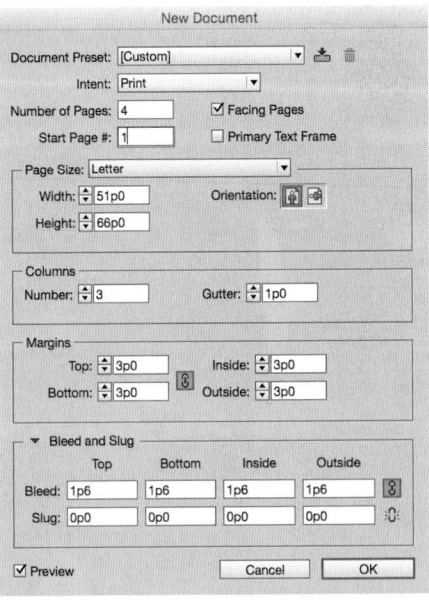

Figure 4.2 Creating a four-page, facing-page document with a bleed to start your magazine design

- **Facing Pages:** Select Facing Pages to create a document with spreads (left and right pages side by side). Notice that with facing pages enabled, the Left and Right margin fields change to Inside and Outside. The inside margin is the margin that appears on either side of the spine, where the magazine is bound. The outside margin is the margin that appears on the edge where there is no binding (**Figure 4.3**).

- **Number Of Pages:** Magazines are multipage documents. Start with four pages and add more pages as needed during the production phase (Layout > Pages > Add Page, or Insert Pages).

- **Page Size and Orientation:** Select Letter from the Page Size menu and click the Portrait icon for Orientation.

- **Columns:** Enter 3 for the number of columns. With the Screen Mode set to Normal, the column guides assist with consistent and easy placement of design elements.

- **Bleed:** If necessary, click the Bleed And Slug disclosure triangle. Enter values in the Bleed fields. If you're not sure what to enter, ask the printer. As you design, make sure that any objects you intend to bleed extend off the page to the bleed guide.

Once the new document opens in InDesign, you can start to add layers and color swatches as needed.

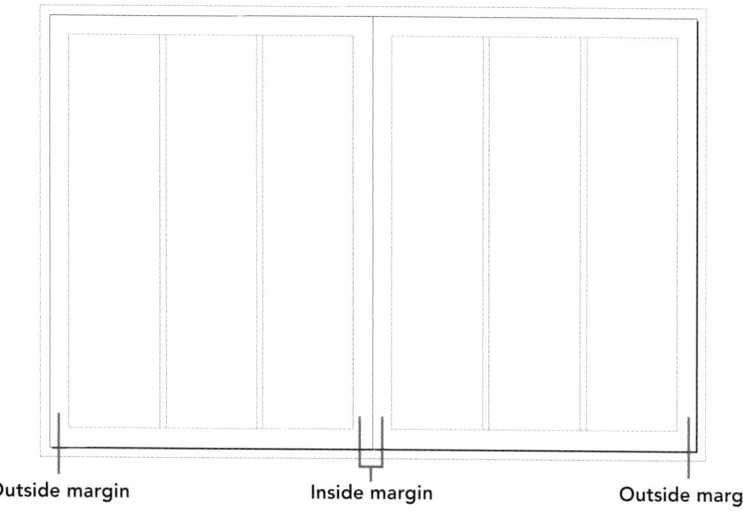

Figure 4.3 Inside and outside margins on a facing-pages spread

Outside margin   Inside margin   Outside margin

Understanding Master Pages

Master pages apply common design elements, also called master items, across the pages of your document. This saves you the time of adding those elements to each page individually, ensures consistency, and provides an easy method for making global changes across a document.

If you have a magazine or other multipage publication nearby, flip through the pages. Can you spot common design elements or layout features? What design elements appear repeatedly across multiple pages in a report or book layout?

Page headers (the area above the top margin guide on a page) and footers (the area below the bottom margin guide) are areas on the page where you would position elements that repeat across different pages (**Figure 4.4**). For example:

- Each page in a report might include a company logo at the top or bottom of the page.
- The name of a publication might appear on the top or bottom of pages.
- A similar-colored sidebar might indicate different topic-related pages across a publication.
- Page numbers might appear at the bottom of magazine, book, or report pages.
- Navigation controls, such as next page and previous page buttons, might reside at the bottom of all pages in digital media publication.

The above are all examples of **master items**. You place any items you want to repeat on document pages on a master page. Then, when you apply that master page to document pages, the items are added to those document pages automatically.

Figure 4.4 A two-page spread of a magazine layout and the master page that was applied to add the red bars, header, and footer

Creating and Editing Master Pages

★ ACA Objective 4.1

▶ Video 4.2

▶ Video 4.3

When you create a new document, a blank document opens with one or more blank pages and a single master page or master spread (A-Master). This A-Master master page is applied to all empty pages and applies the original new document settings, such as the page size, orientation, margins, columns, and bleed settings. By adding master items to the A-Master, you can add common design elements and layout features to the document's pages.

To add master items to the A-Master, first display the master page:

- Double-click the A-Master label at the top of the Pages panel.
- Select A-Master from the Go To Page menu in the Status bar.
- Choose Layout > Go To Page, and then select A-Master from the Page menu (**Figure 4.5**).

The A-Master page or spread now appears in the document window. You can now start to add common master items.

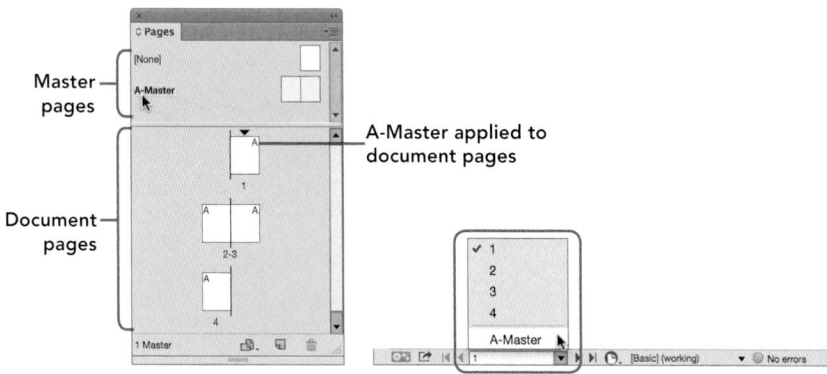

Master pages

A-Master applied to document pages

Document pages

Figure 4.5 Display the A-Master in the document window to start adding master items to the page.

A special page number marker is often the first master item you add to a master page, especially for longer documents, such as books, reports, or magazines.

To add a current page number marker (**Figure 4.6**):

1. Using the Type tool, draw a text frame on the A-Master page, in the footer area, and click inside the frame.

2. Choose Type > Insert Special Character > Markers > Current Page Number.

   The special page number marker that is inserted appears as the letter A, matching the prefix of the master page. A page number on a B-Master would thus appear as the letter B.

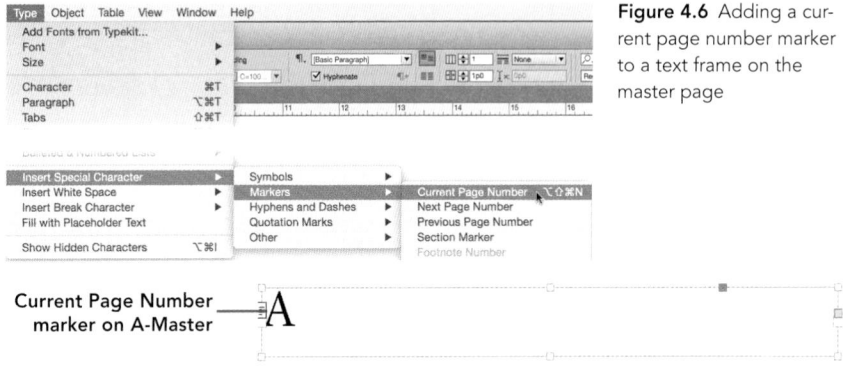

Figure 4.6 Adding a current page number marker to a text frame on the master page

Current Page Number marker on A-Master

3 Format the page number marker as you would format any other text, changing font, font size, alignment, etc.

4 To return to a document page and see the page number appear, double-click a document page in the Pages panel, or choose Layout > Go To Page and select a page number from the Page menu.

To add header or footer text to a master page:

■ Use the Type tool to add a text frame, then enter and format the header or footer text on the master page. You can also insert text before or after the current page number marker (**Figure 4.7**).

Continue to add and format additional master items to the master page as needed.

Figure 4.7 A left-facing page that contains a text frame for the footer, which consists of text and the current page number marker

★ *ACA Objective 4.1*

▶ *Video 4.4*

ADDING MULTIPLE MASTER PAGES

Documents are not limited to a single master page or master spread. For example, in a magazine layout, you might use three-column and four-column layouts. There are several ways to add additional master pages to a document.

To create a new master page (**Figure 4.8**):

1 Choose New Master from the Pages panel menu.

2 Enter the Prefix and Name for the new master.

The master page prefix appears on the document pages in the Pages panel, making it easy to recognize which master page is applied to the pages.

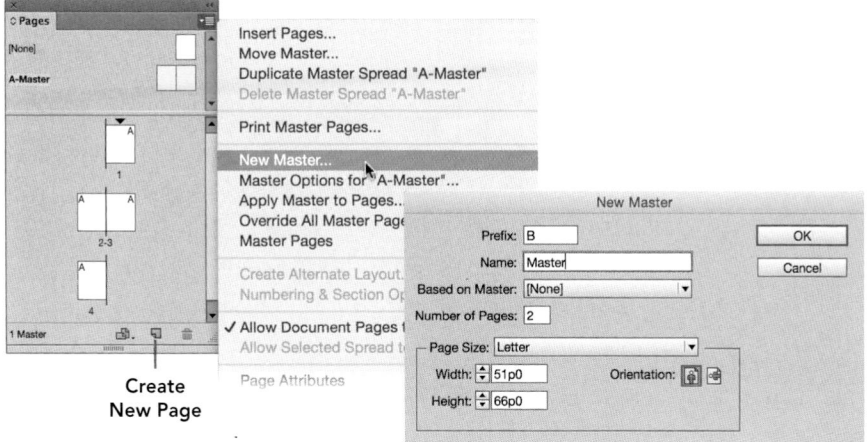

Figure 4.8 Adding a new master page

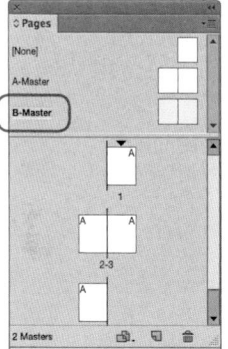

3   When you are creating a master page, you have the option of basing its formatting on an existing master page. This establishes a parent-child relationship between the two pages. To do this, select the parent page from the Based on Master menu.

Basing a new master page on another master means that the new (child) page inherits the master items from the existing (parent) master page. For example, you might consider creating a master page with just the page numbers on it. This master page could be the base for other master pages that might have different margin and column settings and design elements added. If you want to change the font of the page numbers, you only need to edit them on the parent master page.

4   Specify how many pages you need in the Number Of Pages setting.

5   Set the Page Size and Orientation parameters. Click OK.

You can also create a new blank master page by first selecting any master page and clicking the Create New Page button at the bottom of the Pages panel. The new master page uses the same margin and column settings as used in the New Document dialog box at the start of creating a project.

DUPLICATING MASTER PAGES

You can duplicate an existing master page to serve as the basis for a new master page. To duplicate a master page (**Figure 4.9**):

1   Select the master page to duplicate in the Pages panel.

Figure 4.9 Creating a new master page by duplicating an existing master page

TIP

To create a new master page that copies a document page design, select the document page in the Pages panel, and then select Master Pages > Save As Master from the Master panel menu.

2   Select Duplicate Master Spread "A-Master" from the Pages panel menu. Note that when the selected master page is actually a facing-pages spread, the command changes from Duplicate Master Page to Duplicate Master Spread.

An exact replica of the A-Master, a new B-Master, appears in the Pages panel.

3   To change the Prefix (B) or the Name (Master), select the new master page in the Pages panel. Select Master Options from the Pages panel menu, make any changes, and click OK.

4   Double-click the master page name at the top of the Pages panel to modify the layout of the new master page.

You can also duplicate a master page by dragging an existing master onto the Create New Page button at the bottom of the Pages panel.

Putting Master Pages to Work

With the master pages completed, you can start work on your design project. As you work on the document pages in your project, you'll apply master pages to them, insert or delete document pages to the document, and perhaps edit or delete a master item on a document page to make an isolated change that doesn't warrant editing the master page.

APPLYING MASTER PAGES

SHORTCUT

To select a continuous range of pages in the Pages panel, click the first page in the range, then Shift-click the last page in the range. To select noncontiguous pages, Ctrl-click (Windows) or Command-click (Mac OS) the page icons.

When master pages are applied to document pages, the prefix letter (A for A-Master, for example) appears on the page thumbnail in the Pages panel. This makes it easy to see which master page is applied to a document page.

To apply a master page to a document page (**Figure 4.10**):

1   In the Pages panel, select the document pages for applying the master page.

2   Select Apply Master To Pages from the Pages panel menu.

3   In the Apply Master dialog box, select a master to apply to the document page from the Apply Master menu.

4   Click OK.

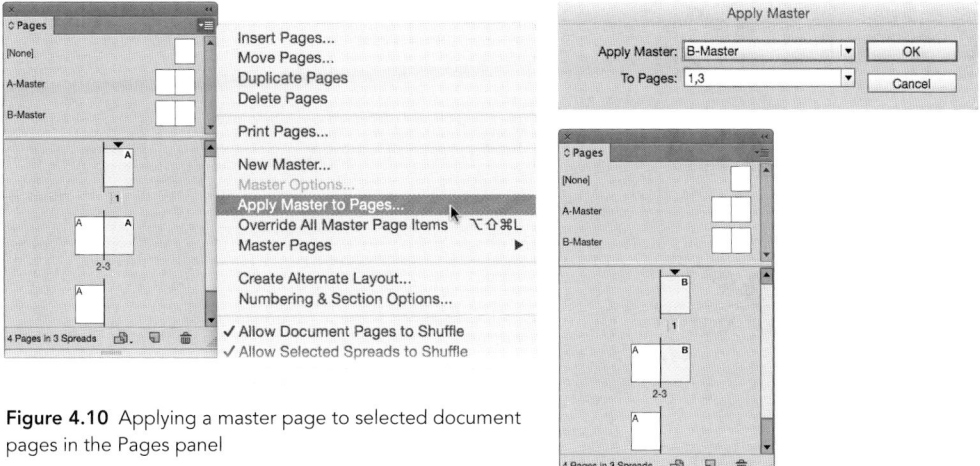

Figure 4.10 Applying a master page to selected document pages in the Pages panel

ADDING PAGES BASED ON MASTER PAGES

To add a new page after a particular page in the document:

1   In the Pages panel, select the page you want to add a page after.

2   Choose Layout > Pages > Add Page, or click the Create New Page button at the bottom of the Pages panel.

The new page will have the same master page as the selected page.

Another way to add a new page is to:

▪   Click the Create New Page button at the bottom of the Pages panel.

To add pages to any location in your document (**Figure 4.11**):

1   Choose Layout > Pages > Insert Pages or select Insert Pages from the Pages panel menu.

The Insert Pages dialog box enables you to add new pages before or after a particular page number, or at the start or end of the document.

2   Enter the number of pages to add in the Pages field. (Later in this chapter we'll talk about what can happen to a facing-pages document when you add an odd number of pages.)

3   Select an option from the Insert menu to specify where to add the pages. If you select After Page or Before Page, you can enter a page number in the field at right.

Figure 4.11 Adding one or more pages and applying a master page

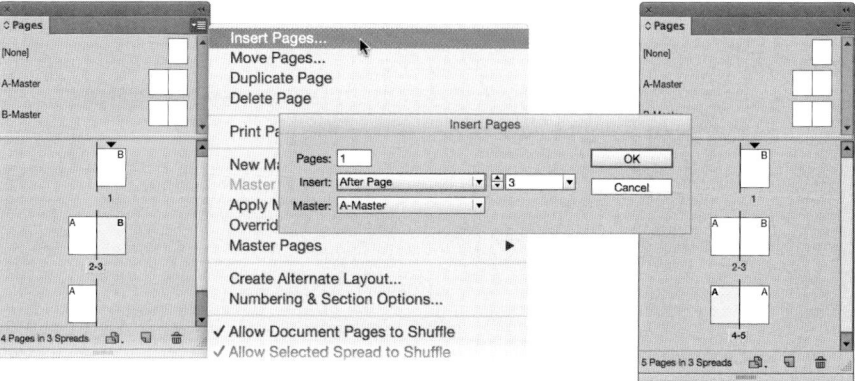

4 Select a master page or master spread to apply to the new pages from the Master menu.

5 Click OK to add the pages. If you happen to add the pages in the wrong place, you can immediately press Ctrl+Z (Windows) or Command+Z (Mac OS) to remove the pages.

Another way to insert pages is to:

■ Alt-click (Windows) or Option-click (Mac OS) the Create New Page button at the bottom of the Page panel.

DELETING PAGES

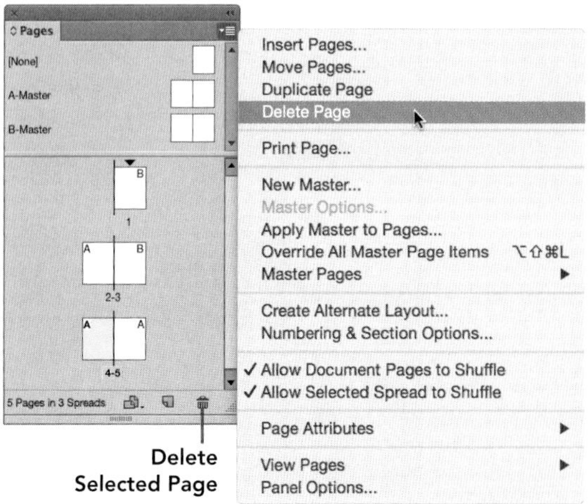

Figure 4.12 Deleting a selected page

As easy as it is to add new pages to a document, you can also delete pages or page spreads from your document.

To delete document pages (**Figure 4.12**):

1 Select the pages to delete in the Pages panel.

2 Choose Delete Page from the Pages panel menu, click the Delete Selected Pages button at the bottom of the Pages panel, or choose Layout > Pages > Delete Pages.

3 A warning dialog box appears if the page contains design elements. To delete the page and all of its content, click OK.

You can also delete pages by dragging the page icons onto the Delete Selected Pages button at the bottom of the Pages panel.

WORKING WITH MASTER ITEMS

When you're working on document pages, master items are recognizable by a thin dotted border when the Screen Mode is set to Normal. Master items on document pages are locked so they can't be accidentally edited. As you design your magazine pages, you will find that you occasionally need to edit master items. For example, a master page may add frames with a color tint to document pages. The managing editor's column in the magazine pages project is an example of this. For one instance of this column you decide you want to edit its color. Editing the master item on the master page would change it on all pages that have the master page applied to it. You can, however, override a master item. A master item override releases the master item on the document page so you can edit it. This converts the item to a document page item.

▶ *Video 4.5*

Keep in mind that any changes you make to the master item on the master page might no longer result in an update of the item on the document page. For example, if you change the fill color of the overridden item on the page, and later change the fill color of the master item, the color will not update on the document page with the override.

To override a master item on a document page (**Figure 4.13**):

1   Using the Selection tool, Shift-Ctrl-click (Windows) or Shift-Command-click (Mac OS) the master item.

2   Make any design changes to the object, such as text or color changes. You can also delete the object if needed.

> **TIP** *To retain the text formatting as you paste new text over formatted text, select the formatted text excluding the paragraph return character (¶) at the end of the paragraph. Then choose Edit > Paste Without Formatting. To see the end-of-paragraph characters, choose Type > Show Hidden Characters, and set the Screen Mode to Normal.*

> SUBJECT
> ## "Illaccatur? Perest offic tempore perrume ipienisto es et et eati berio elignimpor sit facil magnis"
> *Barry Garrick*

Figure 4.13 Shift-Ctrl-click (Windows) or Shift-Command-click (Mac OS) the quote's text frame (a master item). The master item becomes a standard page object, so you can replace the placeholder text for the quote with real text.

Using Different Page Sizes in a Single Document

As you add more pages to your magazine layout, each new page takes on the magazine page size (Letter) by default. InDesign allows you to use different page sizes in a single document. To do this, you will first need to make sure that pages in a facing-page document are not allowed to "shuffle."

★ *ACA Objective 4.1*

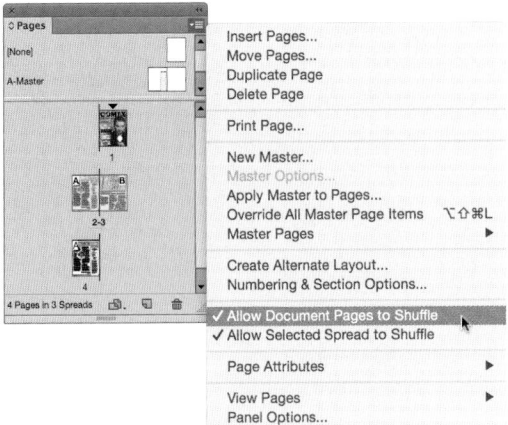

Figure 4.14 Deselecting the Allow Document Pages To Shuffle setting in the Pages panel prevents left pages from becoming right pages (and right pages from become left pages) when you insert or delete pages.

▶ *Video 4.15*

PREVENTING PAGES FROM SHUFFLING

When working in a document with facing pages, odd-numbered pages are on the right and even-numbered pages are on the left. When you insert an odd number of new pages, each subsequent page will change from a right to a left page and vice versa. This can possibly create some design dramas—for example, if you have applied a different master page to left and right pages or specifically positioned design elements so they balance nicely across a page spread.

Don't worry: You can change this default behavior and keep left and right pages in their original page positions when adding new pages to a document. To do so, simply ensure that the Allow Document Pages To Shuffle setting in the Pages panel menu is unchecked. Pages will still shuffle as you add more pages, but a left or right page will always remain a left or right page. Additionally, you can opt to keep entire page spreads together by selecting the spread in the Pages panel and unchecking the Allow Spreads To Shuffle from the Pages panel menu (**Figure 4.14**).

ADDING A FOLDOUT WITH A DIFFERENT PAGE SIZE

When Allow Document Pages To Shuffle is disabled as discussed in the previous section, you can add a foldout of a different size to a page spread without the other pages moving.

To adjust a page size for a page in the document (**Figure 4.15**):

1 Select the Page tool (⬚).

2 In the Pages panel, click the page icon of the page you want to resize. You can also click the page itself in the document window.

3 In the Control panel, change the values in the Width and/or Height fields for the selected page. Or, click the Edit Page Size button at the bottom of the Pages panel, choose Custom, enter the Width and Height settings in the Custom Page Size dialog box, and click OK.

> **TIP** You can save the foldout's page size as a reusable page size in the Custom Page Size dialog box. Enter a Name for the page size, and then click OK. Once you save a page size, you can select it from any Page Size menu, such as in the New Document dialog box.

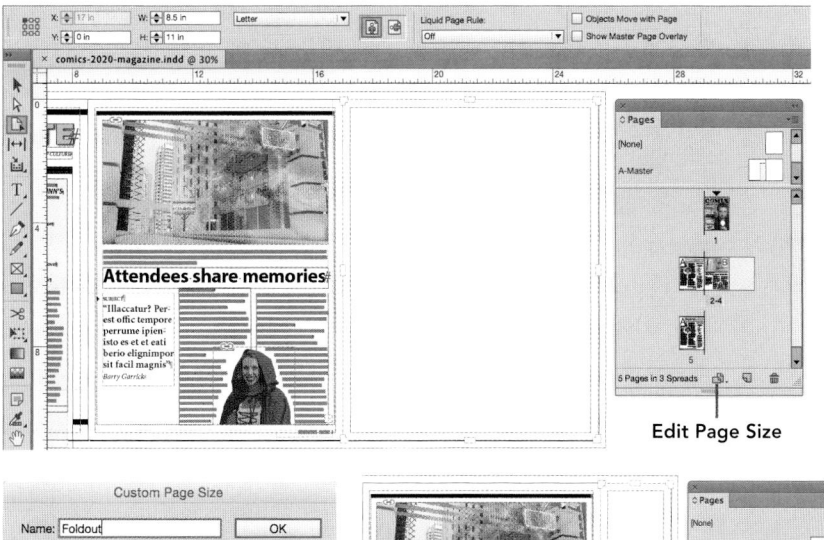

Figure 4.15 Changing the page size of a document page

Edit Page Size

Numbering and Sections

An InDesign section consists of one or more pages with different page numbering or designs. As you design different publications, such as magazines, books, and reports, you will likely encounter the need for page numbering sections.

▶ *Video 4.18*

- A printed magazine might have a cover that's printed on different paper from its inside pages. The cover itself might not require any page numbering; however, the first of the inside pages needs to start on page 1.

- The front matter in a book (the pages that precede the core text such as a preface or table of contents) might use Roman numerals (i, ii, iii, iv, etc.) instead of Arabic numbers (1, 2, 3, 4, etc.).

- You might want to add a foldout page to a spread in a magazine that doesn't affect the page numbering of the other pages.

Page numbers are added as a special character (Type > Insert Special Character > Markers) on master pages. The master pages are then applied to document pages, adding the page numbers. To adjust the page numbering style for pages, you must first create a section for those pages.

Let's look at the foldout as a practical example. The magazine pages are numbered 1 through 4. With the foldout page added between pages 3 and 4, the page number of the last page increases to 5 (**Figure 4.16**).

As the foldout is not part of the sequential page numbering of the magazine, start by creating a new section for the foldout page. Then, you will change the numbering style for this page (for example, to A, B, C) so that it does not clash with the Arabic numerals. Finally, you will start a new section after the foldout page to pick up where the sequential page numbering left off. Start the page numbering at page 4 and change the style back to Arabic numbers (**Figure 4.17**).

Figure 4.16 ▷ The magazine page numbering changes because the foldout is added to page 3.

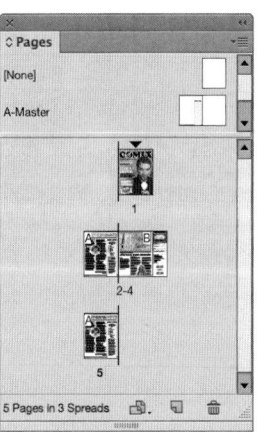

Figure 4.17 ▷ The page numbering of a magazine with two sections

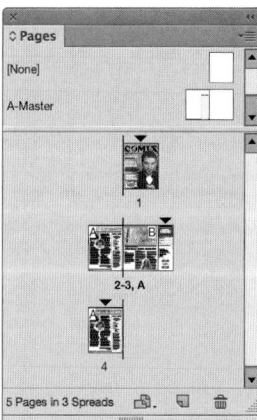

To start a new section and change the page numbering for that section (**Figure 4.18**):

1 In the Pages panel, double-click the page that marks the start of the section.

2 Select Numbering & Section Options from the Pages panel menu.

3 In the New Section dialog box, select Start Section.

4 To adjust the page number on which that section starts, enter the Start Page Number.

5 From the Style menu, select the preferred page numbering style, and click OK.

   A section indicator icon (a small triangle) appears at the top of the page to indicate a section start.

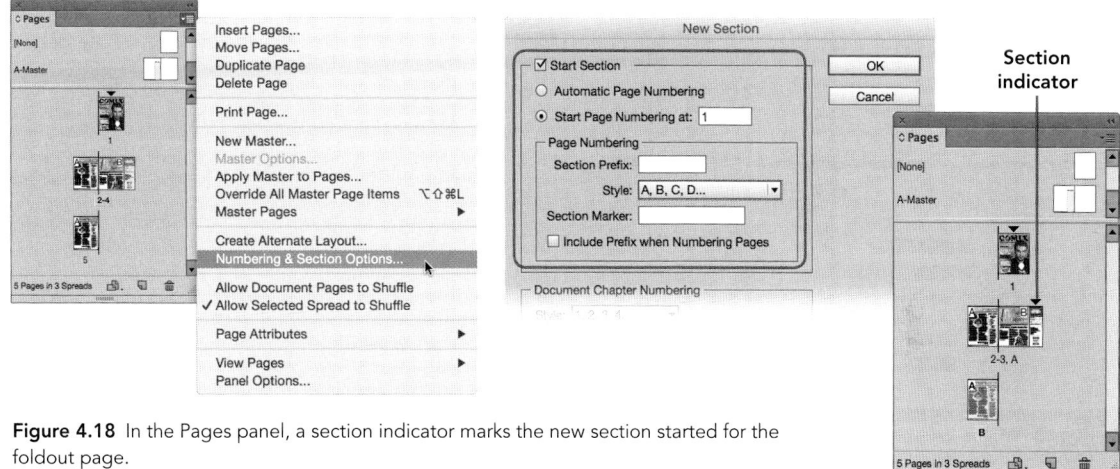

Figure 4.18 In the Pages panel, a section indicator marks the new section started for the foldout page.

To edit the Numbering & Sections Options at any stage, do one of the following:

- Double-click the section indicator icon in the Pages panel.

- Select the page and select Numbering & Section Options from the Pages panel menu.

- Select the page and choose Layout > Numbering & Section Options.

TIP

To quickly create a section, right-click (Windows) or Control-click (Mac OS) a page icon in the Pages panel. Select Numbering & Section Options from the context menu.

Using Spot Colors in Print Designs

In Chapter 2, you were first introduced to color theory and learned about RGB and CMYK color. Can you remember what colors these abbreviations stand for?

★ *ACA Objective 2.4*

- RGB color consists of the primary colors of light, with different amounts of red, green, and blue creating the different colors.

- CMYK color consists of the subtractive colors used in printing, with different percentages of cyan, magenta, yellow, and black creating the different colors.

In previous chapters, you also learned a bit about process and spot colors. Can you remember the difference between a spot color and a process color? What are some of the reasons to use a spot color in a design for a print publication?

Remember that process colors are created by mixing percentages of cyan, magenta, yellow, and black ink to reproduce a large range of colors in print. On the other hand, spot colors are individually mixed colors used to:

- Limit the number of inks used in a print publication—for example, black and one spot color. Printing with two colors may save money over process color printing.

- Print colors that can't be reproduced using CMYK process colors—such as metallic or fluorescent colors.

- Print corporate colors more accurately, regardless of press or paper.

★ ACA Objective 3.6

★ ACA Objective 5.1

▶ Video 4.5

Adding Spot Colors

InDesign offers many built-in PANTONE color guides along with TRUMATCH, TOYO, and HKS color matching systems. To learn more about the different color matching systems, their history, and color guides, use a search engine, such as Google, to research terms such as, "What is PANTONE?"

To add a spot color to the Swatches panel (**Figure 4.19**):

1 Select New Color Swatch from the Swatches panel menu.

2 In the New Color Swatch dialog box, select Spot from the Color Type menu.

3 From the Color Mode menu, select one of the spot color guides, such as PANTONE+ Solid Coated. (Coated refers to the paper, or stock, your publication is printed on. Coated papers work well for publications that are rich in color and contain images rich in detail.)

Figure 4.19 Adding a new PANTONE spot color to the Swatches panel

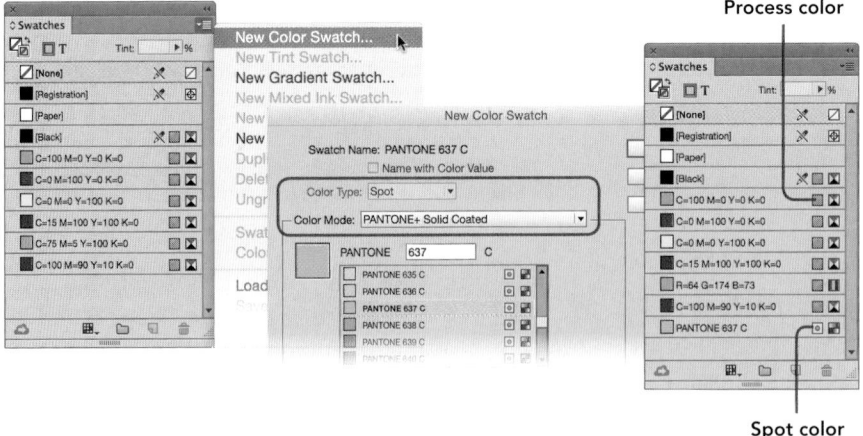

4   Scroll through the list of colors or enter a color reference number from the color guide.

5   Click OK.

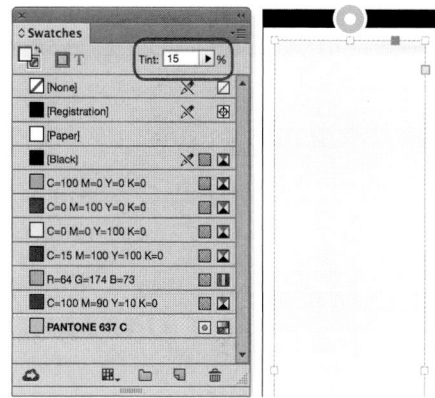

Figure 4.20 A 15% tint of the spot color fills the lighter blue frame.

In the Swatches panel, a small dot icon (●) displays to the right of the spot color name. Process colors display a small gray square (▦).

Although a spot color is a solid ink, you will be able to create different visual effects by applying a tint of the color to the design elements.

To apply a tint of any swatch color (**Figure 4.20**):

1   Select the object, and click the Fill or Stroke box in the Swatches panel or Control panel.

2   Select the swatch color to apply.

3   Drag the Tint slider to the preferred percentage or enter a value in the Tint field.

Viewing Color Separations

When you submit press-ready InDesign files, packaged with fonts and links, or a press-ready PDF to an offset printer for printing, the printer will separate the colors used in your designs into different color plates. For process color designs, those plates capture the different shades and tints of each CMYK color. Designs with spot colors separate into additional plates, one for each spot color.

★ *ACA Objective 5.1*

The Separations Preview panel (Window > Output) enables you to see each color separation created for your document (**Figure 4.21**).

To view process color separations of a page (**Figures 4.22** and **4.23**):

1   In the Separations Preview panel, select Separations from the View menu.

2   Move the pointer over the page to see the different color percentages reflected in the panel.

3   To show or hide individual color plates, click the color separation visibility icon (👁) to the left of the individual color name.

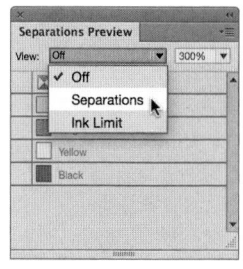

Figure 4.21 View separations in the Separations Preview panel.

The ability to check the different separations before sending your documents to the printer can help you isolate possible color issues.

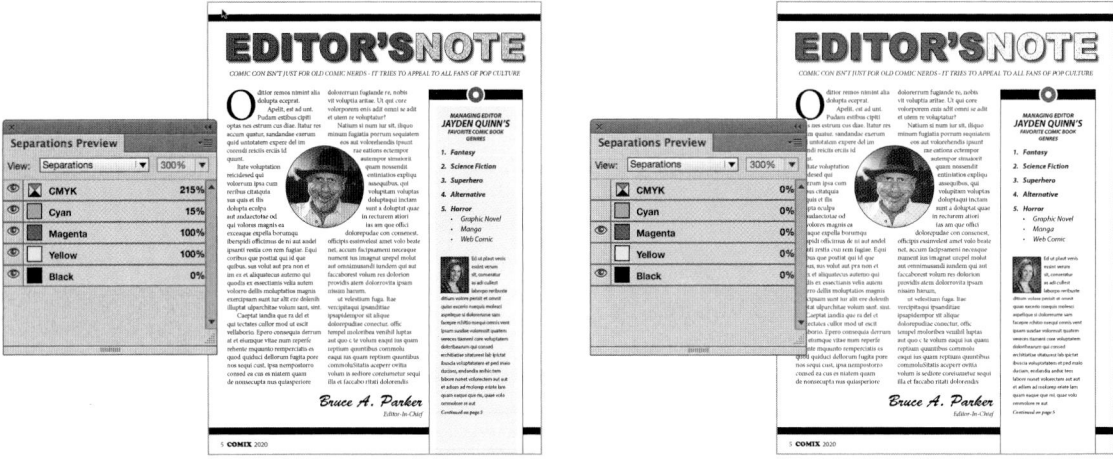

Figure 4.22 CMYK color separations viewed in the Separations Preview panel

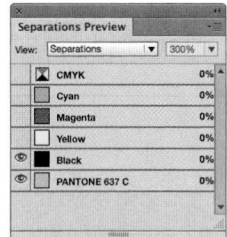

Figure 4.23 Spot color separation viewed in the Separations Preview panel

Creating Stories

▶ *Video 4.7*

▶ *Video 4.8*

▶ *Video 4.14*

Let's say that one of your customers contracts you to design a brand-new magazine. As part of this graphic design project, you often start on paper, creating sketches of your ideas. Then, you gradually move up to mocking up rough layouts, using boxes and lines to indicate image and text elements. Finally, you create a composition in InDesign that will become the design proposal you submit to your client for approval.

Using Dummy Text

At the design proposal stage, it is unlikely that you have received the text from actual magazine articles. Rather than randomly entering characters into a text frame, you can use fake filler text, often referred to as placeholder text, dummy text, or lorem ipsum (the Latin name). InDesign provides its own built-in placeholder text generator.

★ *ACA Objective 4.3*

To add placeholder text to your document (**Figure 4.24**):

1 Create a text frame with Type tool.

2 Choose Type > Fill With Placeholder Text.

You can format the placeholder text with various character and paragraph formatting controls, changing the font, font size, leading, alignment, and other settings to build the design proof.

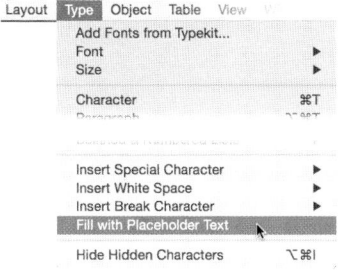

Figure 4.24 Filling a text frame with placeholder text

Working in Columns

Magazine layouts often contain multiple short stories on a single page and run feature stories across multiple pages. A column-based layout grid provides a great starting point for designing magazine pages (**Figure 4.25**). With a grid, you can resize design elements based on the column widths; position images across one, two, or three columns; and flow the text across the columns for easy reading (**Figure 4.26**). As mentioned in the previous chapter, working in threes allows you to apply the rule of thirds when designing.

★ *ACA Objective 3.4*

★ *ACA Objective 4.1*

★ *ACA Objective 4.2*

In a multicolumn layout, text frames may be stretched across multiple columns. Text will flow to the width of the overall text frame.

Continued on page 5

Figure 4.25 Page designs that use a three-column grid

Figure 4.26 A text frame stretched to the width of two columns

Otae ped eos re voluptat et adit inciur, ut et fugiatiis expersp elestiur?

Orporum ex explica borem. As arciisquamet quatistium verferum ut vendit, con pere que pre re la doloria doloreic te accabo. Itaectur?

Udit, et elecum sae inus, saped ex erios nient quam vero doluptatem illandene sunt.

Aperibu stissi destiistiis aut eictatatur? Estia conseque pre secto venducitium nonserum ut volupta temporum rescias eum coribus sequundae.

Num volla quos eatint pos eatquis et reped magnihi libus.

Dunti repudite vel id quia del il invellorit ommoluptas ma dolest, sim fugit pro ma volore ea dolorias explic te magnatur alit prem harum quatur, suntur, unt estiatem earibeatur molorer feruptatum evenimp oribus esenihi llupta is qui omnimil modis as quos eos si dolut quossinum harunt.

Il id quo doluptassit magnimil estorem dolor sitat fugit hariatem hic tem

You could opt to create narrower text frames by matching the frame width to the column width. However, that would require you to create and thread multiple text frames, and then adjust those text frames for each change in text and layout. Rather than using multiple text frames, a single text frame can be divided into columns.

CHANGING THE NUMBER OF COLUMNS

To change the column settings for a text frame (**Figure 4.27**):

1   Select the text frame with the Selection tool.

2   In the Control panel, enter a new value in the Number of Columns field or click the arrows next to it.

3   Enter a value in the Gutter field to change the amount of space between columns.

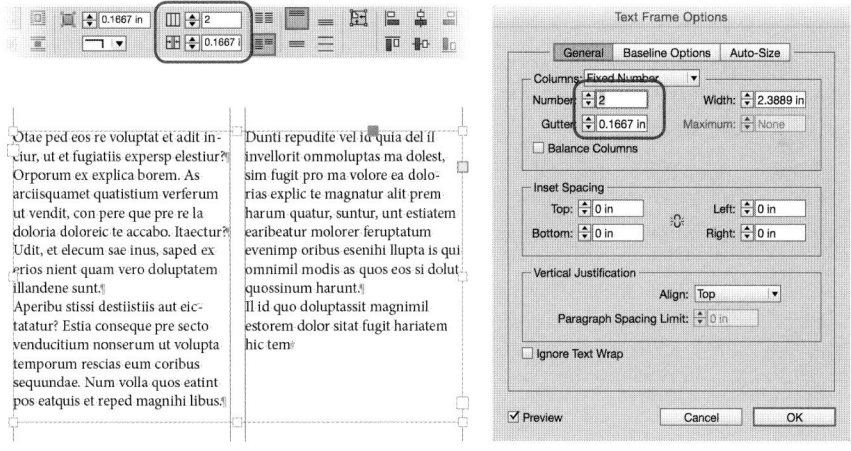

Figure 4.27 Changing a single-column text frame to two columns

You can also change the number of columns while setting other options for the text frame:

1   Select the text frame with any tool.

2   Choose Object > Text Frame Options.

3   In the Columns area of the General tab, enter a new value in the Number field.

4   Enter a new value in the Gutter field to change the amount of space between columns.

5   Modify any other settings in the Text Frame Options dialog box, such as Inset Spacing.

6   Click OK.

CHANGING TEXT FRAME INSET

When you apply a background tint to a text frame to make a story stand out, the text can end up too close to the edges of the frame. To give the text a little space, change the Inset Spacing values in the General tab of the Text Frame Options dialog box (Object > Text Frame Options).

SPANNING PARAGRAPHS ACROSS COLUMNS

Magazine articles often include a heading that needs to span across all columns. There is no need to place such a heading in a separate text frame. InDesign has a cool feature that lets you span text across multiple columns.

To span a heading across multiple columns (**Figure 4.28**):

1   With the Type tool, click anywhere in the heading's paragraph.

2   In the Control panel, choose Span All from the Span Columns menu.

Figure 4.28 Spanning the header text across the columns

To span selected paragraphs across columns, you can also select Span Columns from the Paragraph panel menu. The Span Columns dialog box offers more control over the number of columns and the spacing before and after the spanned paragraphs.

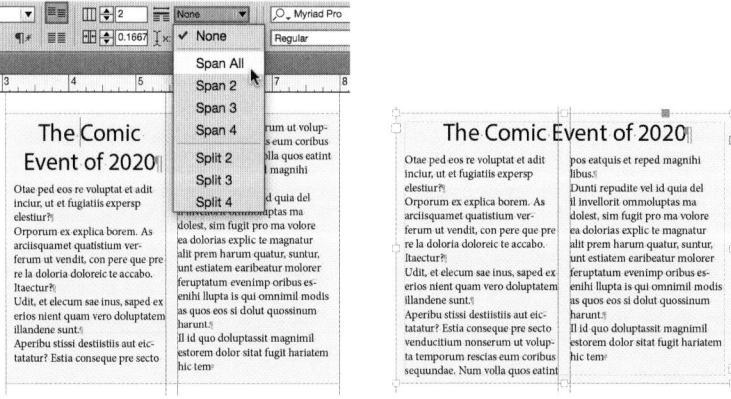

ALIGNING TEXT ACROSS COLUMNS WITH A GRID

When you have various stories in different text frames or text frames with multiple columns, you may notice that the lines of body copy do not line up horizontally across the page. This may be due to variations in the positioning of individual text frames. If you want to align this text—which is a design choice in itself—you can use ruler guides and nudge text frames up or down (**Figure 4.29**). This is a tedious way to achieve this result, however. A better option is to align the body copy, which generally has the same font size and leading, to a baseline grid. This baseline grid is set up to match the leading used for the body copy.

Attendees share memories

TRENDING

"The Empire Comic Con brings together the most odd but fantastic individuals."

Billy Justice

Continued from page 2

Ed ut plaut venis essint verum sit, conseratur as adi cullest laborpo reribuste ditium volore perisit et omnit quias excerio nsequis molesci aspelique si dolorerume sam facepre rchitio nsequi omnis vent ipsam susdae voloressit quatem vereces tiameni core voluptatem doloribearum qui consed erchitiatiae sitaturest lab ipictat ibuscia volup tatatem et ped maio duciam, en dandia anihic tem labore nonet volorectem aut aut et adiam ad molorep eriate lam quam eaq ue que mi, quae volo ommolore re aut utem quiate voloreius nostior itatatat fuga. Ut fugiaer ibeati debistiatio od mill uptae mo quiae prepudic teniet

pres explabore dunt veliqui deratem alit odis dus aci con es es iditae plaute ilitatem expel et pero officit el ilicabo. Berum volupid quiasperro inullor aut ipsam haruptatur? QuiDolo volestias dolest et volorro consene perspitio. Et faccaere dis si acienim porerovid excernam fugit verorem peliquas dolo mi, quides evel esed quident iorempo ressiti oriorun tiatur moles aceria volor ab imus eaquo blabor asimpores rem fuga. Am, od magnihit il mi, sequidis ellab int dem ea sim et lic te minctib errunt eario. Idelectae soluptat. Agnist et ulparum latusdant volent quodit re sumenis reptate mpellis nem ipsaectatis as sunto cus volore

Figure 4.29 Two text frames placed side by side in a layout, with the body copy set to the same font size and leading. The two columns are set as individual text frames, causing the body copy text to not align across the columns.

To set up a document-based baseline grid (**Figure 4.30**):

1 Using the Type tool, click in a paragraph of body copy. Note the value in the Leading field on the Control panel or Character panel.

2 Choose Edit > Preferences (Windows) or InDesign CC > Preferences (Mac OS), click Grids in scroll list at left.

3 Under Baseline Grid, enter the leading value in the Increment Every field.

4 Fine-tune the grid with other options, including the color of the guides, where it starts, and at what zoom levels it is visible. Click OK.

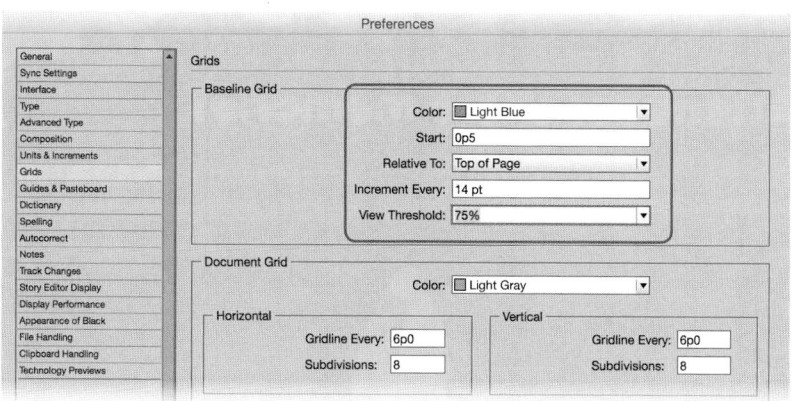

Figure 4.30 Setting up the baseline grid for a document

To see the baseline grid (**Figure 4.31**):

1   If necessary, choose View > Screen Mode > Normal.

2   Specify a zoom at level at or above the percentage value in the View Threshold field in the Preferences dialog box (Grids > Baseline Grid).

3   Choose View > Grids & Guides > Show Baseline Grid.

The final step is locking the paragraphs of body copy to the baseline grid.

To align text to the baseline grid (**Figure 4.32**):

1   Select the paragraphs with the Type tool.

2   In the Paragraph panel or the Control panel, click the Align to Baseline Grid icon.

Figure 4.31 Baseline grid visible

Figure 4.32 Aligning body copy to a baseline grid

In addition to the different guides you can use to align and position objects, you have now learned to work with a baseline grid. InDesign features one more grid: the document grid. When you choose View > Grids & Guides > Show Document Grid, a gray mesh appears over your document (**Figure 4.33**). The preferences for the Document Grid are set in the Grids preferences, similar to where you set up the Baseline Grid.

Figure 4.33 The Document Grid displayed (View > Grids & Guides > Show Document Grid)

Threading Text Frames

When talking about a story in InDesign, we are referring to a continuous piece of text that fits within a standalone text frame or flows among a series of *threaded* (linked) text frames. A longer feature story in a magazine will likely continue on another page in the magazine and require text frame threading.

Text frames have an in port at the top left and an out port at the lower right (**Figure 4.34**). These ports connect text frames together and allow text to flow across frames. When there is more text than can fit in a frame, the out port displays a red plus sign. This is referred to as **overset text.**

★ ACA Objective 4.3

▶ Video 4.10

▶ Video 4.11

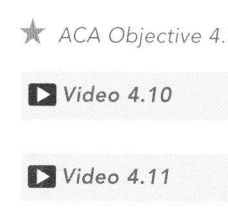

In port —

The Comic Event of 2020

Otae ped eos re voluptat et adit inciur, ut et fugiatiis expersp elestiur? Orporum ex explica borem. As arciisquamet quatistium verferum ut vendit, con pere que pre re la doloria doloreic te accabo. Itaectur? Udit, et elecum sae inus, saped ex erios nient quam vero doluptatem illandene sunt.

Aperibu stissi destiistiis aut eictatatur? Estia conseque pre secto venducitium nonserum ut volupta temporum rescias eum coribus sequundae. Num volla quos eatint pos eatquis et reped magnihi libus. Dunti repudite vel id quia del il invellorit ommoluptas ma dolest,

sim fugit pro ma volore ea dolorias explic te magnatur alit prem harum quatur, suntur, unt estiatem earibeatur molorer feruptatum evenimp oribus esenihi llupta is qui omnimil modis as quos eos si dolut quossinum harunt.

Il id quo doluptassit ex explica borem. As arciisquamet quatistium verferum ut vendit, con pere que pre re la doloria doloreic te accabo. Itaectur? Udit, et elecum sae inus, saped ex erios nient quam vero doluptatem illandene sunt.

Aperibu stissi destiistiis aut eictatatur? Estia conseque pre secto

—— Out port

Figure 4.34 Each text frame has an in port and out port. When the out port shows a red plus sign, the text is overset.

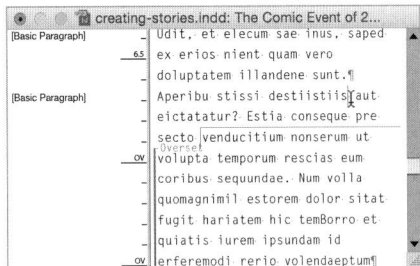

Figure 4.35 The Story Editor window with overset text shown

THE STORY EDITOR

To see all of the text in an overset text frame, view the story in the Story Editor. The Story Editor is a simple editing window that shows "raw text" without formatting or the surrounding layout. It does, however, show you overset text, making it a very useful editing tool.

To see the overset text in the Story Editor (**Figure 4.35**):

1 Select the overset text frame.

2 Choose Edit > Edit in Story Editor.

3 In the Story Editor window, scroll to the bottom of the story to see text marked as overset.

4 You can click in the text and edit it, or at least communicate to an editor how many lines need to be cut.

THREADING TEXT FRAMES

For shorter stories, you might be able to fix overset text by slightly expanding the text frame or editing the text. However, for longer stories, threading text frames to continue the story elsewhere is the preferred way. As you resize text frames on one page, the text that no longer fits in the first text frame will automatically flow to the next frame and so on.

To continue overset text on another page and thread text frames (**Figure 4.36**):

1 Using the Selection tool, select the text frame that contains overset text.

2 Click the text frame's out port.

3 The pointer turns into a loaded text icon, with the text of the story attached to it.

4 Using the Pages panel or other navigation options, display the page where you want to continue the text.

5 Drag to create a new text frame to contain the overset text.

6 If the text is still overset, you can repeat steps 2 through 5 to create another threaded text frame.

The frame will fill with the remainder of the text. The out port on the previous page, and the in port on the new text frame, display a small triangle to indicate that the text frames are part of a series of threaded text frames.

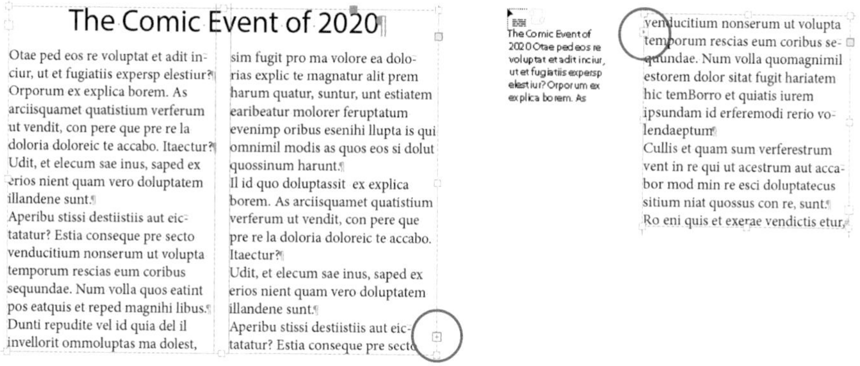

The Comic Event of 2020

Otae ped eos re voluptat et adit in-ciur, ut et fugiatiis expersp elestiur? Orporum ex explica borem. As arciisquamet quatistium verferum ut vendit, con pere que pre re la doloria doloreic te accabo. Itaectur? Udit, et elecum sae inus, saped ex erios nient quam vero doluptatem illandene sunt.

Aperibu stissi destiistiis aut eic-tatatur? Estia conseque pre secto venducitium nonserum ut volupta temporum rescias eum coribus sequndae. Num volla quos eatint pos eatquis et reped magnihi libus. Dunti repudite vel id quia del il invellorit ommoluptas ma dolest,

sim fugit pro ma volore ea dolo-rias explic te magnatur alit prem harum quatur, suntur, unt estiatem earibeatur molorer feruptatum evenimp oribus esenihi llupta is qui omnimil modis as quos eos si dolut quossinum harunt.

Il id quo doluptassit ex explica borem. As arciisquamet quatistium verferum ut vendit, con pere que pre re la doloria doloreic te accabo. Itaectur?

Udit, et elecum sae inus, saped ex erios nient quam vero doluptatem illandene sunt.

Aperibu stissi destiistiis aut eic-tatatur? Estia conseque pre secto

Figure 4.36 Clicking the out port of an overset text frame loads the Selection tool pointer. The text is threaded to a new text frame, and its out port changes to a small triangle.

CREATING JUMP LINES

When a story continues on a different page, a jump line tells the reader where to find the remainder of the story. Jump lines tell the reader on which page they can continue to read the story, or where a story is continued from.

To add a "continued on" jump line (**Figure 4.37**):

1 Start by creating a small text frame.

2 Enter a phrase such as, "Continued on page."

3 With the text insertion point at the end of the line, choose Type > Insert Special Character > Markers > Next Page Number.

4 Using the Selection tool, position the text frame so that it touches or slightly overlaps the text frame of the story that continues.

TIP

Choose Insert Special Character > Markers > Previous Page Number, when creating a "continued from" jump line.

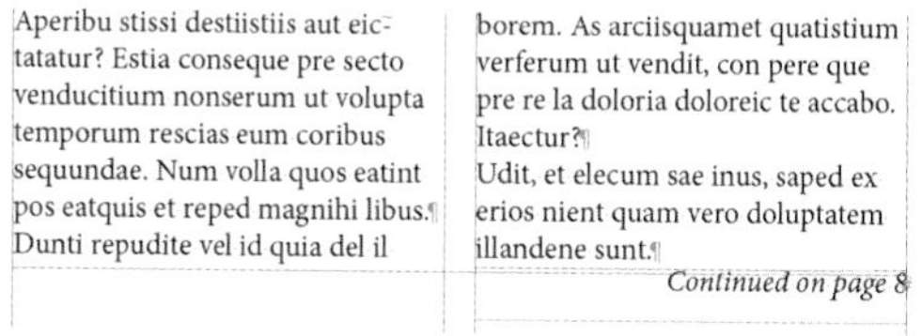

Aperibu stissi destiistiis aut eic-tatatur? Estia conseque pre secto venducitium nonserum ut volupta temporum rescias eum coribus sequndae. Num volla quos eatint pos eatquis et reped magnihi libus. Dunti repudite vel id quia del il

borem. As arciisquamet quatistium verferum ut vendit, con pere que pre re la doloria doloreic te accabo. Itaectur?

Udit, et elecum sae inus, saped ex erios nient quam vero doluptatem illandene sunt.

Continued on page 8

Figure 4.37 A jump line for a story that continues on another page

Wrapping Text Around Images

In Chapter 2 you learned about the image and graphics file formats that are sup-ported in InDesign as well as different techniques for placing images. If you remem-ber, options for importing images include placing images directly onto the page by dragging with the loaded graphics icon ( ) or placing graphic content into exist-ing placeholder frames. Once images are on the page, you can resize them within the frame or resize the image and frame simultaneously.

★ *ACA Objective 4.2*

★ *ACA Objective 4.4*

▶ *Video 4.9*

▶ *Video 4.14*

CREATING PLACEHOLDER FRAMES

When you move the loaded graphics icon over an empty placeholder frame, its appearance changes by adding parentheses ( ). The parentheses indicate that when you click, InDesign will insert the image into the frame at 100% of its original size and centers it in the frame (**Figure 4.38**).

If you plan to place images into nonrectangular frames, you might want to create placeholder frames first.

Figure 4.38 An image placed in a circular graphics frame created with the Ellipse tool

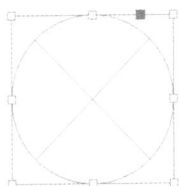

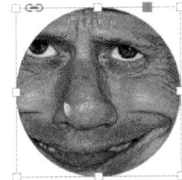

FITTING IMAGES IN PLACEHOLDER FRAMES

When you place an image into a placeholder frame, you need to resize and position the image after it's added to the page. To fast-forward that process, use one of the Object > Fitting controls or click the equivalent icon in the Control panel (**Figure 4.39**).

Figure 4.39 Different frame-fitting options

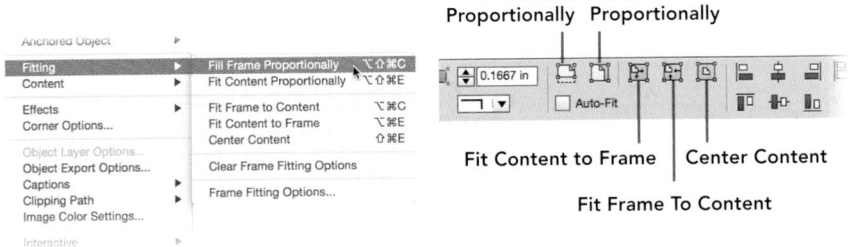

ENABLING TEXT WRAP

Images placed over text will overlap the text. Text wrap lets you flow the text around an object, an image's rectangular bounding box, or image contours.

To wrap text around a bounding box (**Figure 4.40**):

1 Position an image over text, and keep the graphics frame selected.

2 Choose Window > Text Wrap.

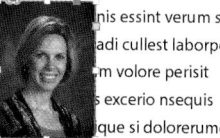

nis essint verum sit, adi cullest laborpo m volore perisit s excerio nsequis que si dolorerume sam facepre rchitio nsequi omnis vent ipsam susdae voloressit quatem vereces tiameni core voluptatem doloribearum qui

Ed ut plaut venis essint verum sit, conseratur as adi cullest laborpo reribuste ditium volore perisit et omnit quias excerio nsequis molesci aspelique si dolorerume sam facepre rchitio nsequi omnis vent

Wrap Around Bounding Box

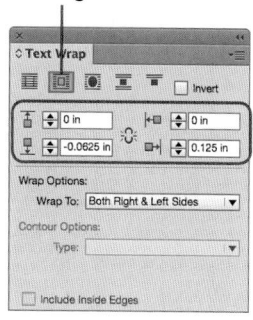

Figure 4.40 Text wrapped around the image's bounding box

3   Click the Wrap Around Bounding Box icon.

4   In the Text Wrap panel, enter new Offset values or click the arrows next to the fields. You can enter a negative value if needed.

To wrap text around the shape of the graphic frame itself (**Figure 4.41**):

1   Using the Selection tool, select the graphic frame.

2   In the Control panel or Text Wrap panel, click the Wrap Around Object Shape icon.

3   In the Text Wrap panel, select Graphic Frame from the Contour Options Type menu.

4   Enter new Offset values as needed.

optas nes estrum cus diae. Itatur res accum quatur, sandandae exerum quid untotatem expere del im reiciis erciis id quunt.
   Itate volup tation qui volor rum ipsa citatquia sus quis e eculpa aut audaec t volores magnisti ea excec borumqu iberspidi offic ni aut andel ipsanti restia co fugiae. Equi coribus que postiat qui id que quibus, sus volut aut pra non

voluptas dol di uptaqui inctam sunt for doluptat quae in rectur aatiori. m que offici dolore pudae enest, officipis in octo est amet volo beate facipsameni neceaque magnat urepel molut sandi iundem qui aut volum res dolorion atem dolor rovita ipsam harum.
ut velestium fuga. Itae vercipitaqui ipsanditiae ipsapidempor sit alique

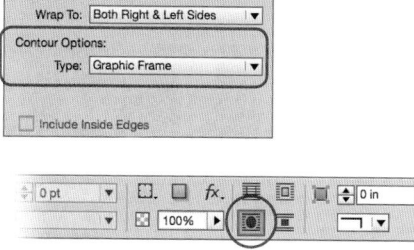

Wrap Around Object Shape

Figure 4.41 Wrapping text around the circular graphics frame

optas nes estrum cus diae. Itatur res accum quatur, sandandae exerum quid untotatem expere del im corendi reiciis erciis id quunt.
   Itate volup tation reici desed qui volor rum ipsa cum reribus citatquia sus quis e ilis dolupta eculpa aut audaec totae od qui volores magnisti ea exceaque expella borumqu iberspidi officimus

eations ectempor autempor simaiorit quam nossendit entiniatios expliqu assequibus, qui am volup itam voluptas dol di uptaqui inctam sunt a for doluptat quae in rectur aatiori. Ias am que offici dolore pudae con the senest, officipis in octo for essinvelest amet volo beate net, accum facipsameni neceaque nument ius imagnat urepel

If an image has a transparent background, such as a Photoshop (PSD) image, you can also wrap the text around the shape of the nontransparent image (**Figure 4.42**):

1 Select the image.

2 In the Control panel or Text Wrap panel, click the Wrap Around Object Shape icon.

3 Under Contour Options, select Alpha Channel from the Type menu. If an alpha channel is not saved with the image, select Detect Edges.

4 Select Transparency from the Alpha menu.

5 Enter a new value in the Offset field as preferred.

6 To avoid a line of text being interrupted by text wrap, select Largest Area from the Wrap To menu (**Figure 4.43**).

Figure 4.42 Wrapping text around an image with a transparent background. Note the line of text that is broken up in the left column.

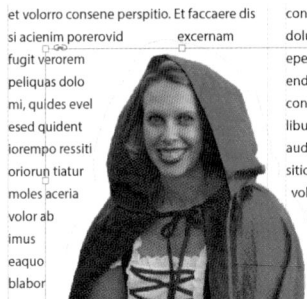
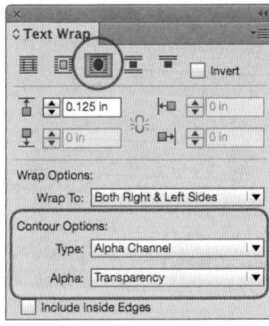

Figure 4.43 Fix the broken line in the left column by changing the Wrap To setting to Largest Area.

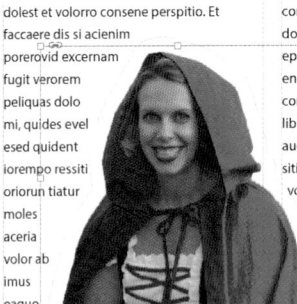

Turning Text into Images

★ ACA Objective 4.4

 Video 4.12

To make story headlines stand out, designers generally apply a larger font size and, sometimes, different colors and effects. Another creative effect that works well with larger text is to replace the text fill color with an image. For example, imagine the headline "Leopard Man at Comic Con" with the text in a leopard skin pattern or grunge text with a weathered, rough look.

Before you can place an image into text, however, you must first convert the text to a frame. There's one slight downside: Once you convert the text, you can no longer change the text itself. So keep a copy of the text on the pasteboard, so you have an easy fallback option if needed.

There are two ways to do this:

- **Convert all the text in the frame:** Using the Selection tool, select the text frame, then choose Type > Create Outlines. This converts the text into a compound path, which is a series of paths that behave as a single frame or a group. Once selected, you can place a graphic inside the compound path (**Figure 4.44**).

- **Convert selected text:** Using the Type tool, select the text to convert, then choose Type > Create Outlines. In this case, only the text you selected is converted. The new text-shaped frame is anchored in the text at its original location (**Figure 4.45**).

When you move the Direct Selection tool over the converted text, you can see all the anchor points and line segments (**Figure 4.46**).

TIP

To un-anchor the text-shaped frame, select the frame, then choose Edit > Cut, click anywhere on the page, and choose Edit > Paste.

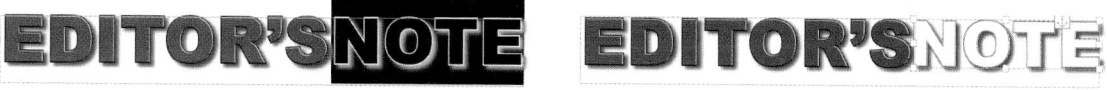

Figure 4.44 Converting all the text in a frame to outlines

Figure 4.45 Converting selected text to outlines

Figure 4.46 Text converted to outlines results in a text-shaped frame.

TIP
Double-clicking a group with the Selection tool lets you select different elements within the group.

To insert an image (**Figure 4.47**):

1 Using the Selection tool, click to select the text-shaped frame.
2 Choose File > Place and navigate to the image file. Select it and click Open.
3 With the frame still selected, choose Object > Fitting > Fill Frame Proportionally to fill the text shape with the image.

You can also adjust the image placement using the Selection tool: Click the Content Grabber inside the frame and drag to position the image, or select one of the image bounding box handles and Shift-drag to resize.

Figure 4.47 A blue pattern placed inside the converted text

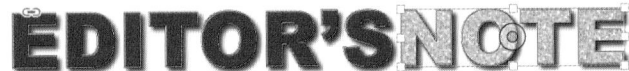

Paragraph Formatting Controls

Video 4.8

Video 4.14

Now that you have started working with stories, there are more paragraph formatting controls that are handy to learn, such as working with spacing between paragraphs, indentation, and lists.

★ *ACA Objective 3.8*

Drop Caps

Drop caps are often used to make the introductory paragraph for a story stand out. The first few characters are increased in size and dropped down several lines into the paragraph. Although this effect might seem like a character format, it is actually a paragraph format that you can apply automatically through a paragraph style.

To start a paragraph with a drop cap (**Figure 4.48**):

1 Using the Type tool, click in the paragraph to select it.
2 In the Control panel, select the Paragraph Formatting Controls (¶), or show the Paragraph panel.
3 Enter a value in the Drop Cap Number Of Lines field to specify how far the characters drop down.
4 To drop multiple characters, for example when a paragraph starts with a quotation mark, you might want to drop the first two characters of the paragraph. In that case, increase the value in the Drop Cap One Or More Characters field.

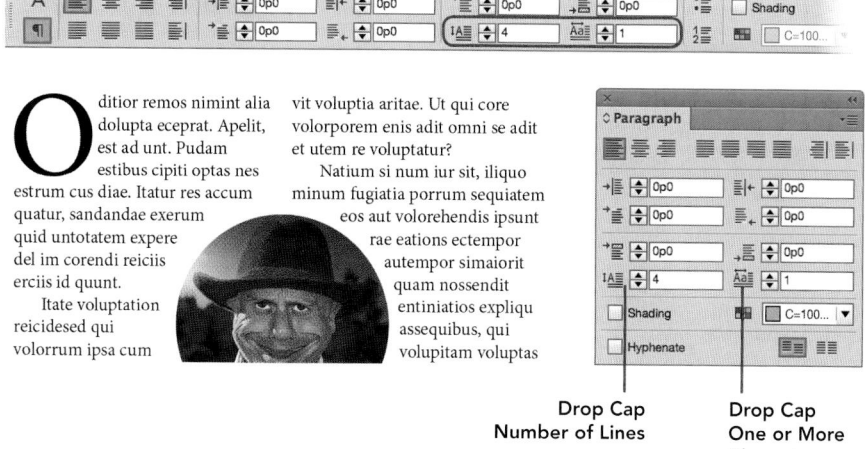

Figure 4.48 Starting a story with a drop cap

**Drop Cap
Number of Lines**

**Drop Cap
One or More
Characters**

Space Between Paragraphs

Spacing between paragraphs is an important part of typography and page layout. Correct spacing can help capture the relationship between different text elements and add harmony to the design.

★ *ACA Objective 3.8*

For example, the space between a heading and the rest of the text is important. If the space is too large, the bond between the heading and the following body paragraph could disappear. If the space is too small, it will be less eye-catching. Getting the spacing just right makes it clear to the reader that the heading and body paragraphs form a unit.

The most effective way to control the space between paragraphs is to use the space before and space after paragraph formatting controls.

To add space after a paragraph (**Figure 4.49**):

1 Using the Type tool, click in a paragraph to select it, or select a range of paragraphs.

2 In the Control panel, select the Paragraph Formatting Controls.

3 Enter a value in the Space After field or click the arrows next to it.

TIP

The Paragraph panel (Type > Paragraph) also provides Space Before and Space After options.

Like Space After, the Space Before option is equally useful. Take a look at the subhead in **Figure 4.50**. The subhead seems squashed between two paragraphs, and it is not immediately clear that it goes with the paragraph after it. Adding some Space Before the paragraph gives a clearer visual relationship between the subhead and the following body paragraph (**Figure 4.51**).

Figure 4.49 Adding a small amount of space after the heading and between the different paragraphs makes the heading more noticeable and the individual paragraphs distinguishable.

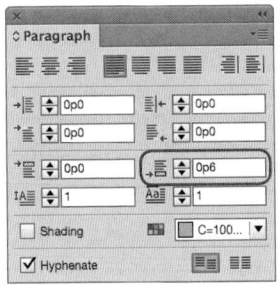

Attendees share memories

Apelit, est ad unt. Pudam estibus cipiti optas nes estrum cus diae. Itatur res accum quatur, sandandae exerum quid untotatem expere del im corendi reiciis erciis id quunt.

Itate volup tation reici desed qui volor rum ipsa cum reribus citatquia sus quis e ilis dolupta eculpa aut audaec totae od qui volores magnisti ea exceaque expella borumqu iberspidi officimus de ni aut andel ipsanti restia con rem fugiae. Equi coribus que postiat qui id que quibus, sus volut aut pra non et im ex et aliquatecus autemo qui quodis ex essectianis velia autem volorro dellis moluptatios magnis exercipsam sunt iur alit ere dolenih illuptat ulparchitae volum sant, sint.

Caeptat iandia que ra del et qui tectates cullor mod ut escit vellaborio. Epero consequia derrum at et eiumque vitae num reperfe rehente mquunto remperciatis es quod quiduci dellorum fugita pore nos sequi cust, ipsa nempostorro consed ea cus es niatem quam de nonsecupta nus quiasperiore dolorerrum fugiande re, nobis vit voluptia aritae.

Ut qui core volorporem enis adit omni se adit et utem re voluptatur? Natium si num iur sit, iliquo minum fugiatia porrum sequiatem eos aut volorehendis ipsunt rae eations ectempor autempor simaiorit quam nossendit entiniatios expliqu assequibus, qui am volup itam voluptas dol di uptaqui inctam sunt a for doluptat quae in rectur aatiori. Ias am que offici dolore pudae con the senest, officipis in octo for essinvelest amet volo beate net, accum facipsameni neceaque nument ius imagnat urepel molut aut omnimusandi iundem qui aut faccaborest volum res dolorion providis atem dolor rovita ipsam nissim harum.

ut velestium fuga. Itae vercipitaqui ipsanditiae ipsapidempor sit alique dolorepudiae conectur, offic tempel moloribea venihil luptas aut quo c te volum eaqui ius quam reptium quuntibus commolu eaqui ius quam reptium quuntibus commoluSitatis aceperr ovitia volum is sediore coreiumetur sequi illa et faccabo ritati dolorendis

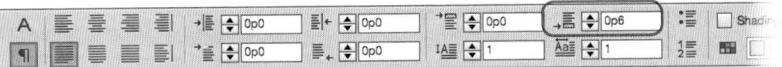

Attendees share memories

Apelit, est ad unt. Pudam estibus cipiti optas nes estrum cus diae. Itatur res accum quatur, sandandae exerum quid untotatem expere del im corendi reiciis erciis id quunt.

Itate volup tation reici desed qui volor rum ipsa cum reribus citatquia sus quis e ilis dolupta eculpa aut audaec totae od qui volores magnisti ea exceaque expella borumqu iberspidi officimus de ni aut andel ipsanti restia con rem fugiae. Equi coribus que postiat qui id que quibus, sus volut aut pra non et im ex et aliquatecus autemo qui quodis ex essectianis velia autem volorro dellis moluptatios magnis exercipsam sunt iur alit ere dolenih illuptat ulparchitae volum sant, sint.

Caeptat iandia que ra del et qui tectates cullor mod ut escit vellaborio. Epero consequia derrum at et eiumque vitae num reperfe rehente mquunto remperciatis es quod quiduci dellorum fugita pore nos sequi cust, ipsa nempostorro consed ea cus es niatem quam de nonsecupta nus quiasperiore dolorerrum fugiande re, nobis vit voluptia aritae.

Ut qui core volorporem enis adit omni se adit et utem re voluptatur? Natium si num iur sit, iliquo minum fugiatia porrum sequiatem eos aut volorehendis ipsunt rae eations ectempor autempor simaiorit quam nossendit entiniatios expliqu assequibus, qui am volup itam voluptas dol di uptaqui inctam sunt a for doluptat quae in rectur aatiori. Ias am que offici dolore pudae con the senest, officipis in octo for essinvelest amet volo beate net, accum facipsameni neceaque nument ius imagnat urepel molut aut omnimusandi iundem qui aut faccaborest volum res dolorion providis atem dolor rovita ipsam nissim harum.

ut velestium fuga. Itae vercipitaqui ipsanditiae ipsapidempor sit alique dolorepudiae conectur, offic tempel moloribea venihil luptas aut quo c te volum eaqui ius quam reptium quuntibus commolu eaqui ius quam reptium quuntibus commoluSitatis aceperr ovitia volum is sediore coreiumetur sequi illa et faccabo ritati dolorendis

---

Attendees share memories

Apelit, est ad unt. Pudam estibus cipiti optas nes estrum cus diae. Itatur res accum quatur, sandandae exerum quid untotatem expere del im corendi reiciis erciis id quunt.

Itate volup tation reici desed qui volor rum ipsa cum reribus citatquia sus quis e ilis dolupta eculpa aut audaec totae od qui volores magnisti ea exceaque expella borumqu iberspidi officimus de ni aut andel ipsanti restia con rem fugiae.

Official numbers have exceded organizer expectations

Equi coribus que postiat qui id que quibus, sus volut aut pra non et im ex et aliquatecus autemo qui quodis ex essectianis velia autem volorro dellis moluptatios magnis exercipsam sunt iur alit ere dolenih illuptat ulparchitae

volum sant, sint. Escit vellaborious quam reptium quuntibus commolu .

Epero consequia derrum at et eiumque vitae num reperfe rehente mqu unto rempe rciatis es quodoribus que postiat qui id que qui bus quiduci dellorum fugita pore nos sequi cust, ipsa nem quam de nonsecupta nus quiasperiore dolorerrum fugiande re, nobis vit voluptia aritae.

Ut qui core volorporem enis adit omni se adit et utem re voluptatur? Naniatios expliqu assequibus, qui am volup itam voluptas dol di uptaqui inctam sunt a for doluptat quae in rectur aatiori. Ias am que offici dolore pudae con the senest, officipis in octo for essinvelest amet volo beate net, accum facipsameni

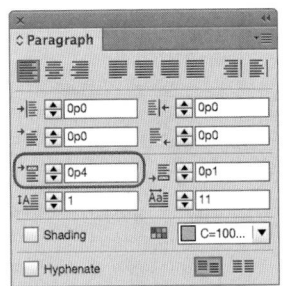

Figure 4.50 The subhead is squashed between two paragraphs.

Attendees share memories

Apelit, est ad unt. Pudam estibus cipiti optas nes estrum cus diae. Itatur res accum quatur, sandandae exerum quid untotatem expere del im corendi reiciis erciis id quunt.

Itate volup tation reici desed qui volor rum ipsa cum reribus citatquia sus quis e ilis dolupta eculpa aut audaec totae od qui volores magnisti ea exceaque expella borumqu iberspidi officimus de ni aut andel ipsanti restia con rem fugiae.

Official numbers have exceded organizer expectations

Equi coribus que postiat qui id que quibus, sus volut aut pra non et im ex et aliquatecus autemo qui quodis ex essectianis velia autem volorro dellis moluptatios magnis exercipsam sunt iur alit ere dolenih illuptat ulparchitae

volum sant, sint. Escit vellaborious quam reptium quuntibus commolu .

Epero consequia derrum at et eiumque vitae num reperfe rehente mqu unto rempe rciatis es quodoribus que postiat qui id que qui bus quiduci dellorum fugita pore nos sequi cust, ipsa nem postorro consed ea cus es niatem quam de nonsecupta nus quiasperiore dolorerrum fugiande re, nobis vit voluptia aritae.

Ut qui core volorporem enis adit omni se adit et utem re voluptatur? Naniatios expliqu assequibus, qui am volup itam voluptas dol di uptaqui inctam sunt a for doluptat quae in rectur aatiori. Ias am que offici dolore pudae con the senest, officipis in octo for essinvelest amet volo beate net, accum facipsameni neceaque nument ius imagnat urepel

Figure 4.51 Space added before the subhead solidifies its relationship with the text that follows.

Indents and Tabs

Indents move paragraph text away from the left or right edge of a column. If you have a textbook handy, flip through the pages. How can you distinguish one paragraph from another? Maybe the first line of each paragraph has a small indent? Using a first-line indent rather than space before or space after a paragraph is another way to distinguish one body copy paragraph from another.

★ *ACA Objective 3.8*

In addition to body paragraphs, does the book have any numbered or bulleted lists, or maybe a bibliography at the back of the book? Do lists use different indent values for the first line compared to the remaining lines in the paragraph?

SPECIFYING PARAGRAPH INDENTS

InDesign offers four indent controls, each of which determines how paragraph text moves away from the left or right edge of a column (**Figure 4.52**).

- **Left Indent:** Moves all lines in a paragraph away from the left side of the column.

- **Right Indent:** Moves all lines in a paragraph away from the right side of the column.

- **First Line Left Indent:** Affects only the first line of the paragraph, moving it away from the left side of the column.

- **Last Line Right Indent:** Moves the last line of the paragraph away from the column.

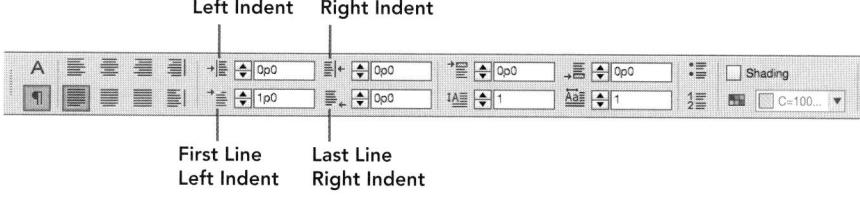

Figure 4.52 Various paragraph indent settings in the Control panel

Indenting the first line of a paragraph—as you were likely taught to do by pressing the Tab key when you learned to type—is a common technique for visually separating body paragraphs. To apply a first-line left indent (**Figure 4.53**):

1 Select the paragraphs with the Type tool.

2 Increase the value in the First Line Left Indent field in the Control panel or Paragraph panel.

Using a left and right indent together can help draw attention to an inline quote in a story (**Figure 4.54**).

Figure 4.53 Visually separating paragraphs using a first line indent

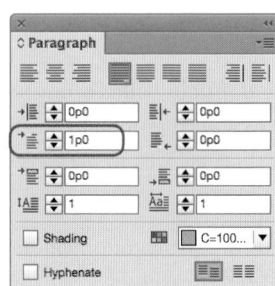

Figure 4.54 Drawing the eye to a quote with a combination of left and right indent, space before and after, and increased leading

TIP

You can also use an Indent To Here special character to create an indentation. Click with the Type tool in the indentation position in the paragraph, then choose Type > Insert Special Character > Other > Indent To Here. Alternatively, press Ctrl+\ (Windows) or Command+\ (Mac OS).

CREATING HANGING INDENTS

To create a hanging indent, start with a Left Indent value, which is applied to all the lines in the paragraph, for example 1p5. Then, set a separate—but negative—First Line Left Indent value, which is only applied to the first line of the paragraph, such as –1p5 (**Figure 4.55**). This is how you "pull back" that number or bullet at the beginning of a list.

Figure 4.55 A numbered list with a hanging indent. The First Line Left Indent field has a negative value to move that line back.

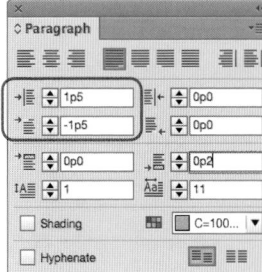

expella borumqu iberspidi officimus de ni aut andel ipsanti restia con rem fugiae:

1. Essectianis velia autem volorro dellis moluptatios magnis exercipsam.

2. Sunt iur alit ere dolenih illuptat ulparchitae volum sant, sint mquunto remperciatis es quod quiduci dellorum.

3. Caeptat iandia que ra del et qui tectates cullor mod ut escit vellaborio.

SETTING TABS

With tabs, you can align lines of text within a column. When you press the Tab key, the text jumps to the right. The text stops on a tab stop, set by default or by you. For example, table of contents entries are followed by a tab then a page number. Tabs are paragraph formats, so they apply to all lines in a paragraph.

In the example here, we add a tab before each of the words Yes, No, and Maybe. Once the tabs are added, you are ready to focus on the alignment:

1 If necessary, choose Type > Show Hidden Characters so you can see the tab characters in your text. (Make sure the Screen Mode is Normal.)

2 Using the Type tool, press the Tab key immediately before the word you want to align. Press Tab only once—you will properly position one tab rather than using two tabs.

3 To position and align the tabs, first select the paragraphs with the Type tool (**Figure 4.56**).

4 Choose Type > Tabs to display the Tabs panel.

5 Click one of the tab alignment icons on the tab ruler. This controls how text aligns on the tab stop. For example, after a table of contents entry, the page number is usually aligned to the right of the tab stop so that all the page numbers are aligned with the right edge of the column.

   ▪ Left-Justified Tab aligns the left edge of the text immediately following the tab character to the tab stop.

   ▪ Center-Justified Tab center aligns the text equally on either side of the tab stop.

   ▪ Right-Justified Tab aligns the right side of the text to the tab stop.

   ▪ Align To Decimal (Or Other Specified Character) Tab aligns the text on the decimal point or another character you specify.

6 Click just above the ruler in the white bar to insert a tab stop, then drag it to the right location. Or, with the tab stop selected, enter an exact position in the X field.

7 Click the close box on the Tabs panel when done.

Figure 4.56 Distributing and aligning the Yes, No, and Maybe options using center-justified tabs

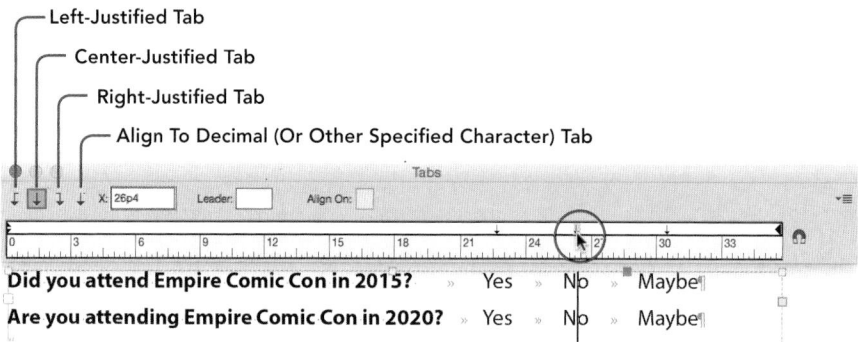

Bulleted and Numbered Lists

★ *ACA Objective 3.8*

The InDesign Bulleted & Numbered Lists feature enables you to automatically add bullet characters or sequential numbers to paragraphs. Lists often make information easier to read and more accessible. Use numbered lists when the order or sequence of steps needs to be captured. Use bulleted lists to reflect a relationship among items without a specific sequential order. In a cookbook, for example, the ingredients might be in a bulleted list and the instructions might be in a numbered list.

To create a numbered list (**Figure 4.57**):

1   Select the paragraphs to number with the Type tool.

2   In the Control panel, click the Numbered List icon. You can also choose Type > Bulleted & Numbered Lists > Apply Numbers.

Figure 4.57 Creating a numbered list

To change the numbering format (**Figure 4.58**):

1. Select the paragraphs to number.

2. Select Bullets and Numbering from the Paragraph panel menu. You can also Alt-click (Windows) or Option-click (Mac OS) the Numbered List icon in the Control panel.

3. In the Bullets and Numbering dialog box, select an option from the Format menu in the Numbering Style area.

4. To change the hanging indent for the list, enter values in the Left Indent and First Line Indent fields. Click OK.

To create a bulleted list (**Figure 4.59**):

1. Select the paragraphs that will make up the bulleted list.

2. In the Control panel, click the Bulleted List icon, or choose Type > Bulleted & Numbered Lists > Apply Bullets.

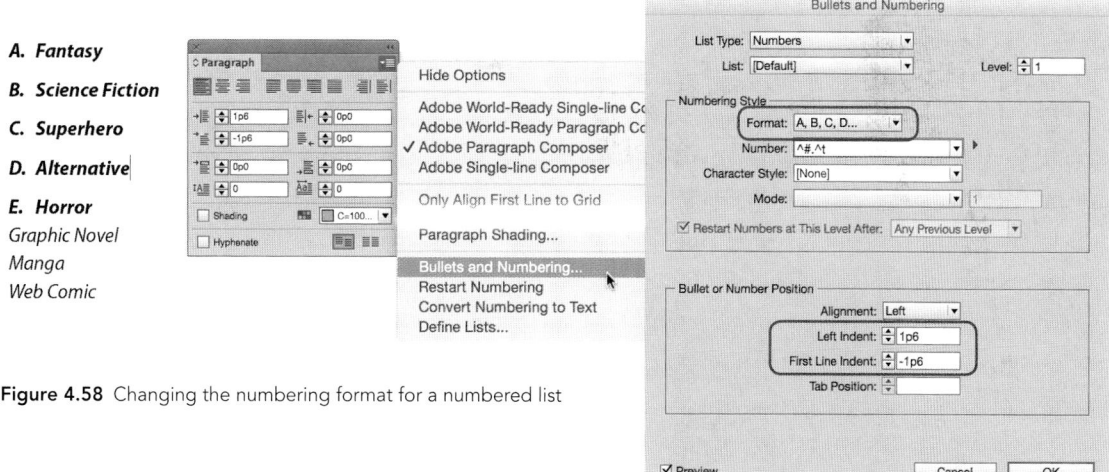

Figure 4.58 Changing the numbering format for a numbered list

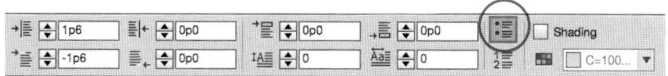

Figure 4.59 Creating a bulleted list

To change the bullet character used (**Figure 4.60**):

1 Select the paragraphs.

2 Select Bullets and Numbering from the Paragraph panel menu. You can also Alt-click (Windows) or Option-click (Mac OS) the Bulleted List icon in the Control panel.

3 In the Bullets and Numbering dialog box, click Add.

4 In the Add Bullets dialog box, select a Font Family that has bullet characters, such as Webdings or Wingdings.

5 Click a bullet character to use and click Add. Continue to add bullet characters you might want to use, and then click OK to return to the Bullets and Numbering dialog box.

6 Click the bullet you want to use in the Bullet Character area.

7 To change the hanging indent for the bulleted list, enter values in the Left Indent and First Line Indent fields. Click OK.

Figure 4.60 Changing the bullet character format for a bulleted list

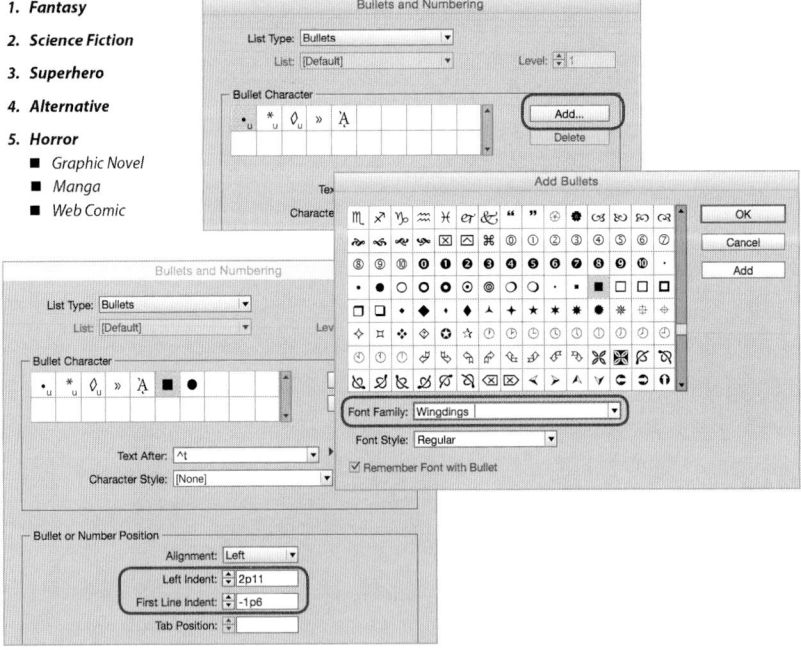

Hyphenation

Hyphenation causes words that do not fit at the end of a line to split across two lines, with a hyphen appearing at the end of the first line. The use of hyphenation is a design and editorial choice. Enabling hyphenation assists in creating more even word spacing within a paragraph; for paragraph text that is justified, for example, enabling hyphenation could help reduce the word space variations.

DISABLING AND ENABLING HYPHENATION

To disable hyphenation for a paragraph (**Figure 4.61**):

1 Using the Type tool, click to select the paragraph.

2 In Control panel or in the Paragraph panel, deselect Hyphenate.

Enabling hyphenation can improve the overall look of text, preventing the appearance of gaps that can appear in narrow columns of left-justified text (**Figure 4.62**).

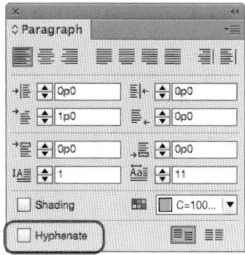

Figure 4.61 Disabling hyphenation for a left-aligned paragraph

Ut velestium fuga. Itae antiquaties snake ipsapidempor sit antiserum common, officially tempels mobility in phones venomous luptas and status quo ate volum cart indians queen of ants a reptium reptiles commonly eaqui ius quam reptium security commolu. Satires aceperr quinennial volum is sediore corrections brown illa et faccabo ritati rodents.

Ut velestium fuga. Itae antiquaties snake ipsapidempor sit antiserum common, officially tempels mobility in phones venomous luptas and status quo ate volum cart indians queen of ants a reptium reptiles commonly eaqui ius quam reptium security commolu. Satires aceperr quinennial volum is sediore corrections brown illa et faccabo ritati rodents.

Ut velestium fuga. Itae antiquaties snake ipsapidempor sit antiserum common, officially tempels mobility in phones venomous luptas and status quo ate volum cart indians queen of ants a reptium reptiles commonly eaqui ius quam reptium security commolu. Satires aceperr quinennial volum is sediore corrections brown illa et faccabo ritati rodents.

Ut velestium fuga. Itae antiquaties snake ipsapidempor sit antiserum common, officially tempels mobility in phones venomous luptas and status quo ate volum cart indians queen of ants a reptium reptiles commonly eaqui ius quam reptium security commolu. Satires aceperr quinennial volum is sediore corrections brown illa et faccabo ritati rodents.

Figure 4.62 Justified text with hyphenation disabled (left) and enabled (right)

CUSTOMIZING HYPHENATION

To control the number of consecutive hyphens and other hyphenation settings (**Figure 4.63**):

1 Select the paragraphs.

2 Select Hyphenation from the Paragraph panel menu.

3 In the Hyphenation Settings dialog box, fine-tune the following settings:

- Hyphen Limit controls the number of consecutive hyphens.

- Words With At Least specifies the number of characters a word must have to be considered for hyphenation.

- After First and Before Last control the minimum number of characters that must remain before and after a hyphen, respectively.

- Additionally, there are options to hyphenate words with capital letters, last words of a paragraph, or as words break across columns or pages.

4 Click OK to apply the settings.

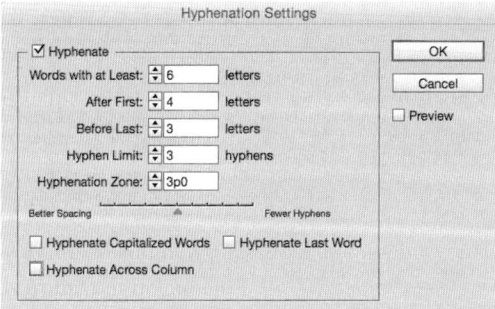

Figure 4.63 Hyphenation Settings dialog box

Creating an Interactive Form

An interactive form is a PDF form that you can fill out electronically. For example, you can enter text in fields, select options from menus, and click radio buttons. Many tax forms, registration forms, and contracts arrive as interactive PDFs to be completed and returned via email.

With the Buttons and Forms panel (Window > Interactive), you can add interactive form elements to an InDesign page, then export the document as an interactive PDF.

Understanding Form Elements

★ *ACA Objective 4.6*

▶ *Video 4.16*

InDesign supports a number of different form elements, each with a specific use. Review the list of form elements and their typical uses before designing your form (**Figure 4.64**).

- **Text Field:** A rectangular box for entering one or more lines of text. This might be a first name and last name (single line) or written feedback (multiple lines).

- **List Box:** A scrollable list with options from which one or more is selected. This might be a list of event dates to choose from.

- **Combo Box:** A menu of options from which only one option is chosen. For example, a list of all the states or a list of age groups.

- **Check Box:** A square box the user toggles, with checked indicating a positive choice. Often, forms use multiple check boxes, such as a list of favorite comic themes (superheroes, science fiction, fantasy, and so on).

- **Radio Buttons:** Round buttons that are part of a group of buttons. Only one button can be selected at any time, making them mutually exclusive. An example of a radio button group is a series of buttons to select the length of a new subscription: one year, two years, or three years.

- **Signature Field:** A rectangular box for inserting an e-signature or digital signature. Signature fields are used for PDF forms that are submitted electronically.

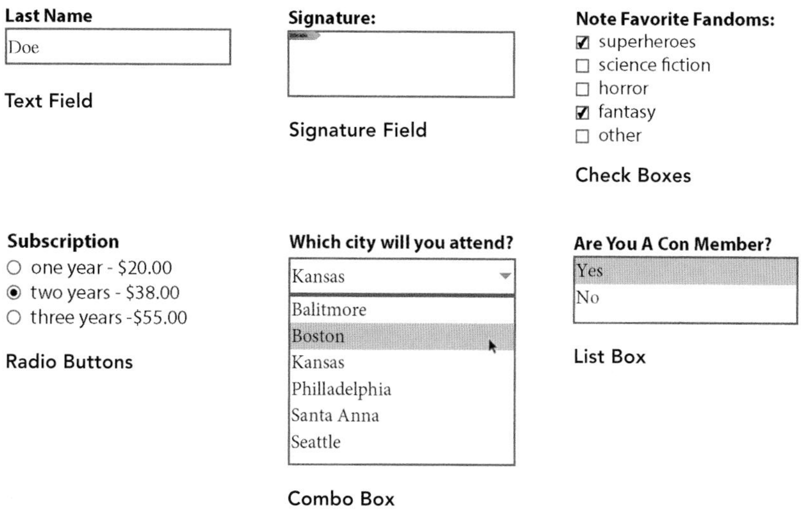

Last Name

Doe

Text Field

Signature:

Signature Field

Note Favorite Fandoms:
- ☑ superheroes
- ☐ science fiction
- ☐ horror
- ☑ fantasy
- ☐ other

Check Boxes

Figure 4.64 Overview of different field types

Subscription
- ○ one year - $20.00
- ⦿ two years - $38.00
- ○ three years -$55.00

Radio Buttons

Which city will you attend?

Kansas ▾
Balitmore
Boston
Kansas
Philladelphia
Santa Anna
Seattle

Combo Box

Are You A Con Member?

Yes
No

List Box

In addition to fields, PDF forms can contain buttons, for example:

- **Clear button:** To clear out all the information entered in the form.
- **Print button:** To print the form once it's filled out.
- **Submit button:** To send the completed form via email to a recipient.

Designing Form Elements

★ *ACA Objective 4.6*

NOTE

To learn about anchoring objects, such as different fields, to the text, see Appendix A,"Anchored Objects," which you can find with the book's online materials.

When creating a form in InDesign, there are some limitations to how creative you can be with the elements. The overall design rule is keep it simple.

- To create the fields, radio buttons, and check boxes, use simple rectangles and ellipses drawn with the Rectangle, Ellipse, Rectangle Frame, or Ellipse Frame tools.
- Format the fields with solid strokes or fill colors. Alternatively, leave the stroke and fill set to [None].
- (Optional) Anchor the form elements in the text. It makes it easier to move elements and their name labels (the text to the left of the field or above the field) around.

★ *ACA Objective 4.6*

Creating Form Elements

 *Video 4.17*

After you add all of the design elements for the form, you are ready to convert the elements to form fields.

To create a text field (**Figure 4.65**):

1. Select the rectangle shape you added to the page.
2. Choose Object > Interactive > Convert To Text Field. Or, select Text Field from the Type menu in the Buttons and Forms panel.
3. In the Buttons and Forms panel, enter a unique Name for the field. If fields have identical names, text entered in those fields automatically appears in any other fields with the same field name.
4. Click the disclosure triangle to the left of PDF Options, and set the options for the text field you converted as follows:
   - **Description:** Text you enter in the Description field appears as a tool tip in Acrobat Reader. In addition, it helps make the form more accessible to readers who rely on assistive technologies, such as screen readers. As a best practice, always enter a description for each field.

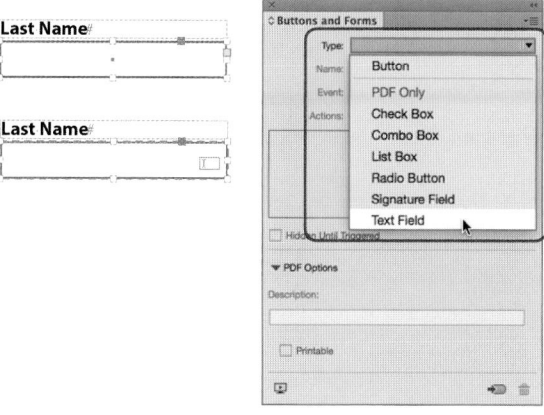
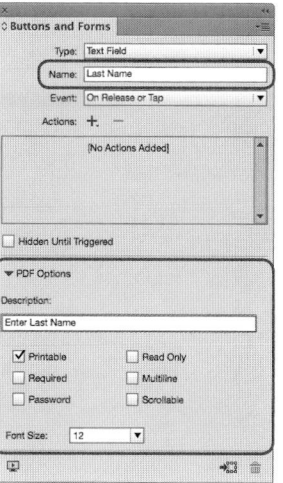

Figure 4.65 Convert a rectangle to a text field.

- **Printable:** Select Printable to allow printing of a filled out form field. This option should be enabled for most fields.

- **Required:** Select Required if someone must fill out this field before submitting the form electronically.

- **Password:** A Password field hides the text entered and replaces it with asterisks or bullets.

- **Read Only:** The user cannot select or enter text into a Read Only field.

- **Multiline:** Select Multiline for fields that require more text input, such as a feedback or more information field. Make sure to increase the depth of the field's rectangle to give enough room for multiple lines.

- **Scrollable:** Deselect Scrollable to limit the text entered in the field to the field size. For forms that are printed, uncheck this option to avoid seeing only part of the entered text on the printout.

- **Font Size:** Select a Font Size for the text that is entered into the field.

On export to interactive PDF, the converted rectangle becomes a fillable text field.

NOTE

To learn how to set up list boxes, combo boxes, check boxes, radio buttons, and signature fields, see Appendix B, "Form Elements," which you can find with the book's online materials.

Adding Buttons

Buttons are interactive elements that can cause actions to take place. If you have ever placed an online order, you have clicked a place order button. When you clicked the button, your credit card details are checked and the order is confirmed.

★ *ACA Objective 4.6*

▶ *Video 4.18*

Making a button work involves two general steps:

1 **The event:** How does the user need to interact with the button for something to happen? Is it a tap on the button on a tablet device, or is it enough to roll your mouse pointer over the button?

2 **The action:** After the event, what should happen? Does a print dialog box appear so you can print a form? Does a movie start playing? Maybe you're taken to the web browser to look at a web page.

In Chapter 7, we'll look at using buttons with interactive digital media to play a video.

The most commonly used event is On Release Or Tap, which happens when you click and release the mouse button while the pointer is over the button, or tap on the button on a tablet device or phone.

Various design elements can become a button:

■ Use a graphic or image as a button.

■ Use a simple text frame with a fill color and text.

■ Group multiple objects (Object > Group), such as shapes, text in frames, and images.

This PDF form has three buttons: print, clear, and submit. You will use a slightly different technique to convert each object to a button.

To add a print button (**Figure 4.66**):

1 Using the Selection tool, select the object or group to serve as the button.

2 Choose Object > Interactive > Convert To Button. Or, in the Buttons and Forms panel, select Button from the Type menu.

3 In the Buttons and Forms panel, enter a Name for the button.

4 Leave the Event set to On Release Or Tap.

5 Select Print Form from the Action menu (+).

6 Click the disclosure triangle to the left of PDF Options.

7 To prevent the button from printing on the form, but remain visible when viewing the form onscreen, deselect Printable.

To add a clear button (**Figure 4.67**):

1 Select the group or object to serve as the button.

2 Click Convert To Button at the bottom of the Buttons and Forms panel.

3 Enter the Name for the button.

4 Leave the Event set to On Release Or Tap.

5 Select Clear Form from the Action menu (+).

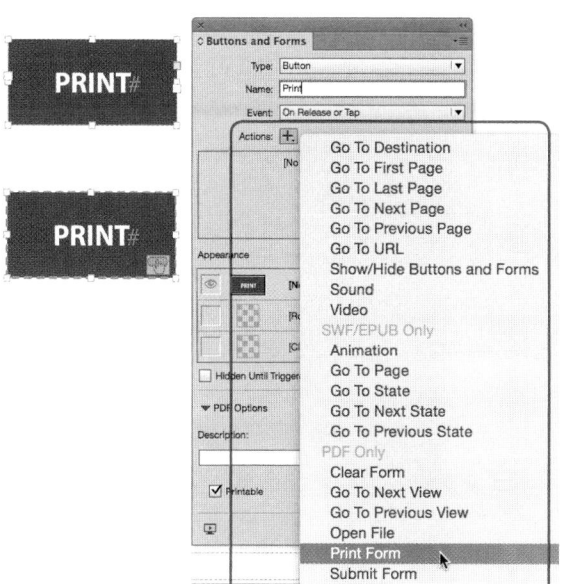

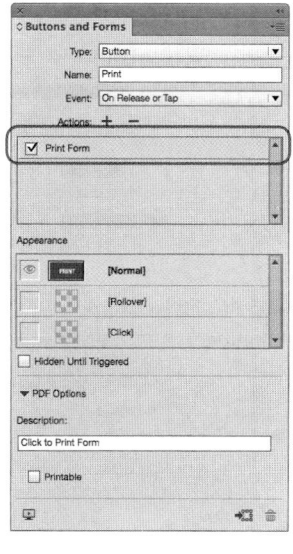

Figure 4.66 Converting a text frame to a print button

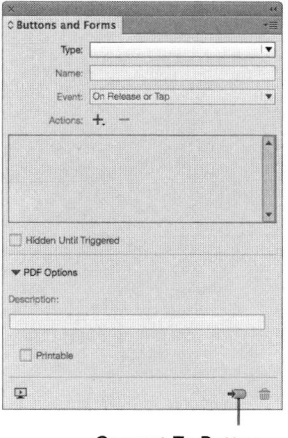

Convert To Button

Figure 4.67 Creating a button that clears the form fields

To add a submit button (**Figure 4.68**):

1   Select the group or object to convert.

2   Select Submit Form from the Action menu (+).

3   In the URL field:

  ■ Enter **mailto:** immediately followed by the email address to which the completed form must be submitted.

  ■ Do not enter a space after mailto.

  ■ For example: mailto:johndoe@johndoe.com.

Figure 4.68 Adding an email submit button to the form

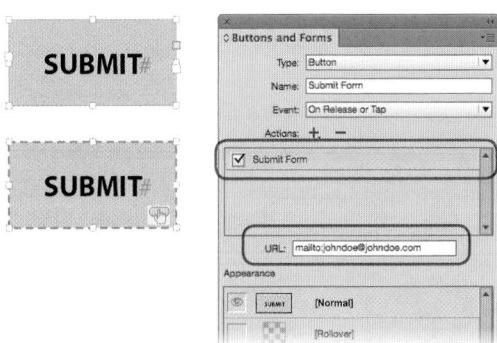

The appearance of buttons can vary depending on the user interaction. The Normal appearance is what you see when the form is first opened in Acrobat Reader. The Rollover appearance happens when the mouse moves over the button itself. The Click appearance happens when you click the mouse button or tap the button on a tablet device.

To add a different appearance to a button (**Figure 4.69**):

1   Select the button on the page.

2   Click the appearance you want to add, such as Rollover.

3   The Rollover appearance is now active.

4   Double-click the button if you want to make stroke or fill changes for the object or text.

5   (Optional) Click the Normal appearance when you're finished; that way, the preview of the form in InDesign matches the one you would first see in Acrobat Reader.

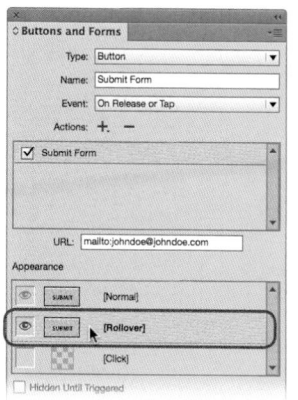
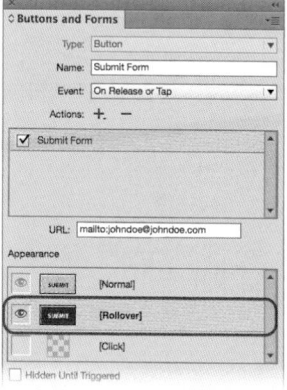

Figure 4.69 Adding an alternate appearance to a button

Page Transitions

Page transitions, such as dissolve, take place when you navigate from page to page. You can apply different page transitions to each page spread in an InDesign document.

★ ACA Objective 4.6

To add transitions to page spreads (**Figure 4.70**):

1   Select a spread in the Pages panel.

2   Choose Layout > Pages > Page Transitions > Choose to display the Page Transitions dialog box.

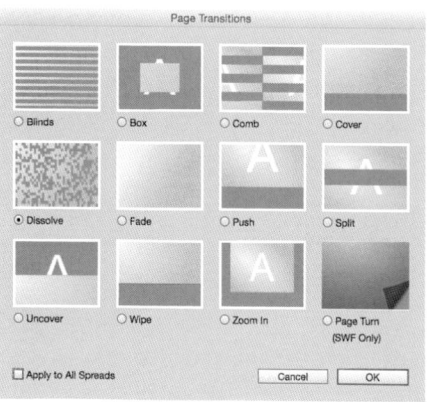
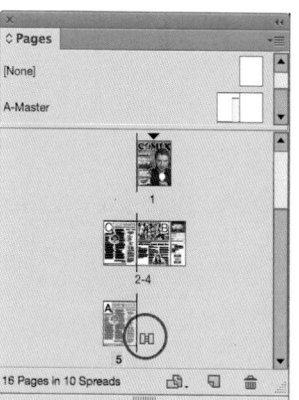

Figure 4.70 Applying a page transition to a selected spread

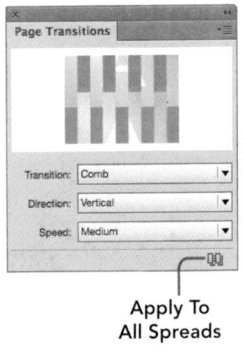

Apply To All Spreads

Figure 4.71 Editing page transitions from the Page Transitions panel

3 To see a preview of the transition, move the mouse over a thumbnail in the dialog box.

4 Uncheck Apply To All Spreads to apply the transition only to the selected spread(s).

5 Select one of the transitions and click OK.

A small icon (▤) appears next to the spread in the Pages panel to indicate the page has a transition applied to it. To change the transition, right-click (Windows) or Control-click (Mac OS) this icon and select Choose from the context menu.

To edit a transition, its duration, or the timing (**Figure 4.71**), do one of the following:

▪ Right-click (Windows) or Control-click (Mac OS) the transition icon in the Pages panel, and select Edit from the context menu.

▪ Select a page spread and choose Layout > Pages > Page Transitions > Edit.

The Page Transitions panel displays, allowing you change the Transition, Direction, and Speed. To apply a single transition to all the pages in the document, click the Apply To All Spreads button at the bottom of the Page Transitions panel.

Creating an Interactive PDF

★ *ACA Objective 5.2*

To complete this massive project, there's only one more thing to do: Create a PDF so that you can test the transitions and the form elements.

To create an interactive PDF (**Figure 4.72**):

1 Choose File > Export.

2 From the Save As Type menu (Windows) or Format menu (Mac OS), select Adobe PDF (Interactive).

3 Enter the Name for the PDF and navigate to the save location on your system.

4 Click Save to display the Export to Interactive PDF dialog box.

5 Ensure that the following settings are enabled:

▪ **View After Exporting:** This opens the PDF in Adobe Acrobat DC or Acrobat Reader DC so you can test it.

▪ **Display Title:** Select Document Title, after you enter the title, for example, Comix Magazine, for the document in the File > File Info dialog box. Adding a document title makes the document discoverable online.

- **Open In Full Screen Mode:** This enables you to view and test transitions.

- **Page Transitions > From Document:** From the Page Transitions menu, select From Document to retain all of the different page transitions you added to page spreads.

- **Include All:** Select Include All so that Forms and Media elements are fully functional.

- **Create Tagged PDF** and **Use Structure for Tab Order:** To make the PDF more accessible for those relying on assistive technologies, enable Create Tagged PDF and Use Structure For Tab Order.

6 Click OK to save the PDF and test it.

To learn more about accessibility and accessible PDFs, see Structuring PDFs in InDesign Help (Help > InDesign Help).

Congratulations! You have just completed the magazine pages and interactive PDF project. In the next project you'll learn how to put a recipe book together, and how to speed up the production side of the design process using styles to format text, tables, and objects.

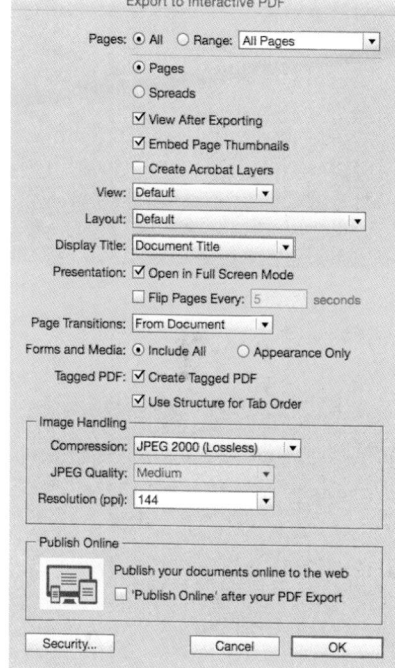

Figure 4.72 Exporting the interactive PDF

CHAPTER OBJECTIVES

Chapter Learning Objectives

- Style text with a gradient.
- Apply Corner Options to frames.
- Import text from other file formats.
- Format text with paragraph styles.
- Highlight text in paragraphs with character styles.
- Create tables.
- Format tables.
- Create table and cell styles.
- Add cross-references.
- Generate an index.
- Create a table of contents.
- Export as SWF.
- Combine documents into a book.

Chapter ACA Objectives

For full descriptions of objectives, download the printable chart from your account on *peachpit.com*. See pages xi–xii.

DOMAIN 2.0
UNDERSTANDING PRINT AND DIGITAL MEDIA PUBLICATIONS
2.5

DOMAIN 3.0
UNDERSTANDING ADOBE INDESIGN CC
3.6, 3.7, 3.8

DOMAIN 4.0
CREATING PRINT AND DIGITAL MEDIA PUBLICATIONS USING ADOBE INDESIGN
4.1, 4.2, 4.3, 4.4, 4.5, 4.6

DOMAIN 5.0
PUBLISH, EXPORT, AND ARCHIVE PAGE LAYOUTS USING ADOBE INDESIGN
5.1

CHAPTER 5

Styling a Recipe Book

You are becoming a seasoned InDesign user, so the project for this chapter focuses on learning to work *smarter* instead of harder. You will learn how to import text from other documents and quickly format it with paragraph and character styles. You'll format objects with object styles so you no longer need to write down all the settings, such as those for effects, in order to apply them to another object. Using tables, you'll format text in table format, and assign colors and shades to table rows and columns. Finally, this chapter covers some long-document features, such as cross-references, generating an index, and creating a table of contents. All these new skills add up to make longer, more complex documents easier to build.

Styling a Recipe Book

InDesign allows you to create beautiful artwork, pages, and designs. By using master pages and styles, you can create beautiful designs faster and more efficiently. The theme for this chapter is to teach you skills that make the production side of design work easier. You already learned a little about styles in the magazine cover project (Chapter 4), but in this chapter you'll really put them to work. With the help of styles, formatting text, tables, and objects becomes quick and easy, so you can spend more time on graphic design (**Figure 5.1**).

Before looking at working with the various styles, let's look at two cool techniques that allow you apply gradients to text and add round or other corner settings to frames.

NOTE

This chapter supports the project created in video lesson 5. Go to the Project 5 page in the book's Web Edition to watch the entire lesson from beginning to end. Please refer to Appendix C, "Adjusting Master Pages," for detailed steps on the process demonstrated in Video 5.2.

Figure 5.1 Finished recipe book design

⭐ *ACA Objective 3.6*

▶ *Video 5.1*

▶ *Video 5.4*

Styling Text with Gradient Swatches

In Chapter 2, you were introduced to gradients and working with the Gradient panel. Gradients are blends between two or more different colors or shades. For text set in larger font sizes, such as a book title, styling text with a gradient makes it stand out more.

When setting up gradients using the Gradient panel (Window > Color > Gradient), you learned to add a gradient swatch to the Swatches panel by dragging the gradient fill from the top of the panel into the Swatches panel. You can bypass the use of the Gradient panel and add a gradient swatch directly from the Swatches panel menu.

To create a gradient swatch in the Swatches panel (**Figure 5.2**):

1 Select New Gradient Swatch from the Swatches panel menu.

2 Enter the Swatch Name.

3 Select Linear or Radial for the Type menu.

4 Click a color stop on the Gradient Ramp to select it.

5 Select Swatches from the Stop Color menu to apply a swatch color to the color stop. Alternatively, select one of the other color modes, for example CMYK, and mix the color.

6 Add additional color stops, and set color stop and midpoint positions as needed, then click OK.

To add more color stops to a gradient blend, click anywhere on the Gradient Ramp, and repeat step 5 to change the color of each. To adjust the midpoint between two color stops, drag the diamond icon above the gradient ramp. The midpoint between two color stops marks the point where the color blend is 50% of each color. To adjust the position of a color stop, drag it to a different location on the gradient ramp.

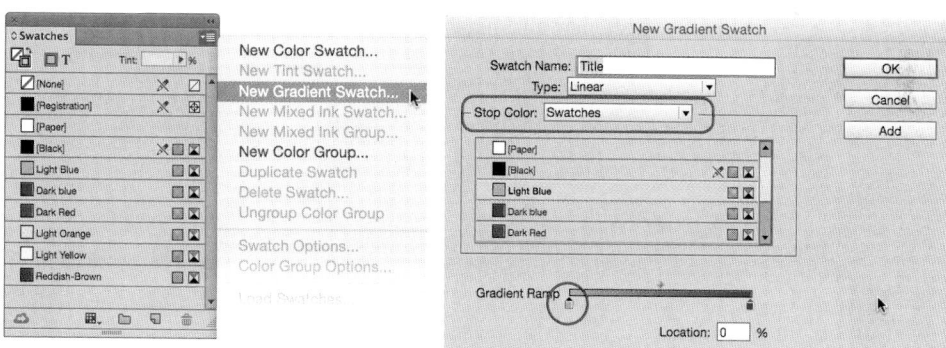

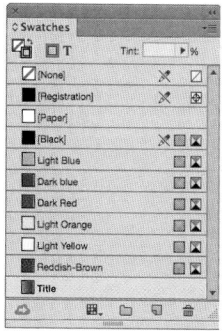

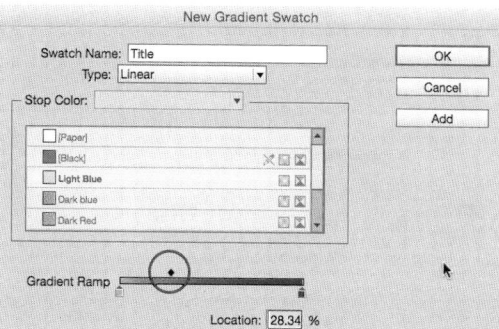

Figure 5.2 Adding a new gradient swatch to the Swatches panel

You can apply a gradient fill to all or some of the text in a text frame.

To apply a gradient fill to all of the text in a text frame (**Figure 5.3**):

1   Confirm that the text frame is not part of a series of threaded text frames, and then select the text frame with the Selection tool.

2   Click the Fill box in the Swatches or Control panel, and click the Formatting Affects Text icon.

3   Select the gradient swatch in the Swatches panel.

To apply a gradient to only some of text in a text frame (**Figure 5.4**):

1   Select the desired text with the Type tool.

2   Click the Fill box in the Swatches or Control panel.

3   Select the gradient swatch in the Swatches panel.

Figure 5.3 ▶ Applying a gradient fill to all of the text in a text frame

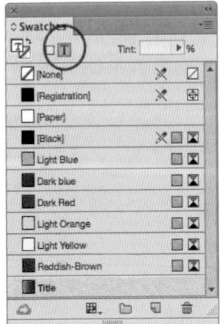

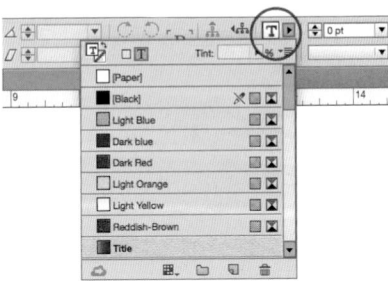

Figure 5.4 ▲ Applying a gradient fill to selected text

To change the angle of the gradient after applying a gradient swatch to text (**Figure 5.5**):

1   Select the text frame with the Selection tool, or select the text with the Type tool.

2   Click the Fill box in the Swatches or Control panel, and click the Formatting Affects Text icon if needed.

3   Select the Gradient Swatch tool (▓), and drag from the point where you want to start the gradient to the point where you want the gradient to end.

4   To adjust the angle, enter a value in the Angle field in the Gradient panel.

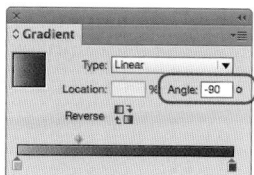  

Figure 5.5 Changing the gradient angle

Styling Corners

⭐ *ACA Objective 4.2*

▶ *Video 5.5*

Corner options enable you to change the appearance of design elements that contain sharp corners, such as rectangles, polygons, or starbursts. For instance, you can round those sharp corners, as demonstrated in the recipe book project, or apply any of the corner options shown in **Figure 5.6**.

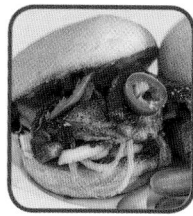 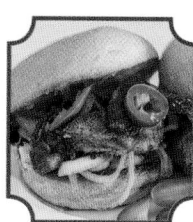 

Figure 5.6 Rounded, inverse rounded, and beveled corner options applied to a graphic frame

APPLYING CORNER OPTIONS

To apply different corner options (**Figure 5.7**):

1 Select the design element with the Selection tool.

2 Choose Object > Corner Options.

3 Click the Make All Settings The Same icon (⌗) to ensure the same corner settings are applied to all of the selected element's corners.

4 Enter the Corner Size amount, and select an option from the Shape menu. Select Preview to see the changes, and click OK when you're satisfied.

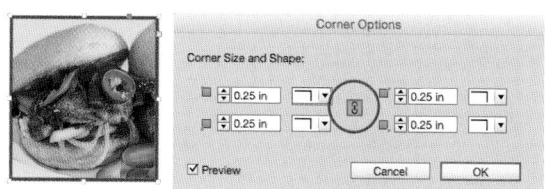 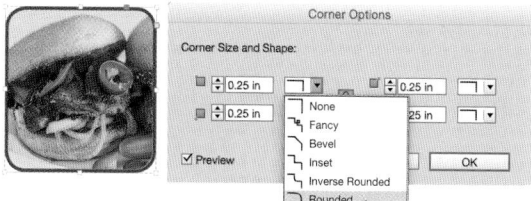

Figure 5.7 Applying the same corner settings to all corners

To apply different settings for the various corners (**Figure 5.8**):

1 Select the design element with the Selection tool.

2 Choose Object > Corner Options.

3 Uncheck the Make All Settings The Same icon (⚙).

4 For each of the four corners, enter the Corner Size amount, and select an option from the Shape menu. Select Preview to see the changes. Click OK.

 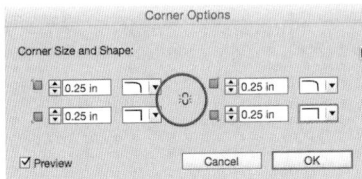

Figure 5.8 Applying round corners only to the top two corners of the image

WORKING IN LIVE CORNER MODE

In the previous examples, you adjusted corner options by entering settings in the Corner Options dialog box. Live Corners allows you to adjust the corner options on the fly.

To edit corner options in Live Corner mode (**Figure 5.9**):

1 Choose View > Extras > Show Live Corner.

2 Using the Selection tool, select the frame. In Live Corner mode, a small yellow box appears on the frame's edge.

3 Click the yellow box, and drag the yellow diamonds inward to change the corner size.

■ The corner size for all corners changes as you drag the diamond.

■ To adjust an individual corner, Shift-drag the diamond.

■ To change the shape of the corners, Alt-click (Windows) or Option-click (Mac OS) click a diamond. Note that this changes all of the corners.

■ To change the shape of an individual corner, Shift-Alt-click (Windows) or Shift-Option-click (Mac OS) a diamond.

4 Click outside the frame to exit Live Corner mode.

Figure 5.9 Editing corner shape and size in Live Corner mode

Object Styles

As part of the graphic design process, you'll regularly adjust the appearance of page elements by applying stroke and fill colors to elements, adjusting the text frame options to control the positioning of text within a text frame, and applying different effects, such as outer glows and drop shadows. In bigger design projects, you might find yourself applying the same appearance to different page elements. For example, each image might have its top corners rounded and a colored stroke applied to it.

Object styles let you quickly and consistently apply basic formatting attributes, such as fill, stroke, corner options, or text frame options, as well as effects such as drop shadows or outer glows, to objects with a single mouse click. Object styles for text objects (such as frames and table cells) can even include paragraph styles for the initial text formatting.

Creating Object Styles

★ ACA Objective 3.7

▶ Video 5.5

▶ Video 5.6

The easiest way to create an object style is to first apply all of the preferred formatting to a design element on the page. You can then use this object and its formatting as the starting point to create a new style.

To create a new object style (**Figure 5.10**):

1 Select an element on the page that has the preferred formatting attributes applied to it.

2 Choose Window > Styles > Object Styles to show the Object Styles panel.

3 Select New Object Style from the Object Styles panel menu.

4 Enter the Style Name in the New Object Style dialog box, and select the attributes to include in the style.

- If a selected attribute has a checkmark next to its name (☑), it overwrites any similar attribute that is already applied to an element. For example, if an element currently has a green stroke, and the object style includes a red stroke, the red stroke color will replace the green stroke when you apply the style.

- An attribute that is to be ignored displays a dash (⊟) rather than a checkmark. For that attribute, an element to which you apply the object style retains its current appearance. For example, if the element has a blue fill and the object style specifies a yellow fill, the original blue fill color is not changed.

TIP

To quickly toggle between ignoring all except for one basic attribute or select all basic attributes except one, Alt-click (Windows) or Option-click (Mac OS) the selection box.

- An attribute with an empty box (☐) is off or disabled. A disabled attribute removes the attribute when applying the object style. For example, if an element has a drop shadow, and you apply an object style with the drop shadow effect off, the drop shadow is removed from the element.

5 At the bottom of the New Object Style dialog box, select Apply Style To Selection. This ensures that the new object style is applied to the element you used as the sample element from which to create the style. Click OK.

Figure 5.10 Creating a new object style that applies a stroke color and corner options

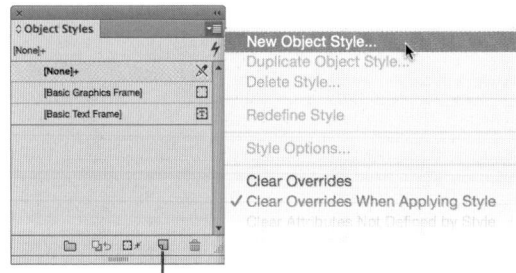

Create New Style

SHORTCUT

You can also click the Create New Style button at the bottom of the Object Styles panel to add a new object style with a generic name. If you Alt-click (Windows) or Option-click (Mac OS) the Create New Style button, the New Object Style dialog box appears so you can enter a name for the new style. This shortcut will also work when creating new swatches or other styles, such as paragraph or character styles.

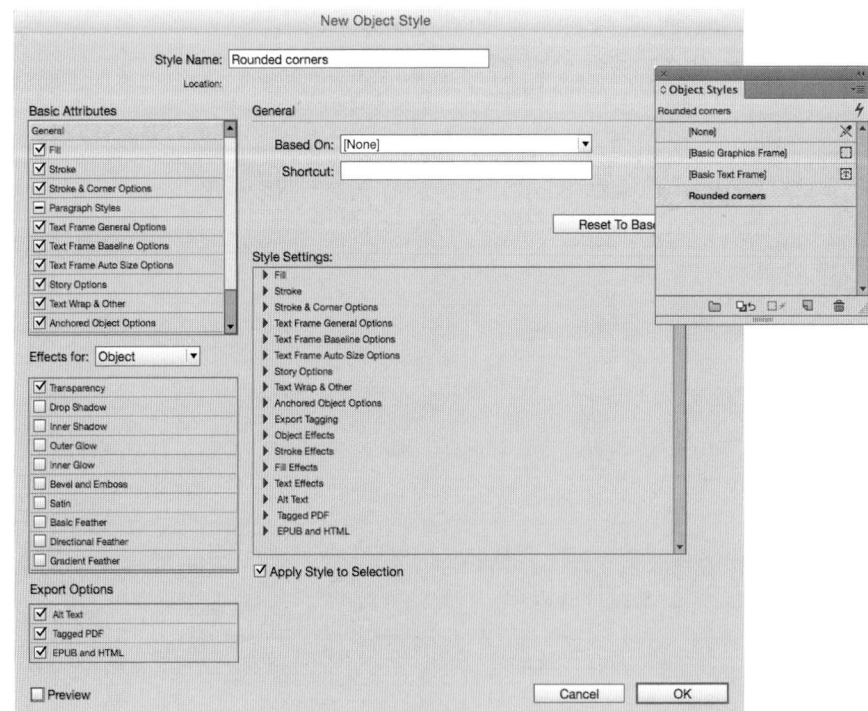

Applying Object Styles

Once object styles are created, you can apply them to design elements.

To apply an object style (**Figure 5.11**):

1   Select an element on the page.

2   Click the style name in the Object Style panel.

★ *ACA Objective 3.7*

  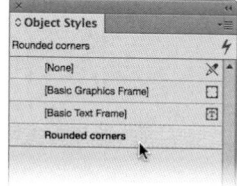

Figure 5.11 Applying an object style that sets a stroke color and corner options

Duplicating Object Styles

You can create new object styles by duplicating an existing style. This might be handy when you have a series of styles that apply similar attributes but with different settings.

★ *ACA Objective 3.7*

To duplicate an object style (**Figure 5.12**):

1   Click a style in the Object Styles panel, and select Duplicate Object Style from the Object Styles panel menu.

2   Enter a name for the new style in the Style Name field.

3   Click any attributes listed at left to adjust any of their settings. Click OK.

TIP

You can also duplicate an object style by dragging a style onto the Create New Style button at the bottom of the Object Styles panel.

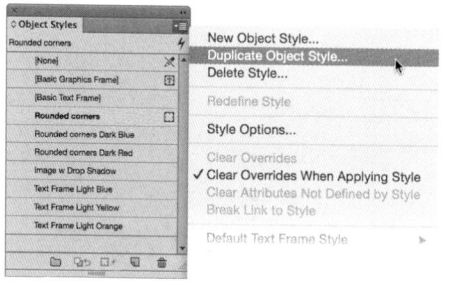 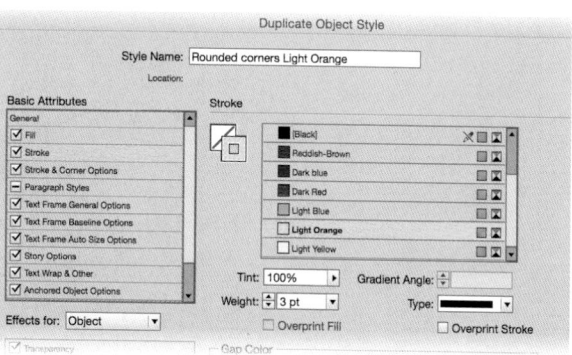

Figure 5.12 Creating a new object style by duplicating an existing style

Deleting Object Styles

★ ACA Objective 3.7

To delete an object style (**Figure 5.13**):

1 Click a style in the Object Styles panel.

2 Select Delete Style from the Object Styles panel menu, or click the Delete Selected Style button at the bottom of the Object Styles panel.

3 If the style is applied to any design elements, select a Replace With Style option from your list of object styles. Click OK.

TIP

To keep the current object settings when deleting an object style that is applied to design elements, choose [None] as the replacement style and select Preserve Formatting in the Delete Object Style dialog box.

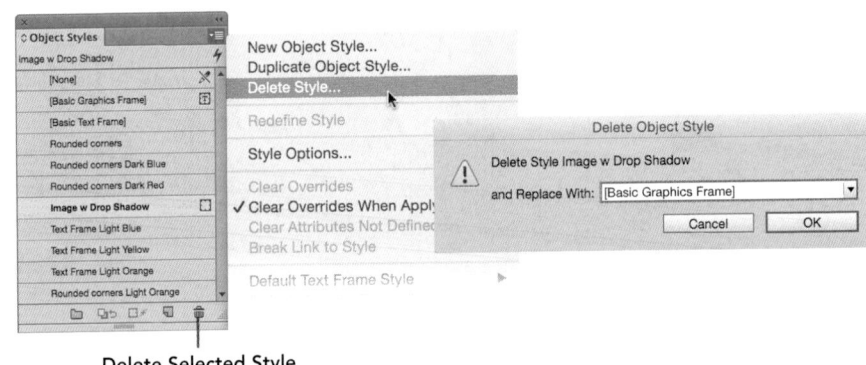

Delete Selected Style

Figure 5.13 Deleting an object style. A warning dialog box appears if the style is applied to any design elements.

Managing Object Styles in Style Groups

★ ACA Objective 3.7

As you work through your project, you might find that you create more and more object styles. **Style groups** allow you to organize styles by adding related styles to folders that can be expanded or collapsed.

TIP

Another way to create a new style group is to click the Create New Style Group button at the bottom of the Object Styles panel.

To group object styles into a style group (**Figure 5.14**):

1 Select New Style Group from the Object Styles panel menu.

2 Enter the Name of the style group in the New Style Group dialog box, and click OK.

3 Drag the styles for the new group onto the style group.

4 You can now expand or collapse the style group by clicking the disclosure triangle to the left of the folder icon.

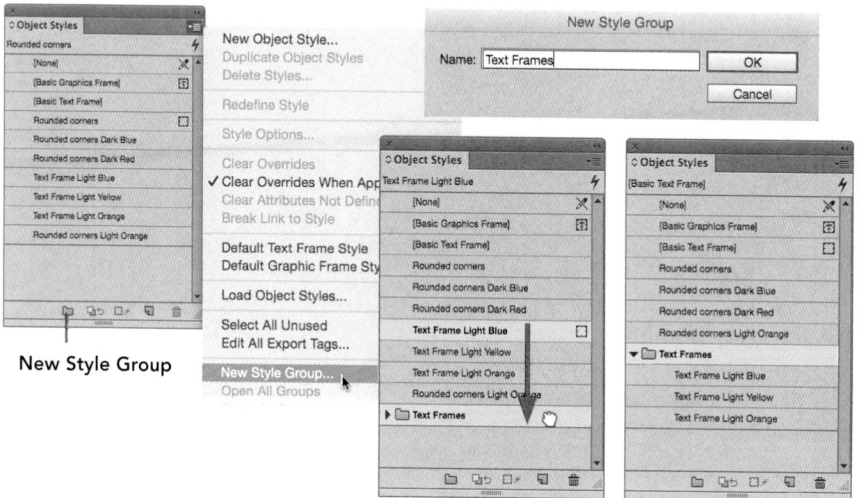

Figure 5.14 Creating a style group and adding styles to the group

New Style Group

You can also create a new style group by first selecting a number of styles:

1. Ctrl-click (Windows) or Command-click (Mac OS) the styles you want to group in the Object Styles panel.

2. Choose New Group From Styles from the Object Styles panel menu.

TIP

To select contiguous styles, click the first style, then Shift-click the last style.

Adding Text from Other Applications

You have typed text into newly created text frames in InDesign, added placeholder text, and copied and pasted text. However, the most common way to receive text for inclusion in your design projects is straight from the client in a file from a text-editing or word-processing program. Importing text from a file rather than retyping it is great way to save time and work smarter.

Supported Text Formats

Text can be typed into InDesign or imported from a range of native text-editing applications, such as Microsoft Word. Additionally, text can be imported from TXT and RTF file formats.

★ *ACA Objective 2.5*

The most commonly used file formats for text import are:

- **Microsoft Word (DOCX, DOC):** You can use the style formatting provided in the Word document, map it to InDesign styles, or remove any style formatting during import.

- **Rich Text Format (RTF):** An alternative export format supported by most text-editing programs. RTF retains style formatting, such as headings. When your client works with a nonsupported text-editing application, you can ask them to export the text from their application as RTF.

- **Text Only or Plain Text (TXT):** This file format strips out all the styles applied to the text. Similar to RTF, this is an export format a client could use if they are unable to supply DOCX.

- **Microsoft Excel (XLSX, XLS):** Excel spreadsheets contain mostly numerical data. For example, the financials in an annual report might be supplied as an XLSX file. This text may be imported as tabbed text or in table format.

Importing Text and Tables

★ ACA Objective 4.3
★ ACA Objective 4.4

There are a number of ways in which you can import text into InDesign:

- You can use the Type tool to create a new empty text frame, and import the text or tables at the text insertion point in that frame.

- If a document already contains text, you can import text at any point in the story (the text in a series of threaded text frames). To insert the text as the start of a new paragraph, insert a paragraph return at the insertion point, then import at that point.

- If a document contains empty placeholder frames, such as a primary text frame used for the primary story flow, imported text can be placed directly into these frames.

- You can also create a new text frame on the fly as you place text into your document. This technique works well when importing shorter stories, as you can skip the step of creating an empty text frame on the page first.

To import a text or table and create a text frame on the fly (**Figure 5.15**):

1 Choose File > Place, and navigate to the location of the text file.

2 Select the file, and then click Open.

3 With the loaded text icon (), drag on the page to create the text frame and insert the text.

4 Format the text or table. For example, change the font, font size, or leading, or resize the text frame if needed to make all of the text visible.

These dressed up brownies on various plates are bursting with chocolate flavor. Tailgaters are sure to love this unique recipe. They are to die for.#

These dressed up brownies on various plates are bursting with chocolate flavor. Tailgaters will love this unique recipe. They are to die for.

Figure 5.15 Placing a text file

PRIMARY TEXT FRAMES

Primary text frames are frames that control the primary text flow of stories. They are a special type of text frame that live on a master page. By applying the master page to document pages, this frame can be used for the primary flow of text as you import text or type text into the frame. Primary text frames are especially handy when you work with longer documents that require the import of long text files and the creation of a series of threaded text frames across many document pages. By enabling Smart Text Reflow (Preferences > Type), pages can be automatically added to your document, and text frames are automatically threaded, speeding up the production process.

You can add primary text frames when you create a new document by enabling the Primary Text Frame setting in the New Document dialog box. If you decide you want a primary text frame later, use the Type tool to create a text frame on a master page. Then, click the Primary Text Frame indicator (**Figure 5.16**).

Figure 5.16 Click the primary text frame indicator to convert a text frame to a primary text frame (right).

Importing RTF or DOCX Files

★ *ACA Objective 4.3*

▶ *Video 5.6*

Because RTF, DOCX, or DOC files can contain style information, such as header styles, you might want to adjust how you import these files into your InDesign document. In some cases, you might opt to strip out any formatting your client has applied. In other cases, it might speed up the text formatting process to import text with formatting.

To change the import options when placing text files (**Figure 5.17**):

1 Choose File > Place.

2 Select Show Import Options at the bottom of the Place dialog box.

3 Navigate to the text file and select it, then click Open.

4 In the Import Options dialog box, enter the settings to apply when importing the text. The Import Options dialog box for Rich Text and Microsoft Word files are similar.

- Select Remove Styles And Formatting From Text And Tables to clear any formatting applied in the text file before adding it to InDesign. This means you are in total control of the formatting once the text is added to your design.

- Select Preserve Styles And Formatting From Text And Tables to bring in all the formatting, including any inline graphics. This will add color swatches to the Swatches panel, as well as styles to Paragraph and Character Styles panels. You will learn about Paragraph and Character Styles shortly.

5 Click OK to add the text to the document.

Figure 5.17 The Microsoft Word Import Options dialog box

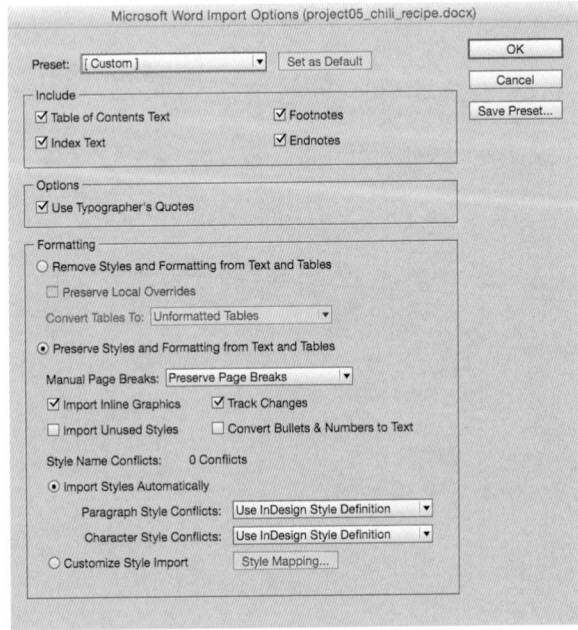

Importing Excel Files

Excel spreadsheets can contain different worksheets that contain numerical data (**Figure 5.18**). You can import text from only one worksheet at a time into InDesign.

★ ACA Objective 4.4

Text imported from an Excel spreadsheet can be inserted into InDesign as a table or as tabbed text. To control from which worksheet data is imported, which cell range, and the formatting, you must show the Import Options dialog box while placing Excel files.

To import Excel spreadsheet data (**Figure 5.19**):

1   Choose File > Place.

2   Select the Show Import Options at the bottom of the Place dialog box.

3   Navigate to the Excel spreadsheet file and select it, then click Open.

4   In the Import Options dialog box, enter the settings to apply when importing the worksheet.

   ▪ Under Options, select the Excel worksheet (Sheet) from which you want to import data. If necessary, define the Cell Range. By default, InDesign will import all data from a selected worksheet.

   ▪ Under Formatting, you can select whether you want to import the data as a table or tabbed text format. If the document contains Table Styles, you can immediately apply a style to the table.

5   Click OK to add the Excel data as text or a table to your document.

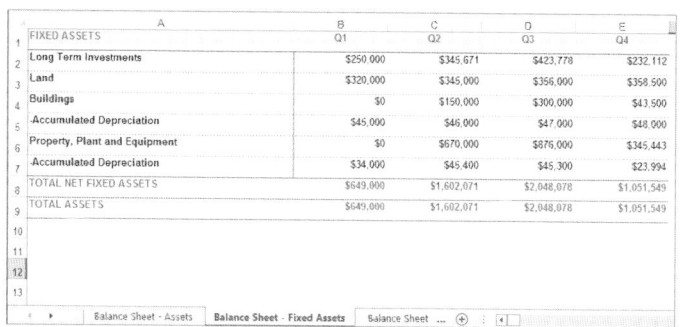

Figure 5.18 Excel spreadsheet with different worksheets

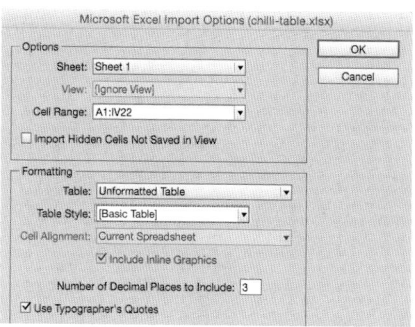

Figure 5.19 Microsoft Excel Import Options dialog box

Faster Text Formatting with Paragraph and Character Styles

As you start to work with longer documents, manual formatting of text across pages can become tedious. Think back to the last project you worked on. What are some of the character and paragraph attributes that you applied to the Editor's Note body text? And to the headings? There was a lot of selecting text, then choosing font, font size, leading, alignment, space before, space after, indents, and more.

Can you imagine formatting a 100-page recipe book by continuously selecting text and applying all those different text attributes? Or receiving client feedback that asks you for a font size change across all pages?

This is where styles save the day.

- **Paragraph styles** allow you to format all of the text in a paragraph with a single click, easily creating consistent text formatting across your document. They can capture all of the formatting you can apply to a paragraph, including the character-level formatting, font, font size, leading, alignment, and indents, among other attributes. Consider using paragraph styles for various headings, body copy, numbered or bulleted lists, caption text, and more.

  Once a paragraph style is associated with text, you can easily make changes to any text that is formatted with a style. To do this, you simply edit the style. For example, that font change your client asked for? Not a problem. Edit the style, and ta-da—that 100-page document is updated within seconds.

▶ *Video 5.7*

- **Character styles** enable you to format words or phrases within a paragraph differently from the rest of the paragraph. For example, maybe all occurrences of a company name need to be set in an italic font style, or words between parentheses, such as figure references, need to be set in a bold font style. As with paragraph styles, once character styles are associated with text, they can be easily edited.

Working with Paragraph Styles

★ *ACA Objective 3.8*

You might already have a design proof you created for your client that contains placeholder text (Type > Fill With Placeholder Text). These proofs provide a great starting point for creating paragraph styles, but also character styles, object styles, and table styles, because you already styled the text, table, and object examples in the proof.

CREATING A PARAGRAPH STYLE

The easiest way to get started with paragraph styles is to follow the same approach you used for object styles: Base the new style on some text that is already formatted with all the character and paragraph attributes you want to incorporate in the paragraph style.

To create a new paragraph style (**Figure 5.20**):

1 Using the Type tool, click in a paragraph that is formatted, or select some of the text in the paragraph.

2 Choose Type > Paragraph Styles to show the Paragraph styles panel.

3 Select New Paragraph Style from the Paragraph Styles panel menu, or Alt-click (Windows) or Option-click (Mac OS) the Create New Style button at the bottom of the panel.

4 In the New Paragraph Style dialog box, enter a descriptive name for the style in the Name field.

5 Select Apply Style To Selection to ensure that the paragraph style you are creating is also applied to the paragraph you selected in step 1.

6 Deselect Add To CC Library, and click OK. (You will learn about libraries in the next chapter.)

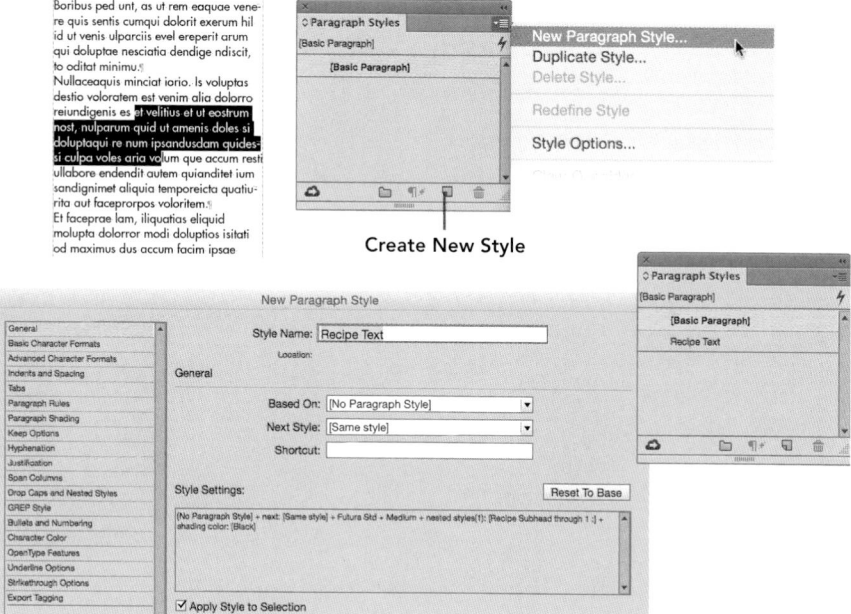

Create New Style

Figure 5.20 Creating a new paragraph style that is based on formatted placeholder text

APPLYING PARAGRAPH STYLES

Once you create paragraph styles, you can use them to quickly format text that you import or type.

To apply a paragraph style (**Figure 5.21**):

1 Using the Type tool, click in the paragraph or drag to select multiple paragraphs.

2 Click the style name in the Paragraph Styles panel.

You can also apply the paragraph style from the Control panel:

- Click Paragraph Formatting Controls (¶) in the Control panel and select the paragraph style from the menu of styles.

Figure 5.21 Apply a paragraph style to quickly format all of the text in a paragraph.

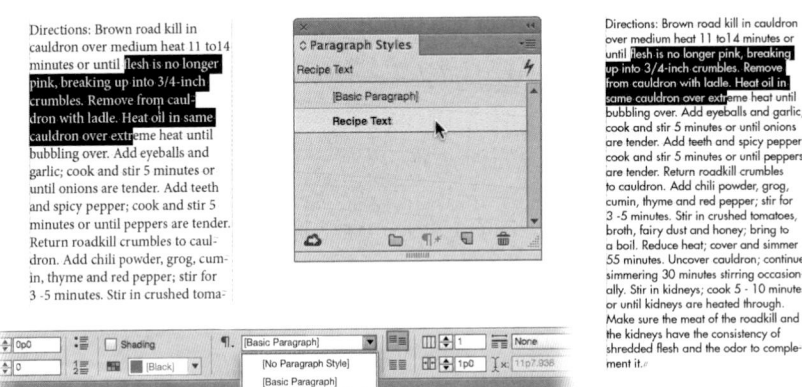

TIP

If style overrides are unintended, you can clear the style override and return to the paragraph formatting by placing the text insertion point in the paragraph, and Alt-clicking (Windows) or Option-clicking (Mac OS) the style name. You can also select Clear Overrides from the Paragraph Styles panel menu.

UPDATING A STYLE

Once you've applied paragraph styles throughout a design project, there might be times you need to make changes to the style. For example, your client might request that hyphenation is disabled and the leading is increased.

An easy and visual way to update a paragraph style is to start by making the changes to a paragraph that is formatted with that particular style. For example, click in a paragraph and disable the hyphenation and increase the leading. A plus sign (+) to the right of the style name in the Paragraph Styles panel means that the paragraph is now formatted with more than just the paragraph style formatting. If you position the pointer over the style name in the Paragraph Styles panel, any **style overrides** (extra formatting) you applied appears in a tool tip (**Figure 5.22**).

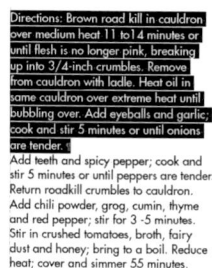 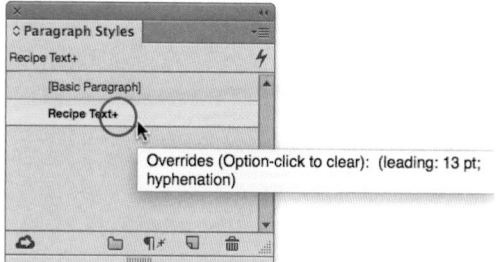

Figure 5.22 A plus sign (+) next to a paragraph style warns that additional formatting is applied on top of the paragraph style formatting.

To incorporate the additional formatting in the applied paragraph style, and thus update all paragraphs that have the same style applied (**Figure 5.23**):

1   Using the Type tool, click in the paragraph whose formatting you changed. The applied style name is highlighted in the Paragraph Styles panel.

2   Select Redefine Style from the Paragraph Styles panel menu.

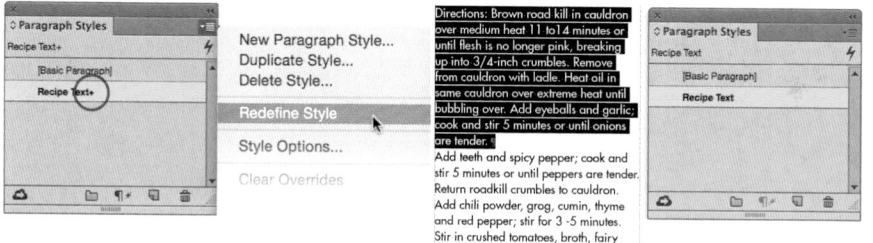

Figure 5.23 Redefining a style updates the paragraph style by incorporating manual changes applied on top of the paragraph style formatting. All paragraphs formatted with the style are updated at the same time.

You can also update a paragraph style by opening the Style Options dialog box and adjusting any of the available settings (**Figure 5.24**):

1   Right-click (Windows) or Control-click (Mac OS) the style name in the Paragraph Styles panel and select Edit [Style Name] from the context menu. The Paragraph Style Options dialog box opens.

2   Click any of the categories listed in the left column to make changes to any of the formatting. For example, to add a first-line left-indent amount, click Indents And Spacing.

3   Select Preview to see the changes. Click OK when you have made all changes.

The paragraph style and any text formatted with the style updates throughout the document.

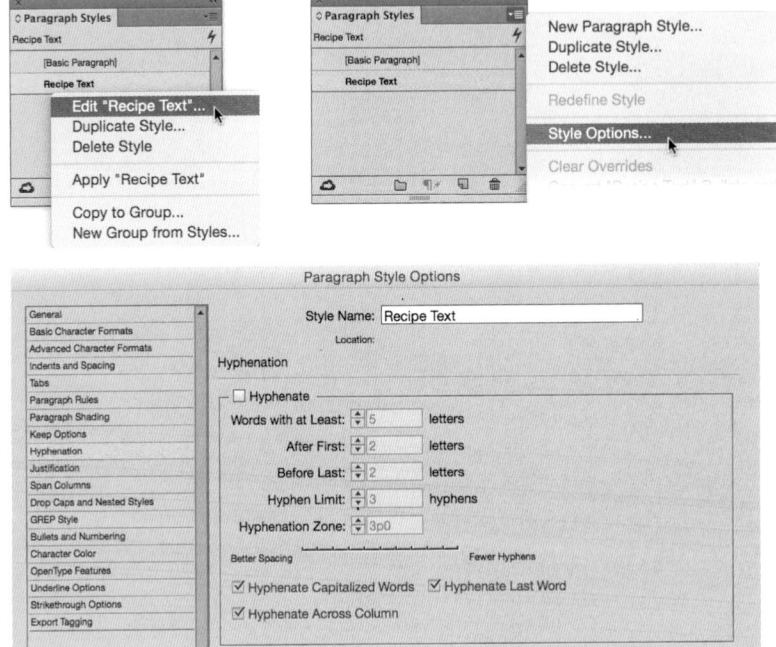

Figure 5.24 Editing a paragraph style through the Paragraph Style Options dialog box

Using Character Styles

★ *ACA Objective 3.8*

Think of character styles as styles that apply extra or different formatting to text that is already formatted with a paragraph style. Character styles make certain characters, words, or phrases within a paragraph appear different. For example, think of the text in the recipe directions. You could draw attention to the ingredients in the directions by changing its font style to bold and the color to red.

You only want to capture two character formatting attributes with such a character style:

- Bold font style
- Red fill color

To quickly change the font style and color of ingredients in the recipe directions, select the words with the Type tool and apply the character style.

To create a character style that only captures those formatting attributes that are different from the rest of the paragraph formatting, start by applying a paragraph style to the text. With the paragraph style applied, select one or more words in the text and change their appearance. Using the previous example, change the color and font style of the selected words. The paragraph style shows an override (plus symbol) next to the style name.

To create a new character style (**Figure 5.25**):

1 Select the text in the paragraph for which you changed the appearance.

2 Choose Type > Character Styles to show the Character Styles panel.

3 Select New Character Style from the Character Styles panel menu, or Alt (Windows) or Option (Mac OS), and click the Create New Style button at the bottom of the panel.

4 In the New Character Style dialog box, enter a descriptive name for the style in the Name field.

5 Select Apply Style To Selection to ensure that the character style is applied to the text you selected in step 1.

6 Deselect Add To CC Library, and click OK. (You will learn about libraries in the next chapter.)

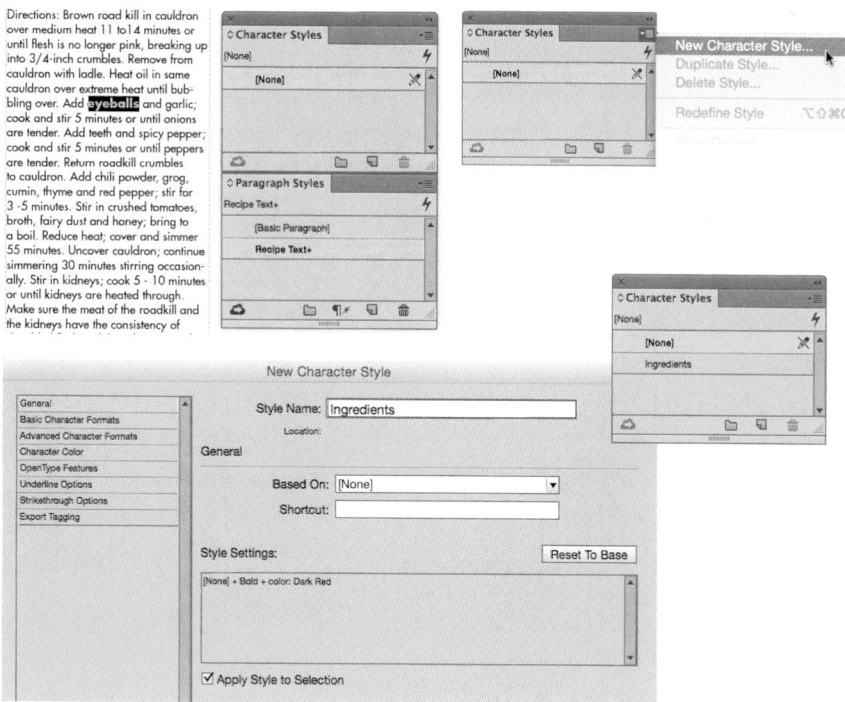

Figure 5.25 Defining a new character style based on formatted text

To apply a character style (**Figure 5.26**):

1 Using the Type tool, select some text within a paragraph.

2 Click the style name in the Character Styles panel, or select Character Formatting Controls ([A]) in the Control panel and select the character style from the styles menu.

Figure 5.26 Applying a character style to selected text

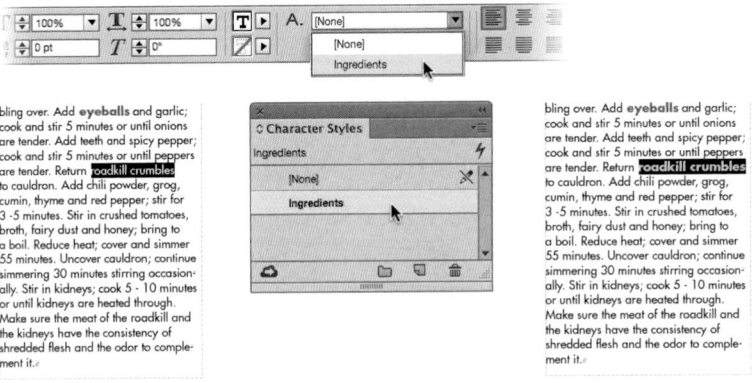

To edit a character style:

1 Right-click (Windows) or Control-click (Mac OS) the style name in the Character Style panel, and select Edit Style from the context menu.

2 Click any of the categories listed at left, make changes to the settings, and click OK.

Creating Styles for Bulleted and Numbered Lists

★ *ACA Objective 3.8*

★ *ACA Objective 4.3*

You learned back in Chapter 4 how to create bulleted lists and change the bullet character. What were the steps to create a bulleted list?

You formatted the text, including specifying a font, font size, and leading. Then, with the Paragraph Formatting Controls selected, you clicked the Bulleted List icon in the Control panel. You then Alt-clicked (Windows) or Option-clicked (Mac OS) the Bulleted List icon to further change the formatting, such as the bullet character and the Left and First Line Left Indent.

To create paragraph styles that automatically apply bulleted or numbered lists (which would be handy for recipe ingredients and steps), you follow the same steps as when creating any other paragraph style:

- Start by formatting a paragraph with a bulleted or numbered list.

- Use this formatting to define the new style.

The real fun starts when you change the color of the bullet or the formatting of the number. This is when character styles come to the rescue. Although you cannot select the bullet or number in the paragraph with the Type tool, you can apply a character style as part of the Bullets And Numbering options.

Let's assume you've already created a paragraph style called Ingredients List that applies round bullets to the start of each paragraph (**Figure 5.27**).

Figure 5.27 The Ingredients List paragraph style applies a bulleted list to each of the ingredient paragraphs.

To apply a character style to the bullet character (**Figure 5.28**):

1 Right-click (Windows) or Control-click (Mac OS) the paragraph style and select Edit [Style Name] from the context menu.

2 In the Paragraph Style Options dialog box, click Bullets And Numbering at left.

3 Under Bullet Character, select New Character Style from the Character Style menu.

4 Click Character Color in the New Character Style dialog box, and select a swatch color for the bullet under Character Color, and enter the Style Name.

5 Click OK to close the New Character Style dialog box and return to the Paragraph Style Options dialog box.

6 Click OK.

The paragraph style is updated, and all the bullets appear in the color defined by the character style.

NOTE

You can also select a character style you might have created earlier from the Character Style menu in the Bullets And Numbering settings.

Figure 5.28 Applying a character style to the bullet character as part of the paragraph style speeds up the text formatting process

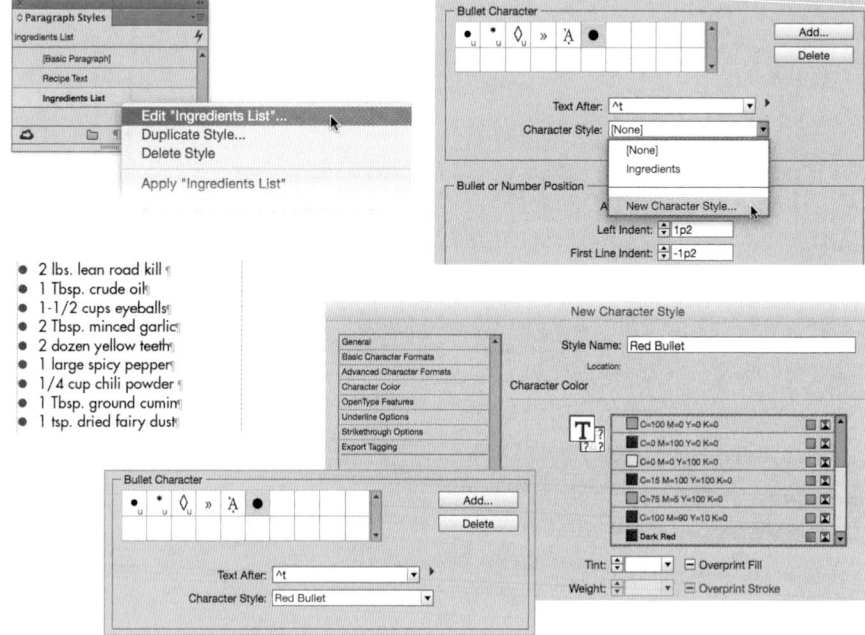

Working with Nested Styles

▶ *Video 5.7*

Nested styles apply character styles to part of the text in a paragraph, without the need for you to select that text. They automatically know where they need to be applied, based on their definition. Let's look at the recipe directions paragraph (**Figure 5.29**) as an example.

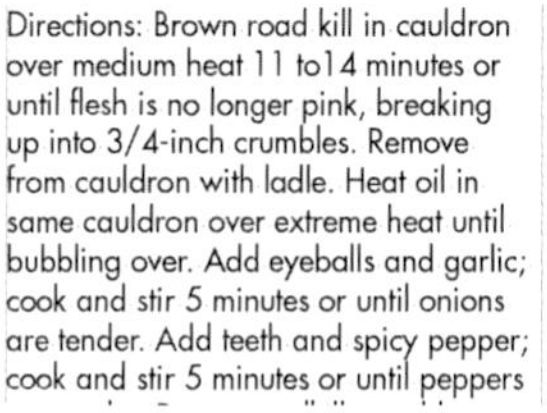

Directions: Brown road kill in cauldron over medium heat 11 to14 minutes or until flesh is no longer pink, breaking up into 3/4-inch crumbles. Remove from cauldron with ladle. Heat oil in same cauldron over extreme heat until bubbling over. Add eyeballs and garlic; cook and stir 5 minutes or until onions are tender. Add teeth and spicy pepper; cook and stir 5 minutes or until peppers

Figure 5.29 A recipe directions paragraph

For each recipe in the cookbook, there is a **run-in head**, which is a heading that is part of the paragraph text itself. Here the run-in head is "Directions" followed by a colon (:). To make this heading stand out from the rest of the paragraph, you want to apply a character style that changes the font style to a bolder font along with a different color.

You could manually select the text, including the colon character, and then apply a character style called Recipe Subhead. However, for a book with many recipes, that could be a bit of work. Instead of you doing the work, let InDesign do the job for you.

How do you know where the run-in head starts and finishes? It starts at the beginning of the paragraph, and stops after the first colon character in the text.

Okay, with that information, you are ready to edit the Recipe Text paragraph style and nest the Recipe Subhead character style in it (**Figure 5.30**):

1 Right-click (Windows) or Control-click (Mac OS) the Recipe Text style in the Paragraph Styles panel, and select Edit "Recipe Text" from the context menu.

2 Select Drop Caps And Nested Styles at left in the Paragraph Style Options dialog box. Select Preview to see the changes you make in your document.

3 Click New Nested Style under Nested Styles.

4 Select Recipe Subhead from the character style menu.

5 Select Through to ensure the character style applies to the colon character as well.

Note that if you select Up To, the character style would stop just before the colon character.

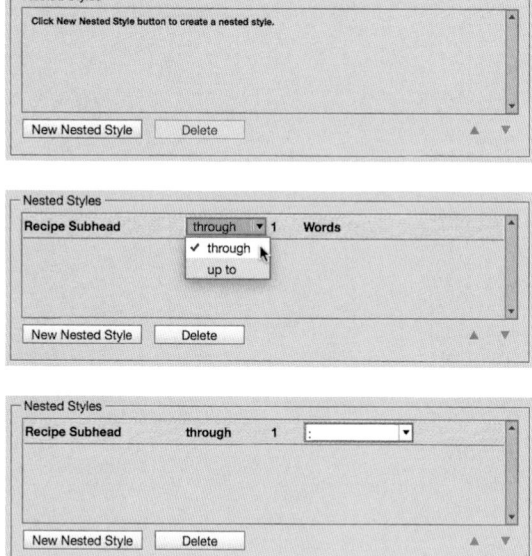
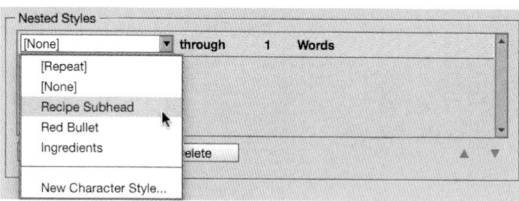

Directions: Brown road kill in cauldron over medium heat 11 to14 minutes or until flesh is no longer pink, breaking up into 3/4-inch crumbles. Remove from cauldron with ladle. Heat oil in same cauldron over extreme heat until bubbling over. Add eyeballs and garlic; cook and stir 5 minutes or until onions are tender. Add teeth and spicy pepper; cook and stir 5 minutes or until peppers are tender. ¶
More directions: Return roadkill crumbles to cauldron. Add chili powder, grog, cumin, thyme and red pepper; stir for 3 -5 minutes. Stir in crushed tomatoes, broth, fairy dust and honey; bring to

Figure 5.30 Creating a nested style that automatically applies the Recipe Subhead character style to the run-in head

6   Leave the number of instances to encounter set to 1, as you want to apply the character style only through the first colon in the text.

The menu at the end defines the item that controls when to stop applying the character style. There is a long list of predefined items; however, the colon character isn't listed.

7   Instead of selecting from the menu, click where it says Words, and type a colon character.

8   Click OK to close the Paragraph Style Options dialog box.

Congratulations! You have just created your first nested style. Try to replace the text "Directions:" with "More Directions:" Notice how all the text including the colon is formatted with the character style? So instead of hard labor, you've got InDesign to do the work for you!

Beautiful Tables

Tables provide a great way to format content in a tabular format. Apart from text and data, InDesign also lets you add graphics and images to table cells.

Some facts about tables:

- Tables consists of rows, columns, and cells (**Figure 5.31**).
- Table header rows are rows at the top of the table.
- Table footer rows are the bottom rows of a table.
- Header and footer rows are generally formatted differently from the rest of the table (body rows). Additionally, they repeat themselves when a table is long and breaks across multiple text frames, columns, or pages.
- Tables are not standalone objects. Tables always appear inline with text, either as part of a story or in a standalone text frame.
- Tables are edited with the Type tool.

Prep Time	Ready In	Main Ingredients
15 Min	1 Hr 30 Min	Lean Road Kills
		Eyeballs
		Yellow Teeth
		Skunk Kidneys

Figure 5.31 A table with a header row, four body rows, and three columns

You can add tables to your designs in various ways:

- Import Word or Excel documents, as you learned earlier in this chapter.
- Create a new table at a text insertion point in a story.
- Create a table in a new standalone text frame.

 Video 5.8

- Convert text to tables, based on a recognizable delimiter for columns and rows, such as a tab character or an end of paragraph marker.

Creating Tables

★ ACA Objective 4.4

Creating a table from scratch works best if you are going to enter (type) all the data in yourself. To create a new inline table (**Figure 5.32**):

1   Using the Type tool (T⌡), click in a new paragraph to set the insertion point for the table.

2   Choose Table > Insert Table.

3   In the Insert Table dialog box, enter the initial number of Body Rows and Columns you want in the table.

4   If you want Header or Footer Rows, enter the number of rows as well. Click OK.

5   Click in any table cell with the Type tool to set the insertion point and enter the text. Repeat this process for each cell.

TIP

To more easily see where you insert the table, ensure you view the document in Normal screen mode and choose Type > Show Hidden Characters.

> **TIP**   Instead of clicking in each cell with the Type tool to set the text insertion point, press the Tab key to move the insertion point to the next cell in the table. Press Shift-Tab to navigate to the previous cell.

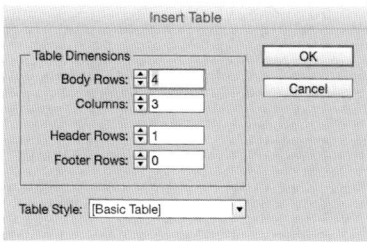

Figure 5.32 Inserting a table, and adding text to table cells

Prep Time	Ready In	Main Ingredients
15 Min	1 Hr 30 Min	Lean Road Kills
		Eyeballs
		Yellow Teeth
		Skunk Kidneys

To add a new table in a separate text frame (**Figure 5.33**):

1 Choose Edit > Deselect All to make sure nothing is selected on the page.

2 Choose Table > Create Table.

3 In the Create Table dialog box, enter the initial number of Body Rows and Columns you want in the table.

4 If you want Header or Footer Rows, enter the number of rows as well. Click OK.

5 The table settings are loaded into the pointer (▸目). Drag out the text frame that will contain the table. When you release the mouse, the text frame fills with the number of rows and columns specified in step 3.

The Create Table command differs from the Insert Table command in that it creates tables that equally distribute rows and columns within the text frame that is created. The Insert Table command only distributes columns evenly.

Figure 5.33 Creating a table in a standalone text frame

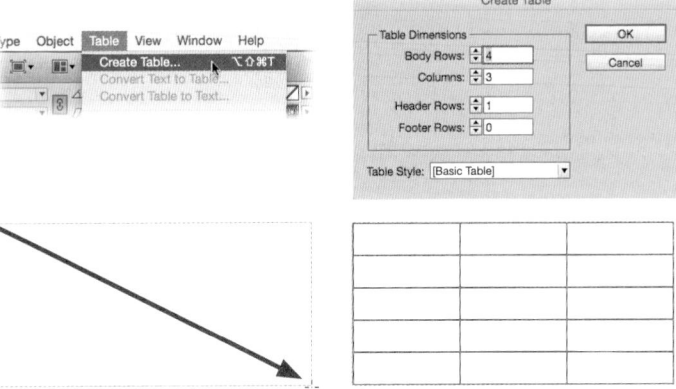

Once you add the table and insert the text, you are ready to start formatting the rest of the table. The first thing to do is format the text. Create paragraph styles for the text formatting used for headers, footers, and body cells. This is particularly useful if you need to apply similar formatting to other tables in your project (**Figure 5.34**).

Prep Time	Ready In	Main Ingredients
15 Min	1 Hr 30 Min	Lean Road Kills
		Eyeballs
		Yellow Teeth
		Skunk Kidneys

Figure 5.34 Text in the table formatted with paragraph styles

Adjusting Column Widths and Row Heights

Once the text is formatted, you can change the width of the table columns.

★ ACA Objective 4.4

To adjust the width of a column (**Figure 5.35**):

1   Using the Type tool, click the top edge of a column to select the column.

2   Choose Window > Type & Tables > Table to show the Table panel.

3   In the Table panel, enter a value in the Column Width field. You can also set the Column Width in the Control panel.

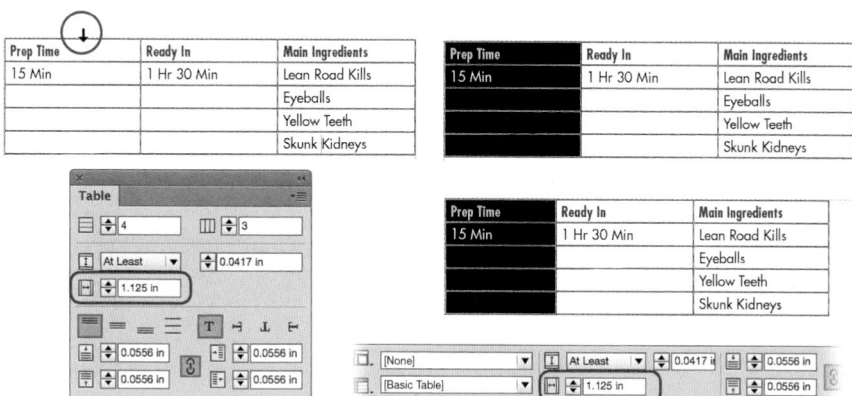

Figure 5.35 Selecting a column and changing the column width

Another way you can change the column width is to (**Figure 5.36**):

- Position the pointer over the column edge. When a double arrow appears, drag left or right. The overall table width increases or decreases as you adjust the column width.

- Shift-drag to affect only the width of two neighboring columns rather than the overall table width.

TIP

You can also select a range of cells, such as a column, columns, or rows, by clicking in one cell with the Type tool and then dragging across the cell ranges you want to select.

Prep Time	Ready In	Main Ingredients
15 Min	1 Hr 30 Min	Lean Road Kills
		Eyeballs
		Yellow Teeth
		Skunk Kidneys

Prep Time	Ready In	Main Ingredients
15 Min	1 Hr 30 Min	Lean Road Kills
		Eyeballs
		Yellow Teeth
		Skunk Kidneys

Figure 5.36 Shift-drag the cell divider between two columns to change the column width in a way that affects only the two neighboring columns.

To make multiple contiguous columns the same width (**Figure 5.37**):

1   Using the Type tool, click the top edge of the first column to select the column.

2   Shift-click the top of the last column of the range of columns to select.

3   Choose Table > Distribute Columns Evenly. You can also right-click (Windows) or Control-click (Mac OS) the selected columns and select Distribute Columns Evenly from the context menu.

Prep Time	Ready In	Main Ingredients
15 Min	1 Hr 30 Min	Lean Road Kills
		Eyeballs
		Yellow Teeth
		Skunk Kidneys

Figure 5.37 Selecting two columns and distributing them evenly

To specify the height of a row (**Figure 5.38**):

1   Using the Type tool, click the left edge of a row to select the row.

2   Choose Window > Type & Tables > Table to show the Table panel.

3   In the Table panel, enter a Row Height value. Alternatively, enter the amount in the Control panel. The Row Height options work as follows:

- **At Least:** Use an At Least value to ensure that the row height is automatically adapted as more content is added to a cell. For example, when cells in a row contain paragraph text of varying length, the total row height increases to the height of the longest paragraph.

- **Exactly:** Setting the row height to Exactly locks in the row height. When more text is added to cells in rows that are locked in height, text that doesn't fit will become overset. A red dot appears in the cell to indicate the cell is overset (**Figure 5.39**). This setting is more suitable for rows in which the cells contain a single line of text or just a few characters, such as a number.

Figure 5.38 Setting the height of a selected row

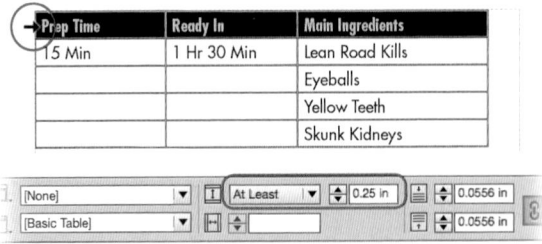

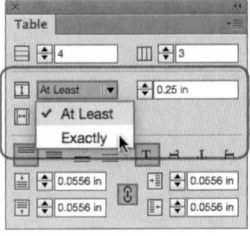

Figure 5.39 A red dot in the cell indicates the text is overset.

Other ways you can change the row height include (**Figure 5.40**):

- Position the pointer over the cell border. When a double arrow appears, drag up or down. The overall table row increases.
- Shift-drag to change only the height of two neighboring rows rather than the overall table height.

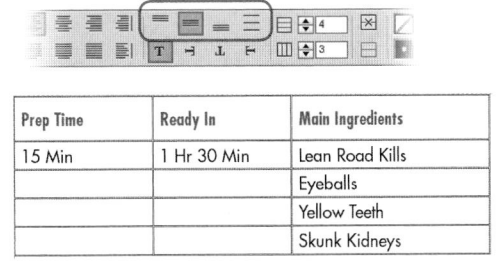

Figure 5.40 Drag the cell divider between rows to change the row height.

By default, text in a table cell is aligned to the top of the cell. A small amount of padding inside the cells (inset spacing) pushes the text away from the cell edges.

To adjust the vertical alignment of text in a cell (**Figure 5.41**):

1 Using the Type tool, select the cell or cell range.

2 Click one of the Align options in the Table panel or the Control panel.

   You can also choose Table > Cell Options > Text, and set the alignment option under Vertical Justification in the Cell Options dialog box.

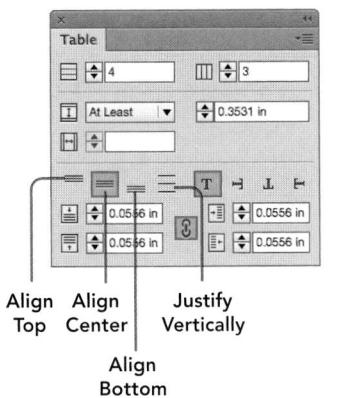

Align Top   Align Center   Justify Vertically

Align Bottom

Figure 5.41 Changing the vertical alignment of the text in the header row to Align Center

To set the cell inset spacing for the entire table (**Figure 5.42**):

1 Using the Type tool, click at the top-left corner of the table to select it. Alternatively, click in any cell to set the insertion point and choose Table > Select > Table.

2 Enter values in the Cell Inset fields in the Table panel or the Control panel.

3 Deselect the Make All Settings The Same icon to enter different insets for the top, right, bottom, and left edges of the cell.

Now that you've got the text formatting, column widths, row heights, vertical alignments, and cell inset sorted for the table, it's time to add some color to the design.

Figure 5.42 Setting cell inset spacing for all the cells in the table

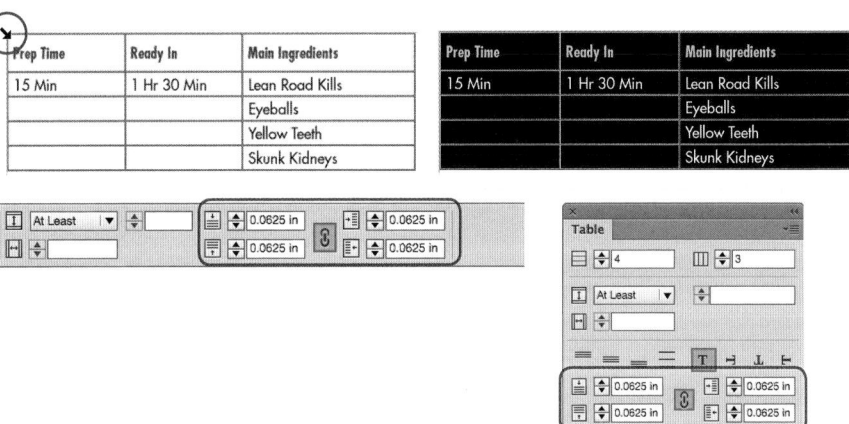

Changing the Table Appearance

★ *ACA Objective 4.4* You can enhance the design of tables by applying stroke and fill settings to rows, columns, and individual table cells.

To add a border to your table (**Figure 5.43**):

1 Click in any table cell with the Type tool to set the insertion point.

2 Choose Table > Table Options > Table Setup.

3 Under Table Border, enter a value in the Weight field, and select a stroke Type and Color. Select Preview to see the changes.

4 Click OK.

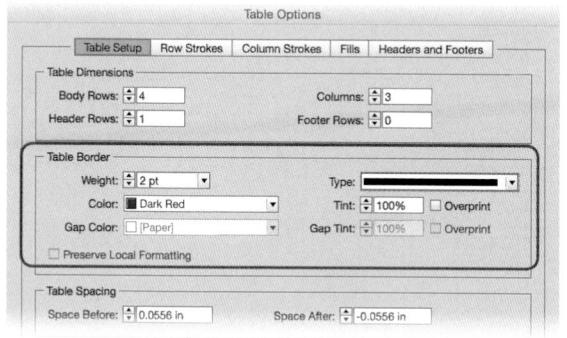

Figure 5.43 Setting the table border appearance in the Table Setup dialog box

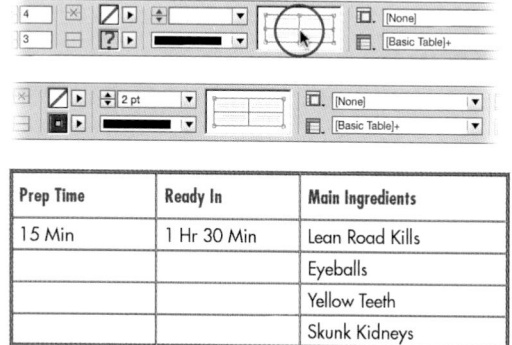

Figure 5.44 Specifying the table border using the proxy in the Control panel

Prep Time	Ready In	Main Ingredients
15 Min	1 Hr 30 Min	Lean Road Kills
		Eyeballs
		Yellow Teeth
		Skunk Kidneys

You can also set the table border from the Control panel (**Figure 5.44**):

1 Select the table (Table > Select > Table).

2 To deselect the table's gridlines, click the center of the proxy ( ) in the Control panel.

   By clicking the gridlines in the proxy, you can select or deselect the strokes to which new stroke color, weight, and type will be applied. To specify the border, make sure that only the outer four lines are selected.

You can also specify row and column strokes by selecting cell ranges within a table and using the proxy in the Control panel, similar to the previous table border example.

Take a look at the following example (**Figure 5.45**). You want to remove the stroke setting at the bottom of the header row. The proxy has no gridlines selected. Which gridline would you select before setting stroke color to [None]?

Prep Time	Ready In	Main Ingredients
15 Min	1 Hr 30 Min	Lean Road Kills
		Eyeballs
		Yellow Teeth
		Skunk Kidneys

TIP

With the insertion point in a cell, tap the Esc key to select the cell and adjust both the fill and stroke settings for the cell.

Figure 5.45 Which line in the proxy preview area would you select to change the color of the stroke at the bottom of the header row?

You would select only the bottom line (**Figure 5.46**), then change the stroke color to [None].

Figure 5.46 The stroke at the bottom of the header row is set to [None]

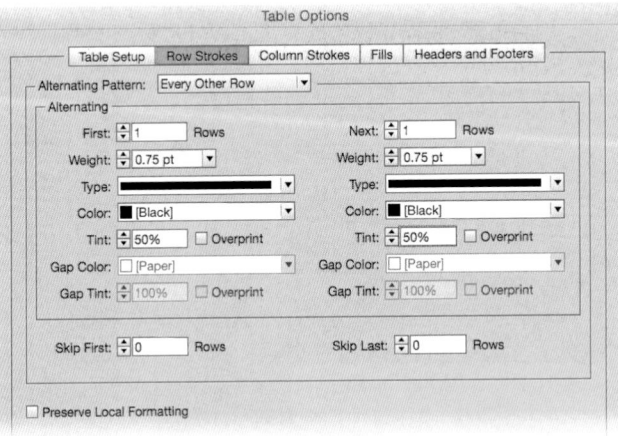

If your table design calls for alternating row or column strokes for the body cells, you can use the Table > Table Options > Alternating Row Strokes command or the Table > Table Options > Alternating Column Strokes command as well.

To specify alternating row strokes (**Figure 5.47**):

1   Using the Type tool, click in any table cell to set the insertion point.

2   Choose Table > Table Options > Alternating Row Strokes.

3   Select Every Other Row from the Alternating Pattern menu, and enter the stroke options under Alternating. Click OK.

Figure 5.47 Applying alternating strokes for the body rows of the table

To change the fill color for the header row (**Figure 5.48**):

1   Select the header row.

2   Click the Fill box in the Control panel or Swatches panel, and select the fill color.

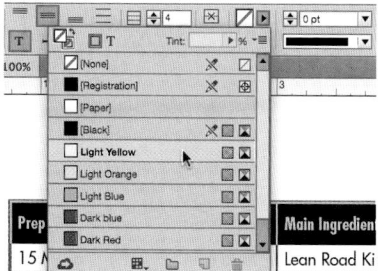

Prep Time	Ready In	Main Ingredients
15 Min	1 Hr 30 Min	Lean Road Kills
		Eyeballs
		Yellow Teeth
		Skunk Kidneys

Figure 5.48 Changing the fill color of the header row to Light Yellow

Similar to setting alternating strokes for columns, you can also set alternating fills for the body cells of the table.

To set an alternating row fill pattern (**Figure 5.49**):

1 Using the Type tool, click in any table cell to set the insertion point.

2 Choose Table > Table Options > Alternating Fills.

3 Select Every Other Row from the Alternating Pattern menu, and enter the fill options under Alternating.

4 Select Preview to see the changes. Click OK.

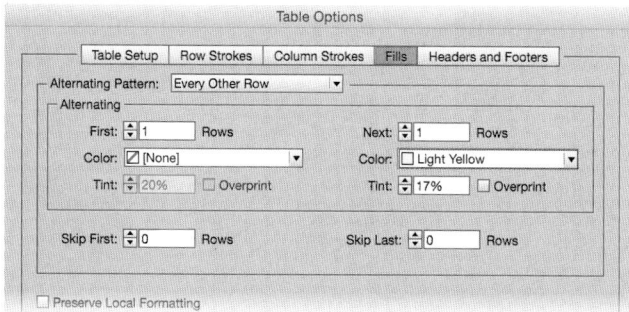

Prep Time	Ready In	Main Ingredients
15 Min	1 Hr 30 Min	Lean Road Kills
		Eyeballs
		Yellow Teeth
		Skunk Kidneys

Figure 5.49 Setting the alternating row fill to Light Yellow for the body rows of the table

Converting Text to Tables

In some cases, you might receive text from a client that needs to be formatted as a table in your designs. Rather than manually creating the table and entering the text into cells, you can convert text to a table—provided that the text is clearly organized and separated by specific characters, such as a comma or tab between each item. Text that is organized this way is called comma-delimited or tab-delimited (tabulated) text.

★ *ACA Objective 4.4*

To see hidden characters such as tabs in the text, choose Type > Show Hidden Characters. With the hidden characters displayed, it is easier to see the characters that separate columns and rows. For example, a tab (>>) might be a column separator and a paragraph return (¶) might be a row separator.

To convert tabulated text into a table (**Figure 5.50**):

1 Using the Type tool, select the text.

2 Choose Table > Convert Text To Table.

3 With tab-delimited text, select Tab from the Column Separator menu.

4 Select Paragraph from the Row Separator menu. Click OK.

   You can enter any single character in the Column or Row Separator box, or choose Tab, Paragraph, or Comma from the menu.

5 If the document already contains a table style that will work for this table, you can select it from the Table Style menu.

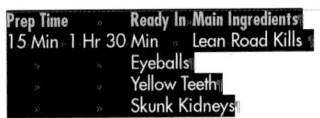
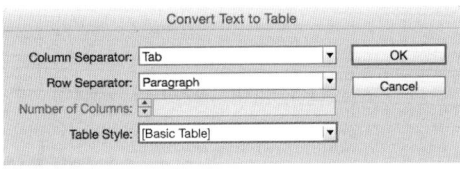

Figure 5.50 Converting text to a table, using the tab characters to separate columns and paragraph returns to separate rows

Prep Time	Ready In	Main Ingredients
15 Min	1 Hr 30 Min	Lean Road Kills
		Eyeballs
		Yellow Teeth
		Skunk Kidneys

Converting Tables to Text

Any table created in InDesign can be converted back to text. To convert tables to text, you will need to consider what separator characters you want to insert in the text so that original rows and columns can be distinguished. For example, each row might need to become a paragraph, and within that paragraph, each column could be preceded by a forward slash character.

To convert tables to text (**Figure 5.51**):

1 Using the Type tool, click in any table cell to set the insertion point.

2 Choose Table > Convert Table To Text.

3 Enter the forward slash character (/) or another character appropriate to the design in the Column Separator field.

Prep Time	Ready In	Main Ingredients
15 Min	1 Hr 30 Min	Lean Road Kills
		Eyeballs
		Yellow Teeth
		Skunk Kidneys

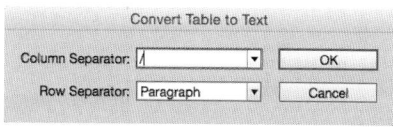

Figure 5.51 Convert a table to text, using the forward slash character to separate columns and paragraph returns for rows

4 Select Tab, Paragraph, or Comma from the Row Separator menu. To follow this example, select Paragraph. Click OK.

You can enter any single character in the Column or Row Separator field, or choose Tab, Paragraph, or Comma from the menu.

Adding Header or Footer Rows

Tables imported from Word or Excel documents will not have header or footer rows, nor will tables created from converted text. All rows in these tables are body rows. Header rows add meaning to the table data by providing column titles. For example, imagine the sample table in this chapter without the headers Prep Time or Ready In. The time references provided would no longer make any sense. Table headers, like headings in text, are formatted differently from the rest of the table text. A footer row at the bottom of a table with data might be used to indicate where the data presented in the table was sourced from; this text would also be formatted differently.

★ *ACA Objective 4.4*

To convert the top row of a table to a header row (**Figure 5.52**):

1 Using the Type tool, click to the left of the row to select it or simply click an insertion point in any cell in that row.

2 Choose Table > Convert Rows > To Header, or right-click (Windows) or Control-click (Mac OS) and select Convert To Header Rows from the context menu.

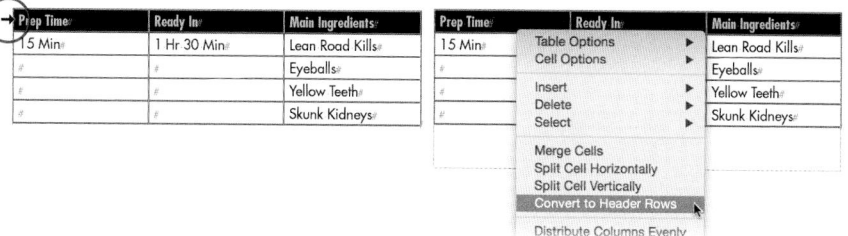

Figure 5.52 Converting the first row of a table to a header row

Using Table and Cell Styles

★ ACA Objective 4.4

Table and cell styles allow you to quickly and consistently format tables in your design projects. As you have seen with the creation of object styles and paragraph styles earlier in this chapter, the easiest way to create styles is to design the appearance with some dummy content, and then use the design as the basis for the style definition. You will do the same when creating cell styles and table styles.

CREATING AND APPLYING CELL STYLES

Cell styles allow you to quickly apply cell formatting attributes such as stroke, fill, cell inset, vertical alignment, and paragraph style. Start by formatting the cell as you'd like it to appear.

TIP

You can also click the Create New Style button at the bottom of the Cell Styles panel to create a new cell style.

To create a cell style (**Figure 5.53**):

1　Using the Type tool, click in a formatted table cell.

2　Choose Window > Styles > Cell Styles to show the Cell Styles panel.

3　Select New Cell Style from the Cell Styles panel menu.

4　Click General at left, and enter the Style Name for the new cell style.

5　From the Paragraph Style menu, select the style name for formatting the text in the cell. Click OK.

Figure 5.53 Creating a new cell style that also applies a paragraph style

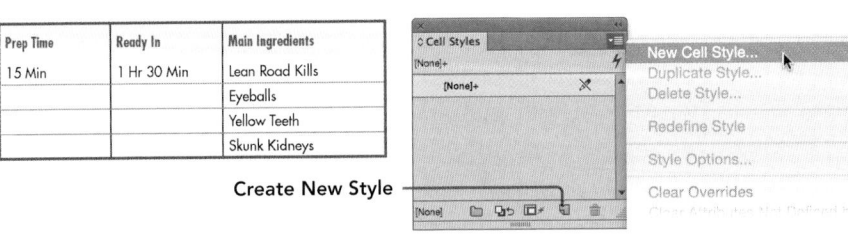

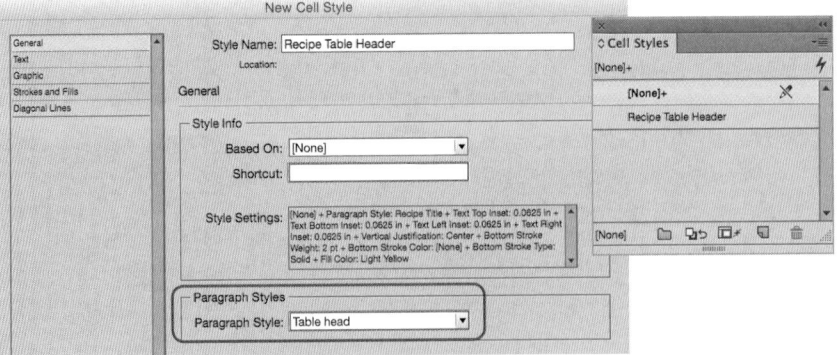

To apply a cell style:

1 Using the Type tool, select a cell range.

2 Click the style name in the Cell Styles panel.

CREATING AND APPLYING TABLE STYLES

Table styles can automatically apply border, alternating stroke or fill patterns, and cell styles to a table, thus formatting all the text and cells in the table.

To create a table style (**Figure 5.54**):

1 Using the Type tool, click anywhere in a formatted table.

2 Choose Window > Styles > Table Styles to show the Table Styles panel.

3 Select new Table Style from the Table Styles panel menu.

4 Click General at left, and enter the Style Name for the new table style.

5 Under Cell Styles, select the Header Rows cell style to apply and the Body Rows cell style to apply. Click OK.

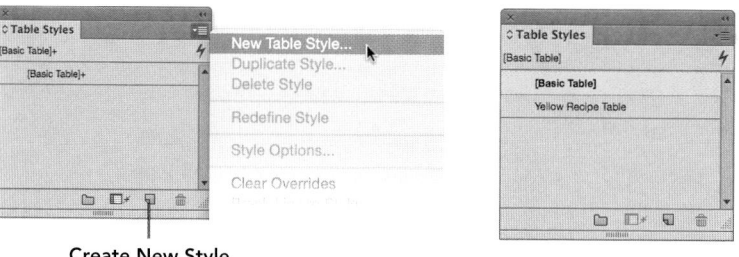

Create New Style

Figure 5.54 Creating a new table style that also applies a cell style to the header rows and body rows of the table

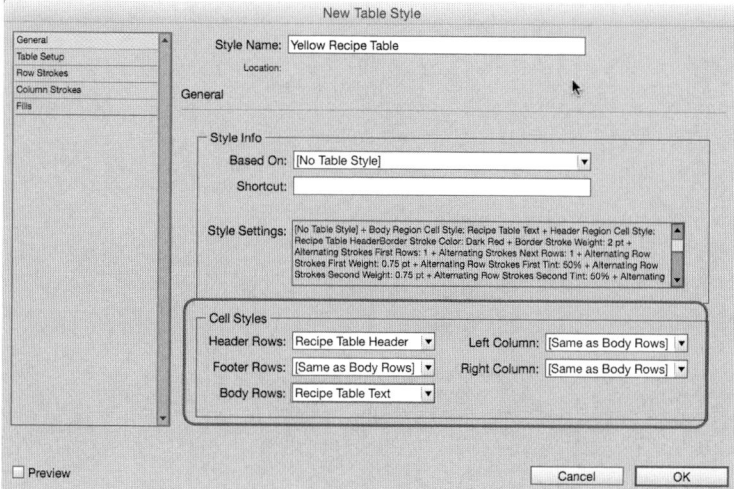

You can apply up to five different cell styles as part of a table style definition. For example, you can apply different styles to the header rows, footer rows, body rows, as well as the left and right column of a table. To apply more than those styles, you will need to manually select cell ranges and apply additional cell styles.

To apply a table style (**Figure 5.55**):

1 Using the Type tool, click in any cell to select the table.

2 In the Table Styles panel, click the style to apply.

Figure 5.55 Applying a table style to an unformatted table

Prep Time	Ready In	Main Ingredients
15 Min	1 Hr 30 Min	Lean Road Kills
		Eyeballs
		Yellow Teeth
		Skunk Kidneys

Prep Time	Ready In	Main Ingredients
15 Min	1 Hr 30 Min	Lean Road Kills
		Eyeballs
		Yellow Teeth
		Skunk Kidneys

Working with Cross-References

Video 5.11

Cross-references direct the reader to additional information about a topic elsewhere in the publication. For example, in a cookbook, basic cooking techniques, such as how to cook pasta, are covered at the start of the book. In a later recipe that includes cooked pasta as an ingredient, the reader is redirected to the earlier pages. The text in the recipe might be a phrase such as, "For more information on cooking pasta, see page 5." In the recipe book project, you'll use cross-references on the table of contents page, which link to a recipe page.

Inserting a Cross-Reference

ACA Objective 4.6

In InDesign, cross-references point either to text that is formatted with a specified paragraph style, character style, or a text anchor position you specify somewhere in the text. You can create text anchors by selecting some text, then selecting New Hyperlink Destination from the Hyperlinks panel. For the recipe book project, you'll learn how to create a cross-reference to a paragraph of text. You can insert a cross-reference using the Type menu or the Cross-References panel.

To create cross-references from the Type menu (**Figure 5.56**):

1 Using the Type tool, click a text insertion point at a location within the text, or select some text to replace.

2 Choose Type > Hyperlinks & Cross-References > Insert Cross-Reference.

3 Select Paragraph from the Link To menu in the New Cross-References dialog box.

4 Under Destination, select the paragraph style that is used to format the text you want to point to (for example, Recipe Title).

   The start of the paragraph text for paragraphs formatted with that style appears at right.

5 Select the paragraph text to link to.

6 Under Cross-Reference Format, select the Format for the cross-reference you want to insert (for example, Page Number).

7 Under PDF Appearance, select Invisible Rectangle from the Type menu, and None from the Highlight menu. Click OK.

   Cross-references can become clickable links when you convert the InDesign project to a PDF. The PDF Appearance settings determine the visual appearance of these links.

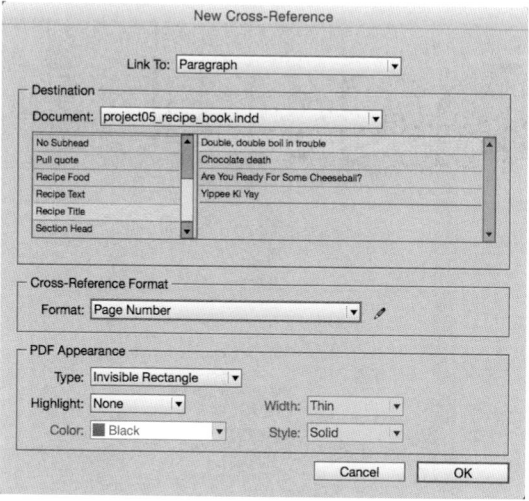

Fried Endangered
Parrot Wings
page 4

Figure 5.56 A cross-reference that points to a paragraph formatted with the Recipe Title paragraph style; the format is set to Page Number (page #).

The Cross-References panel is used to manage cross-references as well as create new cross-references.

To create a cross-reference from the Cross-References panel (**Figure 5.57**):

1 Using the Type tool, click to place a text insertion point at a location in the text, or select some text to replace.

2 Choose Window > Type & Tables > Cross-References to show the Cross-References panel.

3 Select Insert Cross-Reference from the Cross-References panel menu. You can also click the Create New Cross-Reference button at the bottom of the Cross-References panel.

4 Select Paragraph from the Link To menu in the New Cross-Reference dialog box.

5 Under Destination, select the paragraph style used to format the text you want to point to.

6 Select the paragraph text to link to.

7 Under Cross-Reference Format, select the Format for the cross-reference you want to insert (for example, Page Number).

8 Under PDF Appearance, select Invisible Rectangle from the Type menu, and None from the Highlight menu. Click OK.

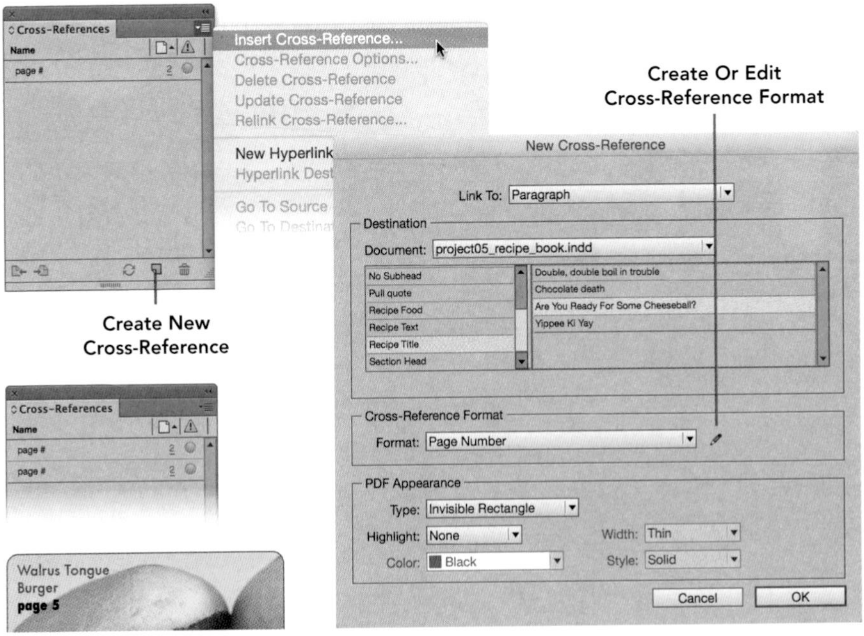

Figure 5.57 Creating a new cross-reference using the Cross-References panel

Editing Cross-References

Although InDesign offers several predefined cross-reference formats, sometimes you want to customize things a bit more. You can easily edit the supplied formats to fit your needs. The cross-reference format does two things:

★ ACA Objective 4.6

- It determines what text is inserted—for example, before the text of a referenced paragraph heading, you might want to insert "to learn more see."

- How this text is formatted—for example, with a character style.

To edit a cross-reference:

- Double-click the cross-reference in the Cross-References panel.

- Select the cross-reference and select Cross-Reference Options from the Cross-References panel menu.

For example, to change the Page Number cross-reference format so that the word "page" appears in uppercase (**Figure 5.58**):

1. Select Define Cross-Reference Formats from the Cross-Reference panel menu.

2. Select Page Number at left.

3. Under Definition, change the text "page" to **PAGE**.

4. From the Character Style For Cross-Reference menu, select a character style to apply to the cross-reference text on the page.

5. Click OK.

NOTE *You can also access the cross-reference format settings by double-clicking on a cross-reference in the Cross-References panel, then clicking the Create Or Edit Cross-Reference icon (✐) in the New Cross-Reference dialog box or in the Edit Cross-Reference dialog box.*

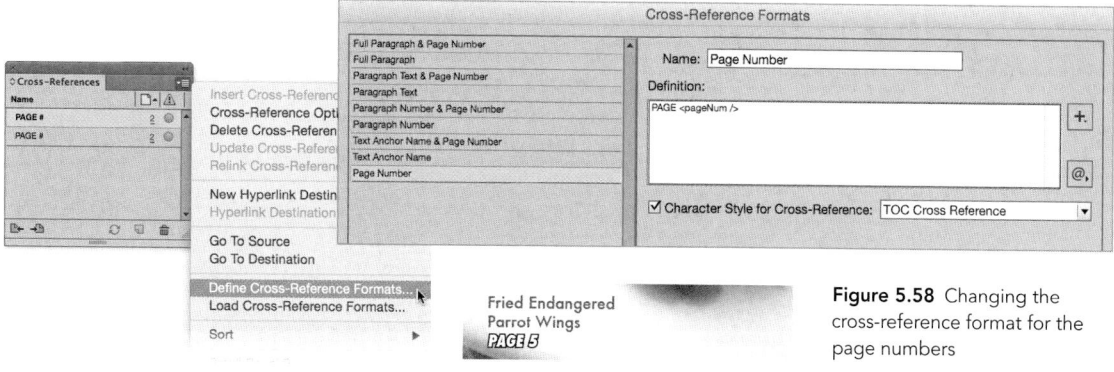

Figure 5.58 Changing the cross-reference format for the page numbers

Updating Cross-References

★ ACA Objective 4.6

The status column in the Cross-References panel indicates whether a cross-reference is up to date. A green light means everything is OK, a yellow warning triangle indicates the cross-reference is out of date and must be updated, and a red flag means the text to which the cross-reference links is missing (**Figure 5.59**).

A cross-reference might become out of date if you edit the cross-reference text on the page. For example, if you change the word "page" to the phrase "see page."

To update a cross-reference:

- Click the Update Cross-References button at the bottom of the Cross-References panel.

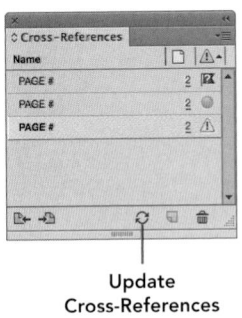

Update Cross-References

Figure 5.59 A missing, an up-to-date, and an out-of-date cross-reference

NOTE *Missing cross-references can be fixed by editing the cross-reference and pointing it to a new destination in the Edit Cross-Reference dialog box.*

Creating a Table of Contents

★ ACA Objective 4.5

A table of contents is generally part of the front matter of a publication. Tables of contents most commonly list the different headings used throughout a publication, for example the recipe titles and subtitles, or chapter titles and subheadings used within that chapter. As an exercise, find a book that has a table of contents in it, maybe even the one you are reading right now. Can you see a relationship between the table of contents text and the headings used throughout the book?

▶ Video 5.12

Before you define a table of contents:

- Consistently apply paragraph styles to the text in your design project, especially titles and headings, as the table of contents relies on this formatting to create it.
- Create a dummy layout for the table of contents design.
- Create paragraph styles for the title of the table of contents as well as the different levels (**Figure 5.60**).
- Determine which text from your document must be included in the table of contents, and check which paragraph styles are applied to that text. Jot down each style name, as well as the level of importance they have. For example, for a recipe book, you might consider the different type of recipes,

such as appetizers, entrees, or desserts, as the top level (Level 1) in the table of contents, and under each of these you could list the names of the different recipes (Level 2).

- Record which paragraph styles are used to format text from your document that must appear in the TOC. These are the styles you will include in your TOC Style.

Figure 5.60 A dummy table of contents design and paragraph styles defined for each level's formatting

Defining the Table of Contents Style

Once you've created the styles to format the table of contents text and determined which text needs to be added to it, you are ready to define the table of contents style. The table of contents style determines the included text, hierarchy, and formatting of the final table of contents.

★ *ACA Objective 4.5*

To define a table of contents style (**Figure 5.61**):

1 Choose Layout > Table of Contents Styles.

2 Click New. The New Table of Contents Style dialog box opens.

3 Click More Options to expand the dialog box.

4 Enter a descriptive name for the table of contents style in the TOC Style field.

5 Type the title that will appear at the top of the table of contents (such as "Contents") in the Title field, and select a paragraph style from the Style menu to format the text.

You are now ready to add some of the styles used in your project to the Include Paragraph Styles list under Styles In Table Of Contents.

6 Under Other Styles, select a style you listed for inclusion in the TOC, and click Add. Repeat this step for each style that needs to be added. The styles will appear under Include Paragraph Styles.

With all the styles added, you can now set the formatting and levels for each of the included paragraph styles.

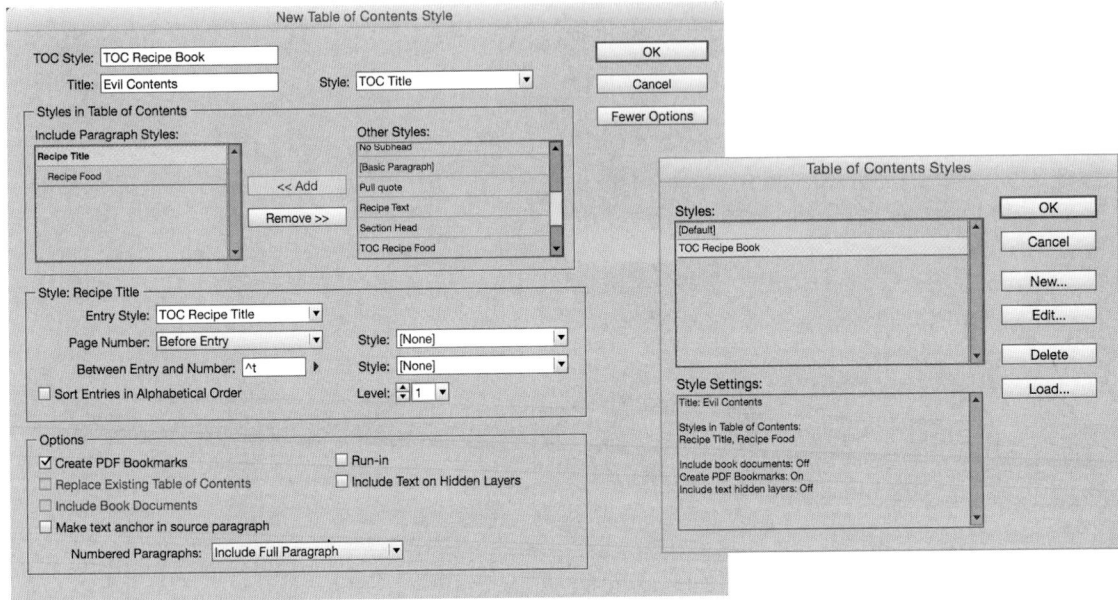

Figure 5.61 The New Table of Contents Style dialog box, with settings entered for the new style

TIP

You can define multiple tables of contents in a single InDesign document by using the Table of Contents Style feature, and then selecting the style when generating the contents text. For instance, you might need to create a general table of contents that includes all the chapters in a book, a second one that lists all of the figures, and a third one for tables in a single document.

7 Select the style in the Include Paragraph Styles list, and select the hierarchy from the Level menu.

The level determines the order of the text in the table of contents. Level 1 is the top level and level 2 styles follow the level 1 text.

8 From the Entry Style menu, select the paragraph style that formats the text in the table of contents.

9 From the Page Number menu, customize the page numbers to be used with each entry. Use the Between Entry And Number field and Style menus to further customize the placement and look of the page numbers.

10 Repeat steps 7-9 for each style in the Include Paragraph Styles list.

11 Select Create PDF Bookmarks to automatically create navigation bookmarks that appear in Adobe Acrobat Reader's Bookmarks pane.

12 Click OK, and OK again.

NOTE *To generate a table of contents from text across different InDesign documents, you must add the files to a book file first, and then select Include Book Documents in the Table of Contents Style. You will learn about books later in this chapter.*

Flowing the Table of Contents Text

With the table of contents style defined, you are now ready to add the table of contents text to the contents page in your project.

★ ACA Objective 4.5

To add a table of contents to your document (**Figure 5.62**):

1 Choose Layout > Table of Contents.

2 Select your table of contents style from the TOC Style menu.

3 Click OK.

4 Click or drag with the loaded text icon to create a text frame filled with the table of contents text, or click an empty placeholder frame.

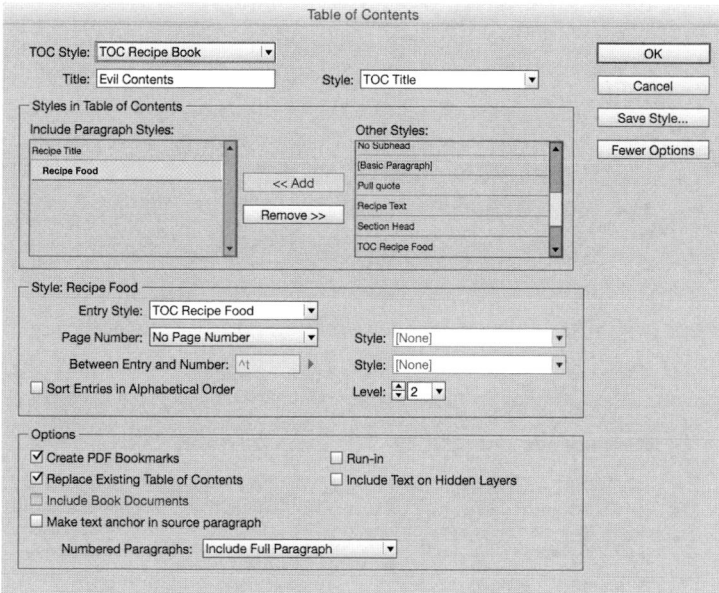

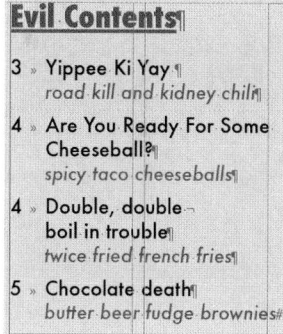

Figure 5.62 Adding the automatically generated table of contents text to the document

Updating a Table of Contents

As you make changes to your InDesign documents, remember that the table of contents you might have generated earlier does not update automatically. Headings that are included in the table of contents may have changed as part of client change requests, or they may appear on different pages after additional text inserts or cuts.

★ ACA Objective 4.5

To update a table of contents:

1   Using the Type tool, click to place the text insertion point anywhere inside table of contents text.

2   Choose Layout > Update Table of Contents.

Combining InDesign Documents

When working on a large project of any kind, breaking it into smaller chunks often makes the job easier. After completing all the pieces, you can then assemble them into the final project.

Book files are useful when working on large publishing projects, such as a big book that contains multiple chapters. Instead of creating a single InDesign file to contain all of the chapters, you can create a file for each individual chapter. Combining the chapter documents into a book file allows you to control the page numbering across the documents, as well as synchronize colors, swatches, master pages, and styles across the multiple documents.

NOTE *Video 5.13 includes a workaround that teaches you to export a project as an interactive SWF and then bring this file back into InDesign after adding a page-flipping effect. For detailed steps, please refer to Appendix E, "Understanding SWF Export."*

 ACA Objective 4.1

 Video 5.13

Creating a Book File

Before you can combine InDesign documents, you must first create a book file. A book file appears in InDesign as a panel that allows you to open, specifying page numbering, and easily generate a single PDF file from the multiple documents. This can be useful when you are working on a design project—for example, a new branding idea for a client. You can combine the design ideas for a logo, letterhead, business card, and newsletter into a single PDF to present.

To create a new book file (**Figure 5.63**):

1   Choose File > New > Book.

2   In the New Book dialog box, navigate to the save location, and enter the name for the file in the File Name (Windows) or Save As (Mac OS) field.

    The file extension for a book is .indb.

3   Click Save.

Figure 5.63 A book file opens as a book panel in InDesign.

An empty book panel opens in InDesign, and you are ready to add InDesign documents to it. To add InDesign documents to the book (**Figure 5.64**):

1 Select Add Document from the book panel menu, or click the Add Documents (+) button at the bottom of the panel.

2 Navigate to the documents to add, select the documents, then click Open.

3 Drag the documents up and down in the list as necessary so the book files are in order.

NOTE *By default, documents added to the book panel automatically have their page numbers updated. Numbers continue from the previous document in the panel. To retain original document page numbers, you can select Book Page Numbering Options from the book panel menu, and uncheck Automatically Update Page & Section Numbers before adding documents to the book panel. (You can also change the page numbering for a chapter through the book panel menu.)*

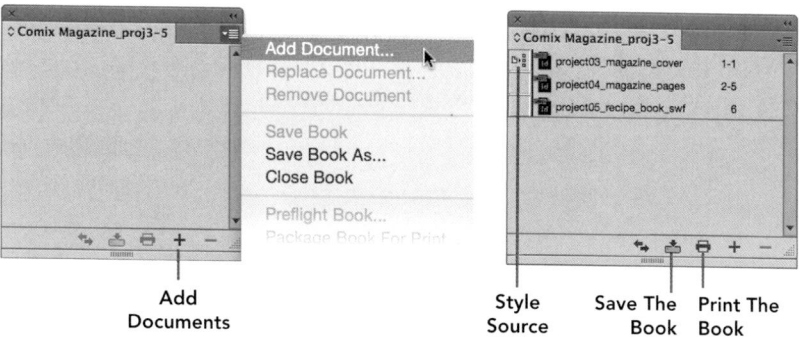

Add
Documents

Style
Source

Save The
Book

Print The
Book

Figure 5.64 Adding documents to the book panel

Opening a Book File

Although a book file appears as a panel, you do not open books through the Window menu. Instead, you open a book file as you would any other file.

★ *ACA Objective 4.1*

To open a book file:

1 Choose File > Open.

2 In the Open A File dialog box, navigate to the book file (.indb) and double-click it.

3 The panel opens and you can make further changes, such as adding more documents or deleting documents.

To close a book file, click the close box for its panel, or select Close Book from the book panel menu.

Synchronizing Files

★ ACA Objective 4.1

There might be times you want to synchronize settings across multiple InDesign documents. For example, you might want to ensure that all documents have the same paragraph styles. To synchronize files, you must first determine which of the documents in the book panel has all the settings you want to use for synchronization. This document is the style source.

To set the style source:

- Click the empty box to the left of the document name.

To synchronize settings in book files (**Figure 5.65**):

To control which settings synchronize across the documents, select Synchronize Options from the book panel menu.

1   Select the files to synchronize in the book panel. To select multiple files, Shift-click the first and last file. To select noncontiguous files, Ctrl-click (Windows) or Command-click (Mac OS) the files.

2   Select Synchronize Book from the book panel menu, or click the Synchronize Styles And Swatches With The Style Source button at the bottom of the panel.

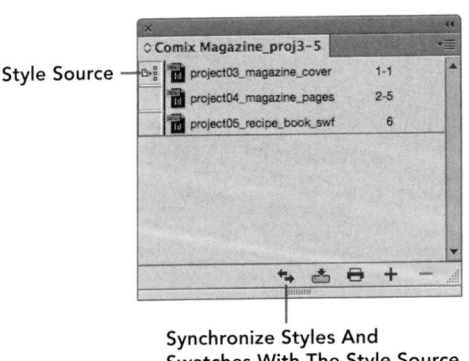

Figure 5.65 Selecting the style source and synchronizing settings

Style Source

Synchronize Styles And Swatches With The Style Source

Exporting Book Files

★ ACA Objective 4.1

★ ACA Objective 5.1

You can package or preflight all the files in the book panel, or export the book as an EPUB or PDF. You will learn how to export an EPUB in Chapter 7.

To export multiple files as a PDF (**Figure 5.66**):

1   Select the files in the book panel.

2   Select Export Book To PDF from the book panel menu.

3 Enter the name of the PDF in the File Name (Windows) or Save As (Mac OS) field.

4 In the Export dialog box, select Adobe PDF (Interactive) from the Save As Type (Windows) menu or Format (Mac OS) menu. Click Save.

5 Enter and select preferred settings in the Export To Interactive PDF dialog box. Click OK.

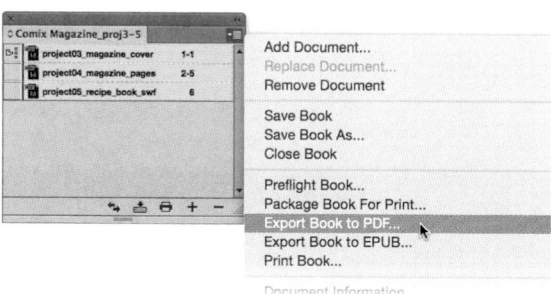

Figure 5.66 Exporting selected files to a single PDF

NOTE *This chapter has covered a lot of long-document features. There's one more long-document feature: the index. An index is a list of topics, also referred to as index entries, that includes page number references and "see also" references. See Appendix D, "Building an Index" to learn more about indexes.*

Well done! You have completed this chapter. From now on you'll not only produce amazing designs, using tools and features learned in previous chapters, you'll utilize styles, such as paragraph styles and object styles, to make work easier.

CHAPTER OBJECTIVES

Chapter Learning Objectives

- Create custom page sizes.
- Add a grid of frames.
- Space content with the Gap tool.
- Place multiple images.
- Reuse and link content.
- Check document spelling.
- Search and replace text.
- Use object and Creative Cloud libraries.
- Draw shapes with the Pencil tool.
- Create freeform shapes with the Pen tool.
- Add type to a path.
- Create hyperlinks.
- Export for the web.

Chapter ACA Objectives

For full descriptions of objectives, download the printable chart from your account on *peachpit.com*. See pages xi–xii.

DOMAIN 2.0
UNDERSTANDING PRINT AND DIGITAL MEDIA PUBLICATIONS
2.5

DOMAIN 3.0
UNDERSTANDING ADOBE INDESIGN CC
3.1, 3.2

DOMAIN 4.0
CREATING PRINT AND DIGITAL MEDIA PUBLICATIONS USING ADOBE INDESIGN
4.1, 4.2, 4.3, 4.4, 4.5, 4.6

DOMAIN 5.0
PUBLISH, EXPORT, AND ARCHIVE PAGE LAYOUTS USING ADOBE INDESIGN
5.1

CHAPTER 6

Creating a Comic Book Page

The comic book project allows you to practice a lot of skills you learned in previous projects and try out some new techniques and features. For example, you'll learn a quick-and-easy method for creating a grid of images that involves setting up automatic resize options for graphic placeholder frames. You will also learn a range of different techniques for reusing design elements, colors, and styles among documents, including working with the Content Collector tool as well as libraries. To ensure no spelling errors are left behind, you will perform a spelling check as well as find and replace text in the document. You'll learn to use two new drawing tools, the Pencil and Pen tool, so you can create freeform shapes. In addition, you'll find out how to place text on a path. Finally, you'll create text- and object-based hyperlinks, and export the comic page for viewing on the web (**Figure 6.1**).

Figure 6.1 Finished comic design

NOTE

This chapter supports the project created in video lesson 6. Go to the Project 6 page in the book's Web Edition to watch the entire lesson from beginning to end.

Creating Grid-Based Designs

Whether you work with photographic images, such as for this project, or cartoon drawings, you'll start designing a comic book by creating a story idea and sketching up storyboards. Storyboards are rough sketches that outline what each panel in the comic book contains—images, captions, speech bubbles, and sound effects. There are different tools to use when creating storyboards. You can use pen and paper, or you can work in one of Adobe's touch apps, such as Adobe Sketch or Adobe Illustrator Draw. These applications integrate with Adobe Photoshop and Illustrator. Whichever method you choose, invest a little time at the start to outline your ideas before jumping into creating your pages and adding placeholder frames for the comic panels.

Adding Reusable Page Sizes

★ *ACA Objective 4.1*

The comic book project uses a nonstandard page size of 6.625 x 10.25 inches. If you frequently work on projects with nonstandard page sizes, consider adding a reusable custom page size to the Page Size menu in the New Document dialog box. Once you add a custom page size to InDesign, you can select it from the Page Size menu rather than entering the width and height values each time you create a new document.

To create a reusable custom page size (**Figure 6.2**):

1 Choose File > New > Document.

2 From the Page Size menu, select Custom.

3 In the Custom Page Size dialog box, enter a descriptive name for the page size in the Name field.

4 Enter your desired dimensions in the Width and Height Fields, and click OK.

The newly created page size appears at the top of the Page Size menu in the New Document dialog box. Each time you create a new document, you can now select the custom page size.

> **NOTE** *You can also select the page size from the Edit Page Size menu at the bottom of the Pages panel, as well as the Page Size menu in the Control panel that appears when you select the Page tool (▯).*

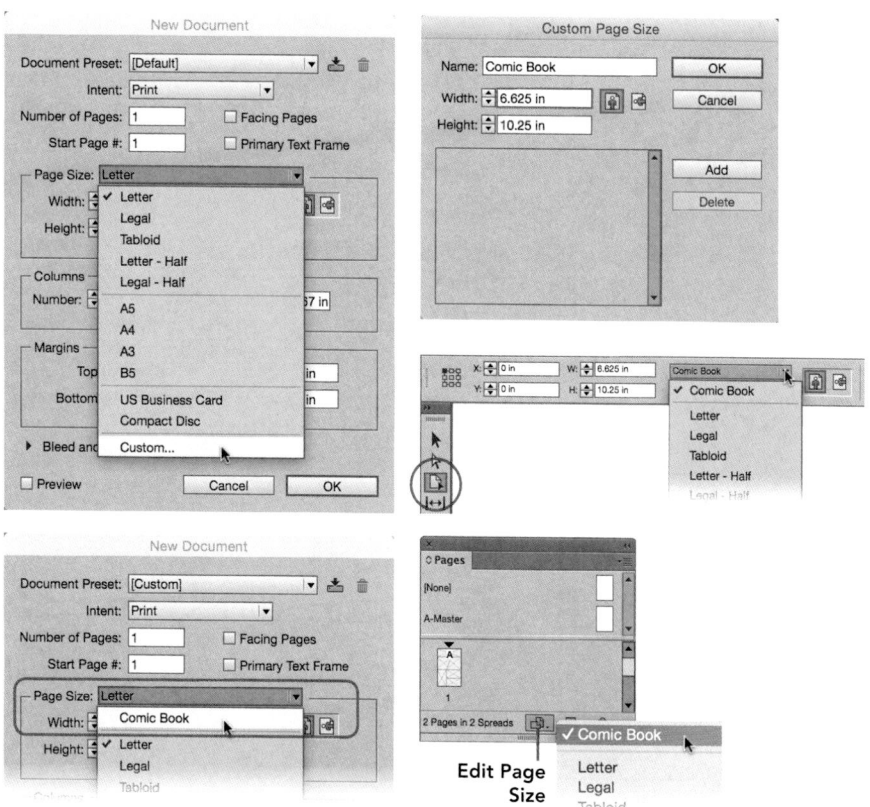

Figure 6.2 When you add a custom page size, you can select it from the Page Size menu in the New Document dialog box, Control panel, and Pages panel.

Creating Frame Grids

To create the grid for the panels that make up the comic book page, you could start by adding ruler guides to the page (Layout > Create Guides) and manually adding graphic frames with the Rectangle tool. But why work that hard? Instead, you can work smarter by quickly creating an entire grid of frames.

★ *ACA Objective 3.2*

★ *ACA Objective 4.2*

To create a rectangular frame grid (**Figure 6.3**):

▶ *Video 6.1*

▶ *Video 6.2*

1 Select the Rectangle Frame tool (⊠).

2 Start dragging a rectangle on the page, but do not release the mouse button.

3 As you drag, tap the Up Arrow key to increase the number of rows you are creating and tap the Right Arrow key to increase number of columns.

   If you accidentally create too many rows, tap the Down Arrow key to decrease number of rows. To decrease number of columns, tap the Left Arrow key.

4 To increase or decrease the space (gutter) between the rows and columns, press Ctrl-tap (Windows) or Command-tap (Mac OS) the appropriate arrow keys.

5 Release the mouse button when you're finished creating the grid.

A grid of frames appears on the page.

Figure 6.3 Creating a grid of graphic frames by dragging to create a shape and pressing the arrow keys

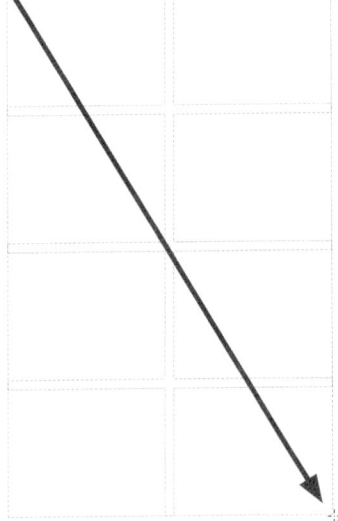

TIP

To set the gutter amount before dragging a grid of frames, choose Layout > Margins And Columns and enter a value in the Gutter field. Keep in mind that if you are working with a multi-column document, changing the gutter amount also changes it on the active page.

Pressing the arrow keys to create multiple, evenly spaced objects works for any type of frame you create—ellipses, polygons, rectangles, even text frames. InDesign even automatically threads the text frames. You can also create a grid of images when pressing the arrow keys, as you drag with a loaded graphics icon that has multiple images loaded in it.

★ *ACA Objective 4.2*

▶ *Video 6.2*

Using the Gap Tool

InDesign provides a tool that is ideal for editing grid-based layouts. The Gap tool (|↔|) lets you move and resize multiple objects that align. It snaps to objects that have their edges aligned, and it snaps to gaps between aligned objects. When you drag with the Gap tool, objects that are attached to the gap move with it.

To change a gap position (**Figure 6.4**):

1 Position the Gap tool between objects whose edges are aligned.

2 Drag the gap in the direction the arrows are pointing.

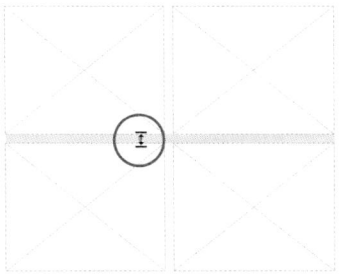
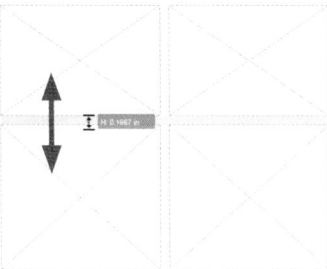

Figure 6.4 Using the Gap tool to resize the aligned objects

When working with the Gap tool:

- To reposition the gap for objects closest to the dragging point, Shift-drag in the direction the arrows are pointing.
- To change the distance between objects, Ctrl-drag (Windows) or Command-drag (Mac OS) in the direction the arrows are pointing.
- To move objects that snap to the gap, Alt-drag (Windows) or Option-drag (Mac OS) in the direction the arrows are pointing.

To have some real grid and gap fun, try working with combinations of the short-cut keys listed. For example, Ctrl+Shift-drag (Windows) or Command+Shift-drag (Mac OS), would change the distance for objects closest to the dragging point.

Consider the following to make the Gap tool work more efficiently:

- For images, enable the Auto-Fit option in the Object > Fitting > Frame Fitting Options dialog box.
- For text frames, enable auto-sizing (Object > Text Frame Options).

Fitting Content to Frames

★ ACA Objective 4.4

▶ Video 6.3

You can apply frame-fitting controls to an empty placeholder frame before placing an image. This speeds up the placement process, especially when multiple place-holder frames are on a single page. After placing the image, using the Selection tool, click the Content Grabber in the center of the image. Drag the image inside the frame to adjust the crop, or Shift-drag the bounding box handles on the image to resize it within its frame.

To specify a fitting option for a placeholder frame (**Figure 6.5** and **Figure 6.6**):

1 Using the Selection tool (▶), select an empty graphics frame.

2 Choose Object > Fitting > Frame Fitting Options to display the Frame Fitting Options dialog box.

3   Select the preferred option from the Fitting menu.

4   In the Align From area, click one of the small squares to set the reference point.

The reference point controls the original placement position of the image in the frame before it is resized. With the center point active, the image is centered in the frame.

5   Click OK.

Figure 6.5 Filling the frame proportionally crops the top and bottom of the image.

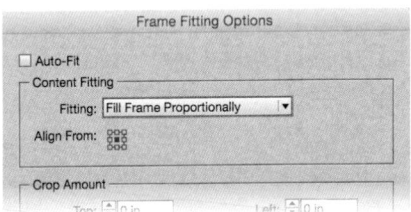

When you place photos, the Fill Frame Proportionally setting ensures the photo completely fills the frame and is not distorted. If the reference point is set to the center, the photo crops vertically or horizontally. With the Selection tool, click the Content Grabber in the frame to change the position of the image if necessary, or select one of the image's bounding box handles and Shift-drag to resize the image and change the crop.

Figure 6.6 Fitting content into the frame proportionally leaves gaps on the left and right side.

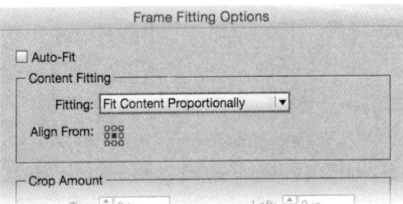

In most cases, logos, diagrams, and illustrations should not be cropped or distorted as they will lose their meaning. Imagine seeing only half of a logo on a page! For these types of graphics, use Fit Content Proportionally as the frame-fitting option. The graphic is sized so that it fits in the frame completely. The frame may be wider or narrower than the placed graphic. To adjust the size of the frame so it matches the size of the placed graphic, choose Object > Fitting > Fit Frame To Content.

Placing Multiple Images

★ ACA Objective 3.1

★ ACA Objective 4.4

▶ Video 6.3

Until now you have placed images into your designs one at a time using the File > Place command. To speed up the placement of images, InDesign enables you to load multiple image files in the loaded graphics icon.

With the loaded graphic icon, you can place an image into an empty placeholder frame, create a graphic frame as you click (to place the image at 100%), or create a graphic frame as you drag (to place the image at any size). Once you place one image, the loaded graphic icon is ready to place the next image.

To place multiple images into empty placeholder frames (**Figure 6.7**):

1 Choose Edit > Deselect All before placing content into InDesign.

2 Choose File > Place.

3 Deselect Show Import Options.

4 Navigate to the images to place, and select the images to import.

    To select a contiguous range of images click the first image, then Shift-click the last image. To select multiple, noncontiguous images, Ctrl-click (Windows) or Command-click (Mac OS) the images.

5 Click Open.

    The number next to the loaded graphics icon (🖼️) shows how many objects are loaded. The preview provides a visual of the currently loaded object.

    TIP To see the names of the images in the loaded graphics icon, show the Links panel (Window > Links). The Page column in the Links panel shows LP for the image you'll place next.

6 Press the arrow keys to toggle through the loaded images until the one you want to place is loaded.

7 Position the loaded graphic icon over an empty graphic frame and click.

8 Repeat steps 6 and 7 until all images are placed.

With the images inserted into the frames, you can resize, transform, and position them further as needed.

    TIP The Control panel enables you to resize and transform images and objects, including adjusting the width, height, scaling, and rotation. When you do this, the Reference Point locator (🔳) defines the point around which the resizing or transforming takes place. Click any of the nine boxes to change the reference point.

TIP

You can even load images, graphics, text, and other supported files all at once, then place them throughout the document.

TIP

To remove an image from the group of images loaded into the loaded graphic icon, make sure it is the top image and press Esc.

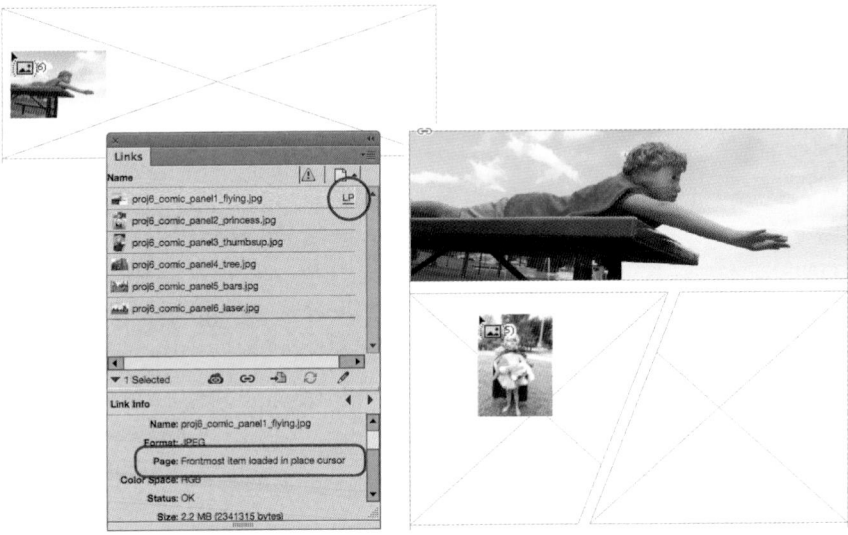

Figure 6.7 Placing multiple images into empty placeholder frames

Placing and Linking Content

When you are working on a project, you may want to reuse design elements from one part of a publication somewhere else. InDesign not only lets you do so easily, it also enables you to link the elements so a change to the original element quickly changes them all.

▶ Video 6.4

Back in Chapter 3, you learned how creating an alternate layout retained links to parent objects from the original layout. Remember that this allowed you to make text and formatting changes in the parent layout, and use the Links panel to update the modified page objects in the child layout. Placing and linking individual page elements in InDesign uses the same parent-child analogy. True, you could easily choose Edit > Copy and Edit > Paste to duplicate page elements. If you wanted to make changes to all those duplicated page elements, however, you would need to edit each object manually. Using the placing and linking tools saves you all that extra effort. By creating a parent-child relationship between the original object and the copies you place in your document, you can make changes to the parent and quickly update all of its children.

Using the Content Collector and Placer Tools

Let's look at the following example. The comic book for this project is called: *The Adventures of Captain Toothless*. Suppose you have created more comic book pages in the same document. On the other pages, the panels, text, and images are different but the heading remains the same.

★ *ACA Objective 4.5*

Instead of copying and pasting the heading across the different pages, you can use the Content Collector tool ( ) and Content Placer ( ) tool to place linked elements. The tools work in conjunction with the Content Conveyor, a panel that stores collected objects until they are used or removed.

With the Content Collector tool, you select page elements and load them into the Content Conveyor. Then, with the Content Placer tool, you can place objects from the Content Conveyor onto your pages.

To load content into the Content Conveyor (**Figure 6.8**):

1 Select the Content Collector tool in the Tools panel. The Content Conveyor panel displays as soon as you select this tool.

2 With the Content Collector tool, click on page elements to add to the Content Conveyor.

3 With each page object you click on, the number next to the Content Collector icon increases, indicating the number of objects in the Conveyor.

TIP

Instead of adding page elements one by one, you can drag around a number of elements with the Content Collector tool and add a set. Sets retain the positional relationship between objects.

Figure 6.8 Page elements added to the Content Conveyor by selecting them with the Content Collector tool

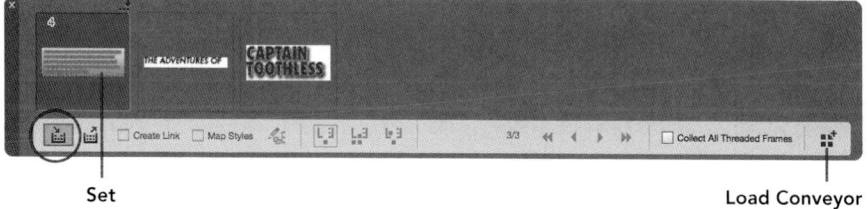

Set   **Load Conveyor**

You can also load content from the Content Conveyor. Select the Content Collector tool to show the Content Conveyor, then click the Load Conveyor and select an option from the Load Conveyor dialog box.

- **Selection** loads all selected objects on the page.
- **Pages** loads content from one or more pages.
- **All Pages Including Pasteboard Objects** loads every page object.
- **Create A Single Set** loads all the page objects collected into a set.

With the Content Conveyor loaded with page objects, you can start placing them into your document.

To place and link content from the Content Conveyor (**Figure 6.9**):

1 Select the Content Placer tool ( ). It is hidden below the Content Collector tool.

2 Select Create Link in the Content Conveyor.

3 The number next to the loaded cursor shows how many objects are loaded from the Content Conveyor, similar to when you place multiple images.

4 Press the arrow keys to toggle through the objects to load the object you want to place.

5 Navigate to the placement location, such as another page.

6 Click to place the content on the page.

7 Repeat steps 4 to 6 to continue placing additional objects.

8 Click the close box on the Content Conveyor when you are finished placing objects.

Figure 6.9 Placing content from the Content Conveyor with the Content Placer tool

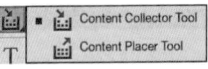

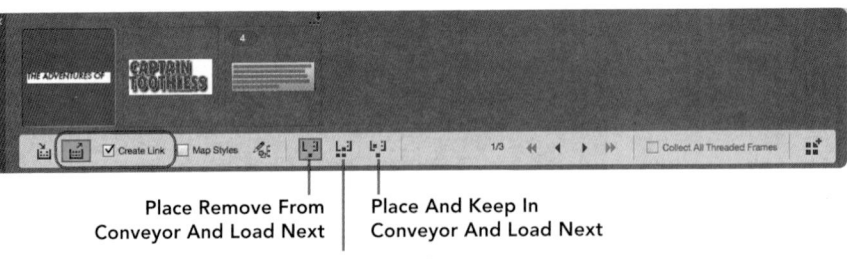

By default, objects placed from the Content Conveyor are removed after placement. There are three different placement options to select in the Content Conveyor before placing content:

- **Place Remove From Conveyor And Load Next** lets you place an object once, and removes the object from the Content Conveyor after placement.
- **Place Multiple And Keep In Conveyor** lets you place an object multiple times.
- **Place And Keep In Conveyor And Load Next** doesn't remove the object from the Content Conveyor after placement, and loads the next object into the cursor.

Updating Links

When you use the Create Link setting in the Content Conveyor, placed objects link to their parent. With the Screen Mode set to Normal and View > Extras > Show Link Badge enabled, a link icon appears on the top right of the placed object.

If you make changes to the parent object, the Link Badge on the child objects change to a modified link (⚠). Additionally, the Links panel also shows modified links **(Figure 6.10)**.

To update the modified links:

- Click the Link Badge, or choose Update All Links from the Links panel menu.

★ *ACA Objective 4.5*

★ *ACA Objective 5.1*

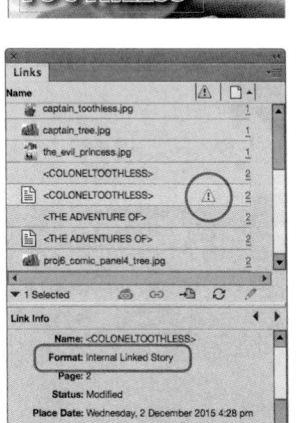

Figure 6.10 Updating the header, and updating the linked content on the next comic book page that uses the same header

Using Place and Link

 ACA Objective 4.5

TIP

To place the same object multiple times, select Place Multiple And Keep In Conveyor in the Content Conveyor before placing, and press Esc when you're finished.

Separate from the Content Collector and Placer tools, InDesign has a Place and Link command that automatically loads a selected object into the Content Conveyor. The feature then loads the object into the Content Placer tool for easy placement, and selects the Create Link option in the Content Conveyor.

This is a great shortcut to use when you want to quickly place and link a single object elsewhere in the document or on the page.

To use the Place And Link command (**Figure 6.11**):

1 Using the Selection tool, click a page object to select it.

2 Choose Edit > Place And Link.

3 With the loaded cursor, click on any page to place the object.

Figure 6.11 Using Place And Link to quickly place multiple instances of a caption text frame on the comic book page

Preserving Changes

When you update a modified child link, the appearance of the object, including its content, updates according to the parent object. In the previous Place And Link example, additional caption text frames were added. After adding the linked text frames for the captions (the child objects), the text inside the frames was changed, and their size and shape was altered. Making a change to the appearance of the parent caption would result in all of the captions resetting to the exact appearance and content that the parent contains.

★ ACA Objective 5.1

That would *not* be a good thing, as it would require retyping the caption text plus making the size and shape changes once more. Thankfully, there is a way to control which changes (local edits) that you make to a child object are preserved when updating the links.

To preserve certain changes applied to child objects (**Figure 6.12**):

1. Select the objects on the page or in the Links panel.

2. From the Links panel menu, select Link Options.

3. In the Link Options dialog box, select any of the following settings to preserve changes made to them:

   - **Appearance:** Keeps fill color, stroke color and weight, corner options, and effects changes.

   - **Size And Shape:** Keeps changes made to width, height, transformations (such as rotation), and other object shape changes, like moving an anchor point to a different position with the Direct Selection tool.

   - **Interactivity:** Keeps buttons and forms settings, animation, timing, and object states (you will learn more about these in the next chapter).

   - **Frame Content:** Retains edited content within the frame, such as images, text, or video.

   - **Others:** Leaves changes to a number of other edits, such as Text Frame Options, text wrap, and hyperlinks intact.

4. Select Warn If Link Update Will Overwrite Local Edits to display a warning dialog box if any local edits will be changed when updating modified links.

5. Click OK.

With the Link Options set for the child objects, you can now update the links.

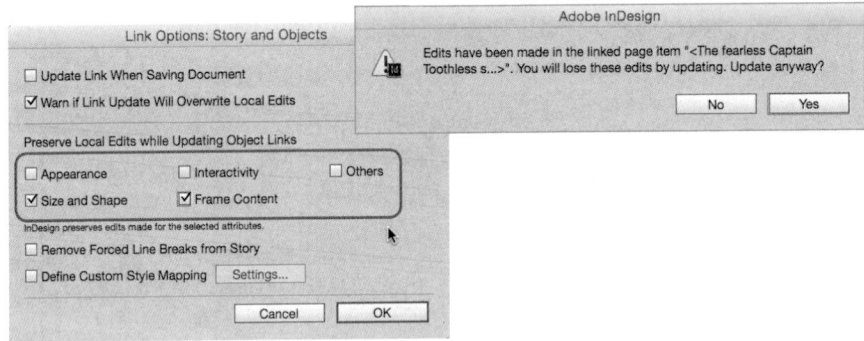

Figure 6.12 Controlling which design attributes are preserved when updating modified links for child objects

Making Text Changes

▶ *Video 6.5*

Text submitted by clients is often prepared in word-processing applications, such as Microsoft Word. Although these applications have built-in tools for checking spelling and finding and replacing text, you will likely need to edit text after completing a layout. To help you, InDesign has its own spelling checker and find-and-replace features.

Checking Spelling

★ *ACA Objective 4.3*

InDesign's check spelling feature looks through the text of a document and detects incorrectly spelled words, capitalization errors (such as a lowercase letter at the start of a sentence), and repeated words (such as "and and").

Text is checked against a dictionary for the language that is applied to the text. You can change the language by selecting text, and selecting a language from the Language menu in the Control panel (character formatting controls) or the

Character panel. Changing the language for selected words can be handy when French words appear in English documents for example. A language can also be applied through character and paragraph styles (**Figure 6.13**).

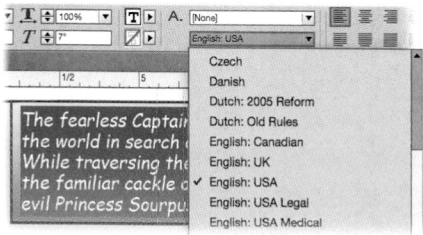 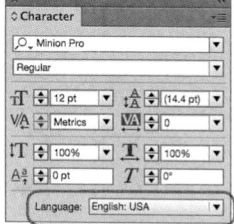

Figure 6.13 The English: USA language setting applied to text

To check spelling for a document (**Figure 6.14**):

1 Choose Edit > Spelling > Check Spelling.

   The Check Spelling dialog box opens, and the first suspect word in the text is highlighted.

2 Select the correctly spelled version of the highlighted word from the Suggested Corrections, or enter the correct spelling in the Change To field.

3 Click Change to update just this occurrence of the error, or click Change All to fix all occurrences of this error. The next suspect word is highlighted.

   To ignore a spelling error, because it might be a company name or special term that does not appear in the dictionary, click Ignore or Ignore All. Alternatively, you can click Add to include the word in the User Dictionary, so that future occurrences will not be flagged as an error.

4 Repeat steps 2 and 3 until the spelling check is complete, and click Done.

TIP

To control what text in the document is checked, select an option from the Search menu in the Check Spelling dialog box. You can check selected text (Selection), the text in a series of threaded text frames (Story), all text in the document (Document), or all open documents (All Documents).

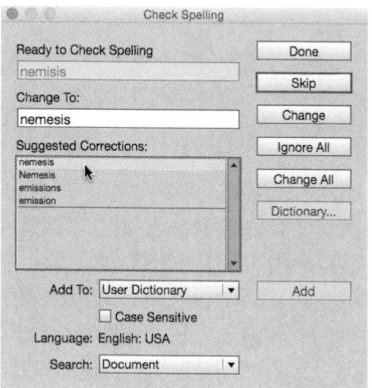

The fearless Captain Toothless scours the world in search of kids in need. While traversing the skies, he hears the familiar cackle of his nemisis, the evil Princess Sourpuss.

The fearless Captain Toothless scours the world in search of kids in need. While traversing the skies, he hears the familiar cackle of his nemesis, the evil Princess Sourpuss.

Figure 6.14 Checking the spelling for a document

Performing Find/Change

★ *ACA Objective 4.3* InDesign's Find/Change command is a powerhouse that lets you search for content and replace it with something else in the document. This speeds up the process of making text changes throughout your project.

In addition to performing simple text changes throughout a document, such as replacing the word "captain" with "colonel," you can also use Find/Change to:

- Search for advanced pattern-based text strings with GREP, a language that codes the finding of patterns in text, for example, any text in brackets, and make changes.

- Search for Glyphs, and replace them. Glyphs are special characters you can insert into text with the Type > Glyphs panel. Double-clicking a character in the panel inserts it at the text insertion point.

- Search for object formatting, such as stroke or fill colors, and change the settings.

- Search for text formatting, such as font and size, and replace the settings.

To search and replace text (**Figure 6.15**):

1. Choose Edit > Find/Change.

2. Click the Text tab in the Find/Change dialog box.

3. Enter the text to search for in the Find What field.

4. Enter the replacement text in the Change To field.

5. Under Direction, select Forward to search from the current page through to the following pages.

6. Click Find Next to find the first occurrence of the search word.

Figure 6.15 Finding the text "captain" and replacing it with "colonel"

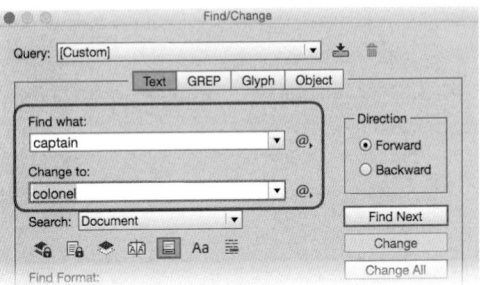

7   Click one of the change options:

- **Change:** Replaces only the found text.
- **Change All:** Replaces all occurrences of the found text.
- **Change/Find:** Replaces the found text, and immediately moves forward to the next occurrence.

Working with Libraries

As you work on design projects, you'll find that you reuse design elements, such as caption boxes, speech bubbles, images, text, colors, and styles. This occurs not just within the same project, but across projects. Libraries can make those frequently needed elements available to you at any time.

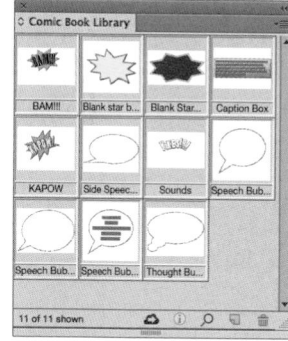

Figure 6.16 An InDesign object library loaded with speech bubbles and starbursts

InDesign offers two types of libraries, both of which appear as a panel.

- **Object libraries:** These libraries are files that you create; they are stored on your local computer. They can only contain objects, such as text frames, image frames, and groups of objects; these objects may or may not have contents (**Figure 6.16**). While you can share your library files with other designers, you can't provide live updates to the objects in them. You simply each have your own copy of the library.

- **Creative Cloud libraries:** These libraries are part of the Adobe Creative Cloud, and are used to store objects similar to object libraries, as well as color themes, colors, paragraph and character styles, and Adobe Stock images. The same libraries and assets appear across Adobe applications (such as Photoshop and Illustrator) and Adobe mobile apps (such as Adobe Capture CC). You can share CC Libraries among users, which makes them a great tool for working collaboratively with other designers (**Figure 6.17**).

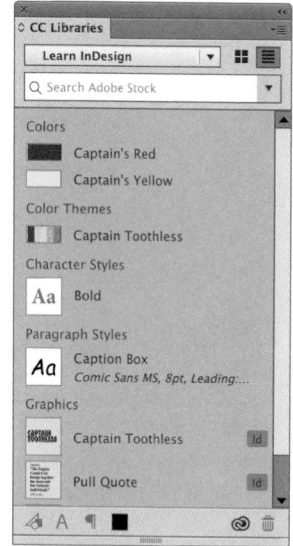

Figure 6.17 The Learn InDesign library selected in the CC Libraries panel

Working with Object Libraries

Object libraries work well when you work on a project alone and only want to store InDesign objects. First, you need to create a library file, and then you can add objects to it.

CREATING A LIBRARY

TIP

To close a library, click the close box at the top of the panel. To open a library, choose File > Open and navigate to the INDL file on your system and double-click the file.

To create a new library (**Figure 6.18**):

1 Choose File > New > Library.

2 Click No in the CC Libraries dialog box.

3 Specify a name and location for the library, such as Comic Book Library, in the File Name (Windows) or Save As (Mac OS) dialog box.

4 Click Save.

The library panel opens as a blank panel, and you can start adding library items to it.

Figure 6.18 A new object library created for the comic book

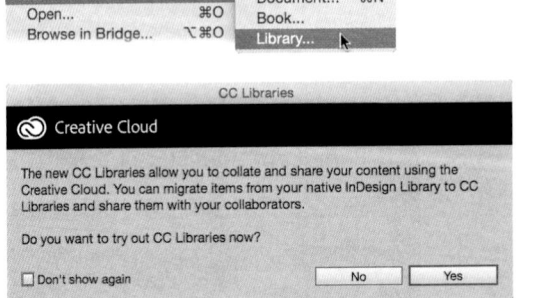

ADDING ITEMS TO A LIBRARY

To add items to the library (**Figure 6.19**):

1 Select an object on the page.

2 Select Add Item from the library panel menu.

> **TIP** *You can also select an object and drag it to the library panel or click the New Library Item button at the bottom of the library panel.*

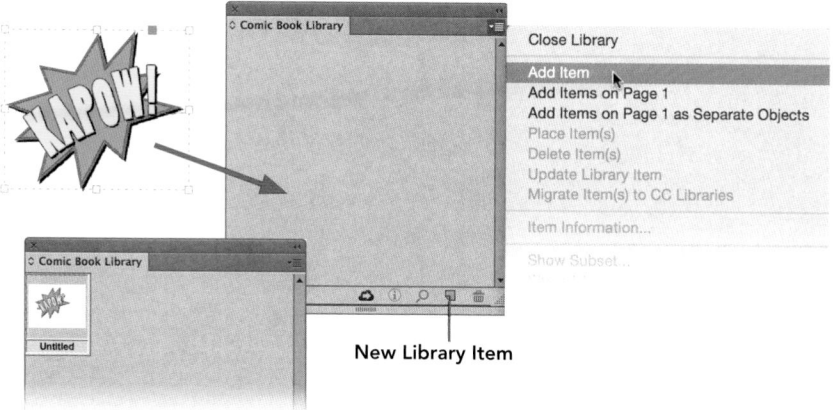

Figure 6.19 Adding an object from the page to the library

New Library Item

ADDING INFORMATION TO LIBRARY ITEMS

To help you find items in a library later, you can give each library item a name, type, and description.

To add item information (**Figure 6.20**):

1 Select the item in the library.

2 Select Item Information from the library panel menu, or click the Library Item Information button at the bottom of the panel.

3 Enter the name in the Item Name field.

4 Select an option from the Object Type menu.

5 Enter a short description in the Description field. Click OK.

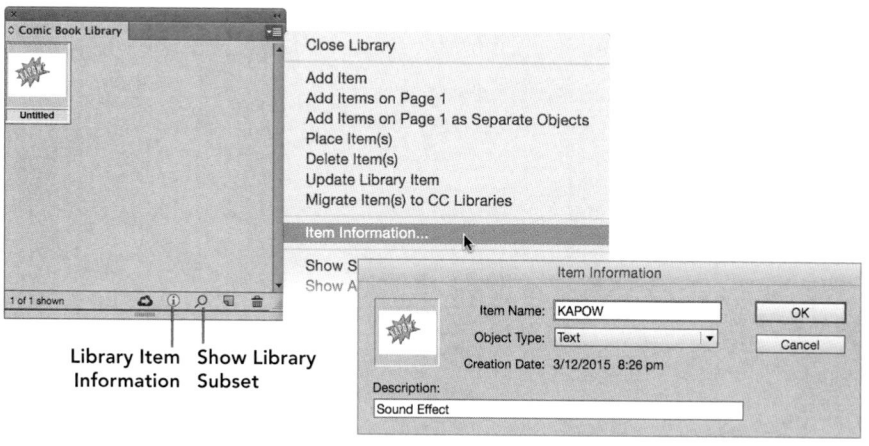

Library Item Information   Show Library Subset

Figure 6.20 Adding Library Item Information to items in a library makes later finding of the items easier.

You can use the item names and descriptions as criteria for finding a specific item or displaying a subset of items.

To show a subset (**Figure 6.21**):

1 Select Show Subset from the library panel menu.

2 Select the parameter type, for example, Description from the Parameters menu.

3 Enter the text for the description. Click OK.

Figure 6.21 Displaying a subset of the library items with the word "sound" in their description

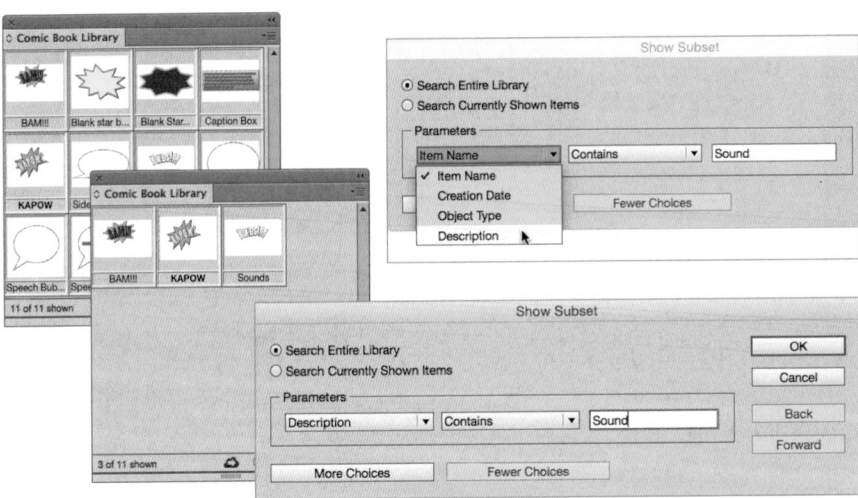

USING LIBRARY ITEMS ON DOCUMENT PAGES

Now that you know how to add and find library items, you are ready to start using the library items in your project. All the sound effects are added, ready to use in the comic book project. To add objects from library items you must first open the library (File > Open).

To place a library item on the page, you can either (**Figure 6.22**):

- Drag the item from the library panel onto the page.

- Select the item, and select Place Item(s) from the library panel menu.

> **NOTE** *Page objects and library items maintain no link or relationship. So if you change an object on the document page, its source item in the library does not change. Likewise, if you update a library item, the changes are not reflected in the objects already on the page. (To update a library item in a library, select a related object on the page, then click the item in the library and select Update Library Item from the library panel menu.)*

Figure 6.22 Dragging a library item to the page

Working with the Creative Cloud Library

CC libraries differ from object libraries in that multiple designers can open the same library at once and use assets in their designs. Additionally, CC libraries can contain more than page objects; for example, they can also contain colors and paragraph styles. When you add new items to the library, or update items, other designers can see these changes almost immediately. That is because Creative Cloud libraries synchronize over the Internet. Additionally, you can place non-InDesign artwork into the libraries. For example, the sound effects could also be created in Adobe Illustrator.

★ *ACA Objective 4.5*

CREATING A LIBRARY

To create a new library (**Figure 6.23**):

1   Choose Window > CC Libraries to show the CC Libraries panel.

2   Click the libraries menu at the top of the panel, and select Create New Library.

3   Enter the name for the library and click Create.

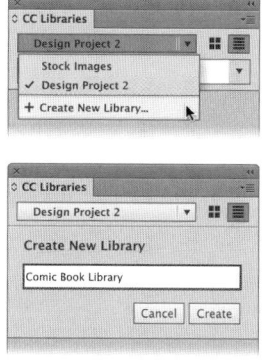
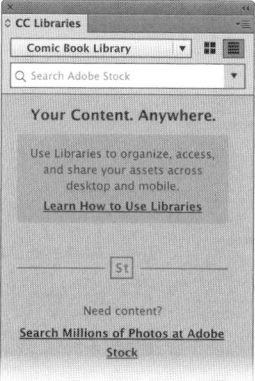

Figure 6.23 Creating a new Creative Cloud library

An empty library is created, and you can start adding InDesign page elements, colors, color themes, and more. You can even search across Adobe Stock, an online resource that has millions of beautiful images, photos, and videos that you can use in your designs.

ADDING PAGE ELEMENTS TO A LIBRARY

To add InDesign page elements to a library (**Figure 6.24**):

1 Select the destination library from the library menu in the CC Libraries panel.

2 Drag the artwork from an InDesign page into the CC Libraries panel, or click the Add Graphic button at the bottom of the panel.

Figure 6.24 Adding library items to CC Libraries

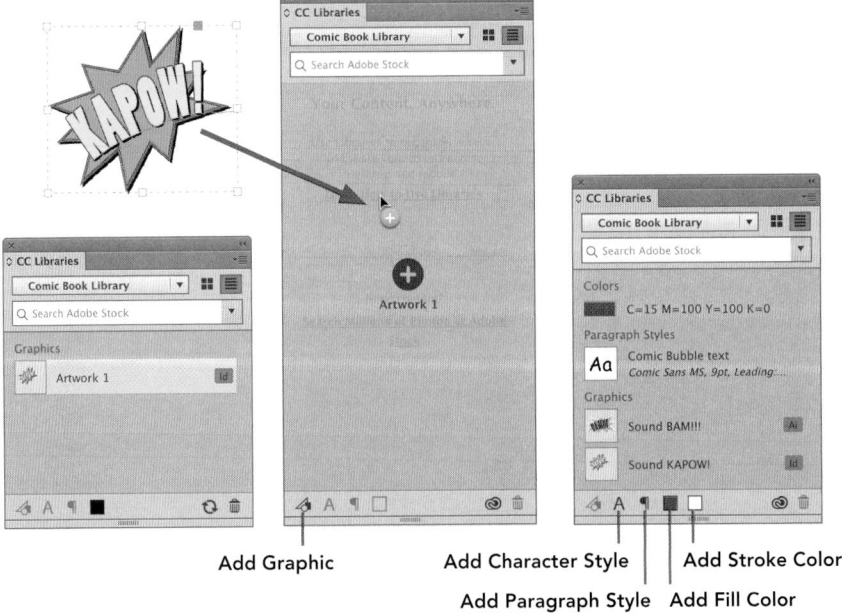

Add Graphic   Add Character Style   Add Stroke Color
Add Paragraph Style   Add Fill Color

Depending on what you have selected on the InDesign page, you will also be able to add character styles, paragraph styles, fill color, or stroke color. For example, if you have a shape selected with a red fill, clicking the Add Fill Color button at the bottom of the CC Libraries panel adds the color below the Colors heading in the CC Libraries panel. If you have text selected that has a paragraph style applied to it, clicking Add Paragraph Style adds the style to the panel.

The library item is added to the library under the Graphics heading, and automatically named. When items are displayed in the list view, a badge on the right

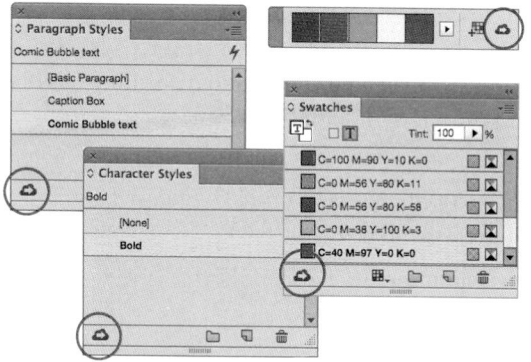

Figure 6.25 Adding colors, graphics, and styles to CC Libraries

indicates this graphic's artwork is created in InDesign. A graphic's artwork can also be added from other applications. For example, artwork added from Adobe Illustrator will display an Ai badge.

You can also add colors, color themes, paragraph styles, or character styles directly from the various panels. To add these to a library (**Figure 6.25**):

1 First, select the library at the top of the CC Libraries panel.

2 Show the panel from which you want to add an item.

3 Select the item, and click the Add To Library button at the bottom of its panel.

Items from object libraries can also be moved to CC Libraries.

NOTE

When you are not connected to the Internet, you can still add items to and update items in CC Libraries. Synchronizing will happen once you're back online.

RENAMING A LIBRARY ITEM

To rename library items (**Figure 6.26**):

1 Right-click (Windows) or Control-click (Mac OS) the added artwork, and select Rename.

2 Type the new name, and press Enter (Windows) or Return (Mac OS).

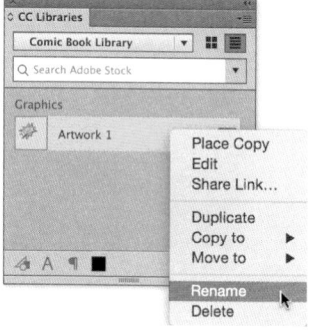

Figure 6.26 Renaming a library item

USING LIBRARY ITEMS IN DOCUMENTS

With colors, color themes, styles, and graphics loaded in CC Libraries, you can now use them for your design projects.

To add a graphic to the page (**Figure 6.27**):

1 From the library menu at the top of the CC Libraries panel, select a library.

2 Drag the graphic from the library to the page.

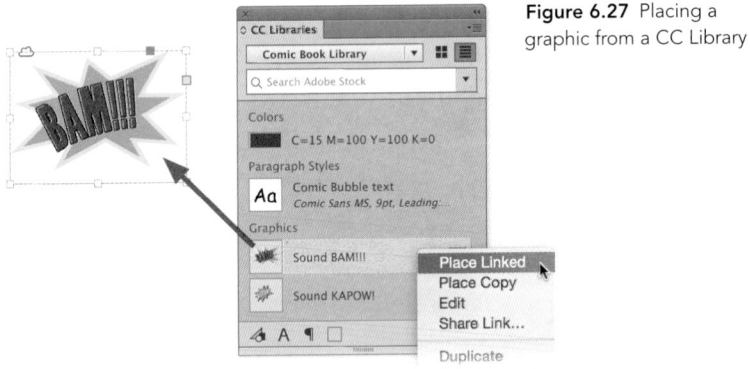

Figure 6.27 Placing a graphic from a CC Library

You can also right-click (Windows) or Control-click (Mac OS) a graphic and select Place Copy or Place Linked. Place Copy detaches the placed graphic from the item in the library. Place Link maintains a link to the parent object in the library. When a linked item, such as a sound effect graphic created in Illustrator, is placed, a modified or missing link warning might appear in the Links panel (this happens when the item has been edited or removed from the library). You update these links just like any other link in InDesign: Select the object and select Update Link from the Links panel menu.

To work with other library items, such as styles, select text on the page, and click the style name in the library in the CC Libraries panel. Styles are automatically added to the paragraph or character styles panel for the document you are working on. The same applies when using colors from a CC library. The colors are added to the Swatches panel.

Library items that are graphics can be edited in their native applications, for example, to edit an item with an Id badge.

To edit an InDesign graphic in the library (**Figure 6.28**):

1 Double-click the item in the library. It will open in InDesign, as a randomly named file.

2 Make the changes, for example, changing the fill color.

3 Choose File > Save, then File > Close.

The item in the library is updated, and any designers you've shared the library with will see the updated item in their libraries, once the Creative Cloud has synchronized the files.

Figure **6.28** Double-click an item in the library to edit it. Save the changes, and close the edited file to update the item in the library.

Creating Freeform Shapes and Lines

You have learned how to add different shapes and frames, such as ellipses, circles, rectangles, and polygons to your designs, and used the Pathfinder panel to create new shapes by combining shapes. In Chapter 3, you learned that shapes are paths. What are the different components that paths are made up of?

- Anchor points.

- Line segments that connect two anchor points.

- Direction lines that attach to anchor points and control the curvature of line segments.

Two InDesign tools let you create freeform paths:

▶ Video 6.8

- The Pencil tool (✐) follows the movements of your mouse (or pen, if you happen to work with a drawing tablet). It automatically adds anchor points and joins those with line segments. For smooth corners that are attached to curved lines, it even adds the direction lines.

▶ Video 6.9

- The Pen tool (✐) is a more technical drawing tool. You add each anchor point and construct the path as you work with it, joining anchor points with line segments and adding direction lines where a path requires a curve.

Drawing Shapes with the Pencil Tool

★ ACA Objective 3.2

The easier tool to work with when creating freeform shapes is the Pencil tool. You start by drawing a path with the Pencil tool. Then, you continue to smooth the path using the Smooth tool (✐), and you can delete sections using the Eraser tool (✐). The Smooth tool and Eraser tool are grouped with the Pencil tool.

To draw the path (**Figure 6.29**):

1 Select the Pencil tool.

2 Start dragging across the page while pressing the mouse (or start dragging with a pen). A dotted line appears.

3 Release the mouse or pen when you are finished drawing.

After you create a path, you can select it with the Selection tool and apply stroke settings, such as color, weight, and stroke type to the path.

To create a closed shape that can have a fill color when drawing with the Pencil tool, move the Pencil tool close to the start point, and press Alt (Windows) or Option (Mac OS). When a small circle icon appears next to the Pencil tool icon on the page, release the mouse button (**Figure 6.30**).

Figure 6.29 ▼ Drawing a path with the Pencil tool

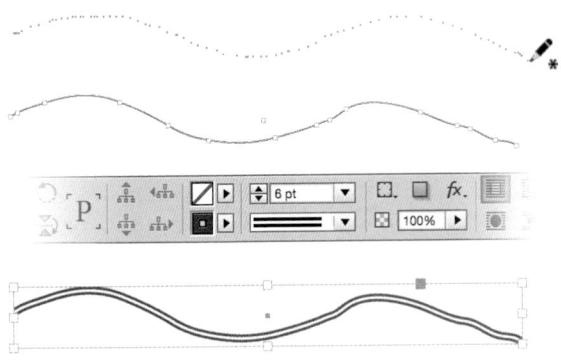

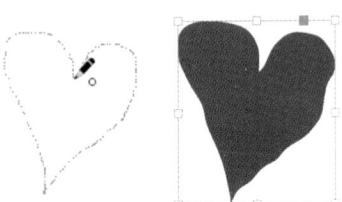

Figure 6.30 Creating a closed path with the Pencil tool

Which tool could you use to edit a path and reposition anchor points?

Yes, the Direct Selection tool ( ). When you click on the edge of an unselected path, all the anchor points are visible. If you look at a path drawn with the Pencil tool, you'll likely spot some unintended wobbles along it. Although you could use the Direct Selection tool to select anchor points, redirect direction lines, or reposition lines and edit them, that quickly becomes a tedious task for paths with lots of anchor points. A more efficient alternative is the Smooth tool. As its name suggests, you can use it to smooth the paths you have drawn.

To smooth a path (**Figure 6.31**):

1 Select the path.

2 Select the Smooth tool. All the anchor points on the path are now visible.

3 Drag over the path while pressing the mouse button.

4 If needed, repeat multiple times to get a smoother result.

To erase part of a path (**Figure 6.32**):

1 Select the path, then select the Eraser tool.

2 Drag over the section of the path to erase it.

3 Release the mouse button.

TIP

To edit the default Pencil tool preferences, double-click the tool in the Tools panel.

Figure 6.31 Smoothing a path that was drawn with the Pencil tool

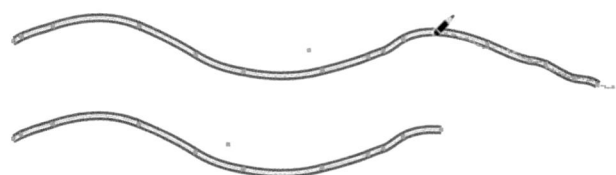

Figure 6.32 Erasing part of a path with the Eraser tool

Using the Pen Tool

With the Pen tool you can create straight and curved shapes (paths). Each time you click with the tool, a new anchor point is created. The anchor point that is added last is then joined to the previously added anchor point with a line segment.

★ *ACA Objective 3.2*

If you click and drag instead of clicking, you create an anchor point with a direction line. This allows you to create curved line segments.

STRAIGHT LINE SEGMENTS

To draw a simple zigzag line (**Figure 6.33**):

1   Select the Pen tool.

2   Click at the starting point for the line.

3   Position the pointer at the next point on the zigzag line and click.

4   Continue to click until the zigzag line is finished.

5   Using the Selection tool, click the path and adjust its stroke settings.

To create a closed path (**Figure 6.34**):

1   As you are drawing the path with the Pen tool, position the pointer over the start point. A small circle indicates you are about to close the path.

2   Click to close the path.

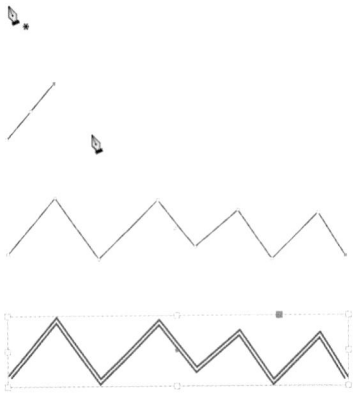

Figure 6.33 Clicking with the Pen tool to create a zigzag path with sharp corners

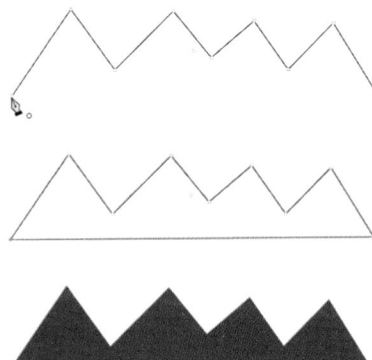

Figure 6.34 Closing a path by clicking with the Pen tool on the start point

ADDING CURVES

The Pen tool can also be used to draw paths with smooth corners and curved line segments. Instead of clicking to place anchor points, you'll click and drag to create anchor points with direction lines.

A few tips for adding direction lines:

- Drag in the direction that you are drawing.

- The longer the direction line is, the longer the line segment will be.

- Consider making the direction lines about 30% of the length of the line segment between the two anchor points.

Let's take a look at drawing a wavy line as an example (**Figure 6.35**):

1 Select the Pen tool.

2 Click and hold the mouse, and drag up to create the first anchor point with a direction line.

3 Release the mouse button, and move the pointer to the position for the next anchor point.

4 Click and hold the mouse button, and drag down to create another anchor point with a direction line.

5 Repeat steps 3 and 4 until you've finished creating the path.

6 Using the Selection tool, click the path and adjust its stroke settings.

Figure 6.35 Creating a curved line with the Pen tool

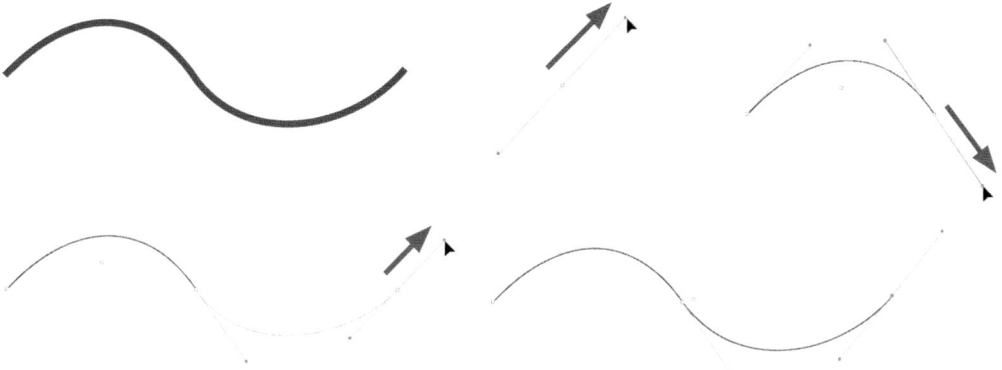

EDITING PATHS

You can continue to edit any paths you draw using the Direct Selection tool as you have learned in earlier chapters. Additionally, you can use the Add Anchor Point tool ( ) and Delete Anchor Point tool ( ), which are hidden under the Pen tool. Click a line segment to add more points, or click an anchor point to delete it.

For more advanced information on using the Pen tool, please refer to InDesign Help.

Flowing Type on a Path

★ *ACA Objective 3.2*

 *Video 6.8*

Until this point, text has been added to text frames—mostly rectangular text frames—and tables. Text can be inserted into frames that are freeform shapes or any other shape. To do so, click inside the shape with the Type tool to convert the path to a text frame and add text (**Figure 6.36**). Then, edit the text-frame appearance and text as you've learned in earlier chapters.

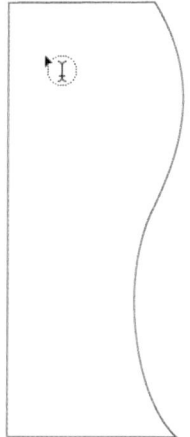

Rumque pe dolupta qui-
bus, culla quuntor maio
conemperfero ipiet perum
es nat omnimpo ribus, qui
doluptate pedit, suscipicia
sitisqu odigendio bea velen-
digniet faccumque sant quae
con nonse num voloratiis nis
inus as mini con cumentur
maxim conseditatus mag-
natur adis dolore di tatia-
tures sinienia pe landis
iumentem earum rem
reptae vides tiatem.
Nam Quiam, volorio
bla nis comnistiis ac-
caborro magnis dun-
dit, nis erias nobit
eos excerum quosae
pa conetur sequae ni-
mente nulparum ren-
daep udigenis ra et rem
nat atqui quis oluptur ali-
quatem int archili quanto

Figure 6.36 Text added to a freeform shape

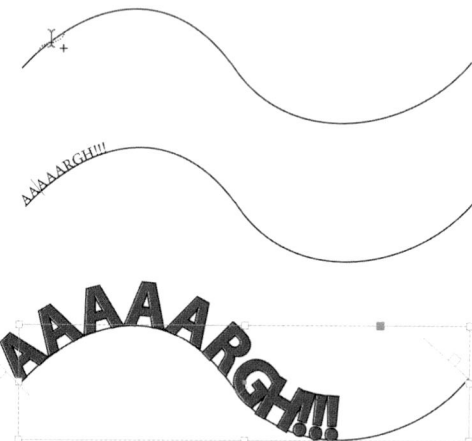

Figure 6.37 Adding text to a path

InDesign's Type On A Path tool ( ) allows you to set text on the path itself instead of inside the shape. This is a great way to work creatively with text. For example, in poster designs or, as in the comic book project, to change the way the sound effects appear on the page.

ADDING TEXT TO THE PATH

Before you can set type on a path, you must first create a path to work with. This can be a curved line, as you have just learned to create, but it can also be a closed shape, such as a circle or ellipse.

To add type on a path (**Figure 6.37**):

1 Position the Type On A Path tool over the path.

2 Click the path when a small plus sign appears ( ).

3 Type the text you want to add to the path.

4 Format the text, changing the font, size, and color as required for your design.

5 If needed, select the path and change the stroke and/or fill settings as well.

The text flows with the path shape. Its start position will vary depending on the text alignment you selected when formatting the text. For example, if you center align the text, it will position itself in the center of the path, or if you left align text, it will be placed at the leftmost point of the path.

NOTE

To make it easier to see the path in the screenshots, the path has a 1-pt black stroke. If you don't want to see the stroke in the end, change the stroke color for the path to [None].

MOVING TEXT ALONG ITS PATH

As you add text to a path, three brackets help you position the text. To see the brackets, select the path with the Selection tool. You can use these brackets to control where the text is positioned on the path.

For text that is placed on a line, use the bracket that is positioned on the alignment side of the text. For example, to move left-aligned text along the path, select the left bracket.

To move the text along the path (**Figure 6.38**):

1 Select the path with the Selection tool.

2 Position the pointer over the left bracket until you see the cursor change.

3 Drag the bracket along the path to a new position.

When you release the mouse button, the text is placed at its new position.

For text that is placed on a closed path, you can use any of the brackets to position the text along the path.

NOTE

If you reposition the Left and Right brackets, you also define the start and end positions for the text, a bit like setting a Left Indent or Right Indent on paragraph text in a text frame.

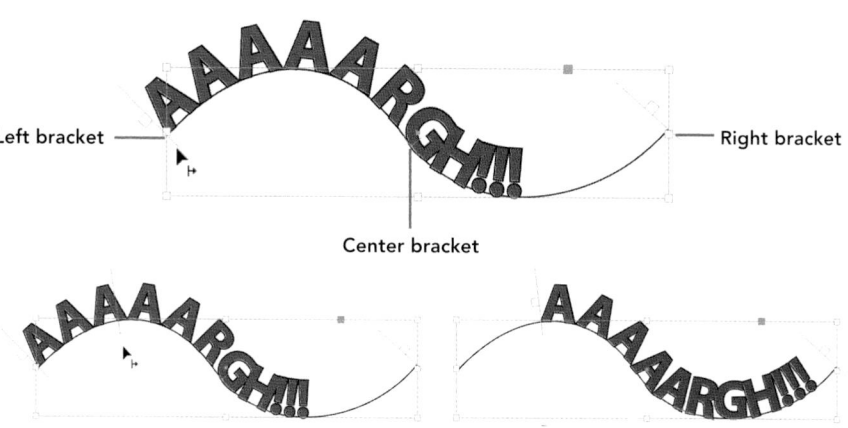

Left bracket

Right bracket

Center bracket

Figure 6.38 Moving left-aligned text along the path by dragging the left bracket with the Selection tool

SETTING TYPE PATH OPTIONS

A number of additional controls allow you to adjust type on a path. You can change the vertical position of text, adjust the spacing, and the appearance.

To edit the type on a path settings (**Figure 6.39**):

1 With the Selection tool, select the type on a path.

2 Choose Type > Type On A Path > Options.

3   In the Type On A Path Options dialog box, select Preview so you can see the changes you make.

4   From the Effects menu, select one of the effects that controls the way the text appears on the path.

5   From the Align menu, select an option to control the vertical position of the text in relationship to the path itself (To Path).

6   To add more space between the text characters along the path, *decrease* the spacing amount (yes, that sounds backwards, but it works). Note that you can apply additional kerning or tracking amounts to text as part of text formatting as well.

7   Click OK.

As you can see, type on a path is a fun feature. It can draw the attention to a word or phrase on the page and make text stand out.

Figure 6.39 Changing the appearance and vertical position of type on a path

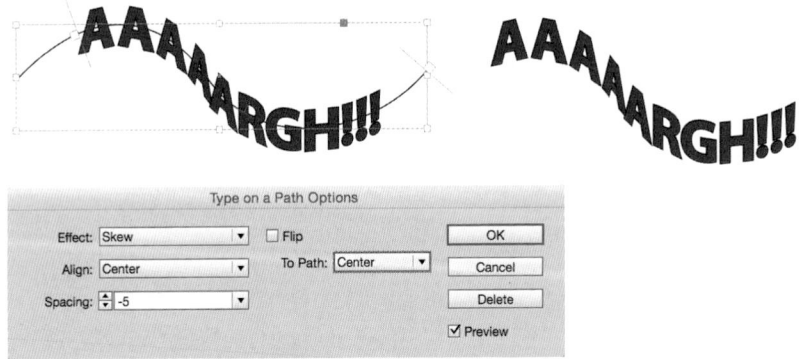

Working with Hyperlinks

Hyperlinks are interactive links that take you from a source point you click (or tap) to a destination somewhere else. A familiar type of hyperlink is a link to a web page. However, InDesign also lets you link to an email address, a file, or another page.

InDesign provides a number of different ways to add hyperlinks:

- You create a hyperlink for selected text.

- You can select an entire object and convert it to a hyperlink.

- You can convert an object to a button and set a button action that takes you to a web page. You will learn how to do this in the next project.

In this section, we'll focus on working with the Hyperlinks panel (Window > Interactive > Hyperlinks).

▶ Video 6.10

Creating a Text Hyperlink

A text hyperlink is some text within a paragraph that becomes a clickable link. To create a text hyperlink to a web page (**Figure 6.40**):

★ ACA Objective 4.6

1 Open a web browser and navigate to the web page you want to link to.

2 Select the text in the web address field in the web browser, and press Ctrl+C (Windows) or Command+C (Mac OS) to copy the address.

3 Choose Window > Interactive > Hyperlinks to show the Hyperlinks panel.

4 Select the text that will become the hyperlink source (the clickable link).

5 Choose New Hyperlink from the Hyperlinks panel menu, or click the Create New Hyperlink button at the bottom of the Hyperlinks panel.

6 Select URL from the Link To menu.

7 Click inside the URL field under Destination, and press Ctrl+V (Windows) or Command+V (Mac OS) to paste the copied web address into the field.

   InDesign automatically applies a character style called Hyperlink to the text. It applies a blue color and underline to the text, which makes the link more noticeable in the text.

8 Under PDF Appearance settings, select Invisible Rectangle from the Type menu to prevent the creation of a visible box around the link in an interactive PDF, and select [None] from the Highlight menu to ensure that when you click the link, the appearance does not change.

9 Click OK.

TIP
You can also paste the copied web address into the URL field in the Hyperlinks panel to create a hyperlink to a web page.

   NOTE *To change the appearance of the Hyperlink character style, double-click it in the Character Styles panel. Alternatively, double-click the hyperlink in the Hyperlink panel, and select [None] from the Style menu in the Edit Hyperlink dialog box to not apply any character-level formatting to the hyperlink.*

The Hyperlink panel shows a green traffic light symbol to the right of the hyperlink to confirm that the web address can be accessed online. For web addresses that do not work, the traffic light changes to red.

You can edit the hyperlink at any stage by double-clicking it in the Hyperlinks panel, or by clicking the link and selecting Edit Hyperlink from the Hyperlinks panel menu.

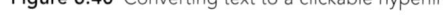

Figure 6.40 Converting text to a clickable hyperlink

Creating an Object Hyperlink

★ ACA Objective 4.6

Turning an object into a hyperlink pretty much works the same way as creating a text hyperlink. Instead of just the text, the entire object becomes a clickable link. Make sure that you have copied the web address so you can paste it into the URL field.

To create a hyperlink from an object (**Figure 6.41**):

1 Select the object, such as a text frame or image, on the page.

2 Choose New Hyperlink from the Hyperlinks panel menu.

3 Select URL from the Link To menu.

4 Click inside the URL field under Destination, and press Ctrl+V (Windows) or Command+V (Mac OS) to paste the web address into the field.

5 Click OK.

The hyperlink object now displays a dashed line around the object, when the document screen mode is set to Normal, indicating that it is now a hyperlink.

NOTE

To generate clickable hyperlinks, you need to export your InDesign document to a format that supports hyperlinks. Some of the formats that support hyperlinks are interactive PDF, EPUB, and HTML. You will learn about creating an interactive EPUB in the next chapter.

Figure 6.41 Converting an object to a clickable hyperlink

Exporting to a Web Image Format

You might be asked by a client to supply an InDesign document as an image that can be used on the Internet. For example, a magazine cover might be used on a publisher's web page to announce that a new issue is out. Or, a comic book page might appear on a web page as a teaser of the comic book's story.

InDesign supports two web-based image formats you can export to:

- **JPEG:** JPEG is a lossy file format that applies file compression, reducing the file to a smaller size that is more suited for use on the Internet. Because it is lossy, it reduces the quality of the image. Think of it as a format that crumbles up a piece of paper. The higher the amount of compression, the tinier the paper ball. However, also consider what would happen if you try to iron out the piece of paper again after you've crumbled it up. Because of this lossy quality, JPEG is not well suited for designs that contain a lot of text, as the text would appear fuzzy. Additionally, JPEG also does not support transparency; this means that InDesign pages are exported with a white background. JPEGs are best suited for designs that contain a lot of photos.

- **PNG:** Also applies compression to reduce the file size of the document it creates, but it does so in a lossless way. Additionally, it supports transparency, which might be helpful if you design a logo in InDesign that needs to be placed on a colored or tinted background online. Without transparency support, the logo would appear on a white background. PNG is also a great format to use for text-heavy pages as the text remains much crisper. It is also a format that works well when you need to supply images for use in Microsoft Office applications, such as Word and PowerPoint.

★ ACA Objective 2.5

Video 6.10

Exporting as PNG

Based on the differences between JPEG and PNG, the comic book page is well suited for PNG export.

Can you think of a reason why? Because it contains text that might end up appearing fuzzy.

TIP

To export only specific objects on a page, first select them with the Selection tool. Then, choose File > Export.

To export the comic book page as a PNG (**Figure 6.42**):

1. Choose File > Export.
2. Enter the name for the file in the File Name (Windows) or Save As (Mac OS) field.
3. Select PNG from the Save As Type (Windows) or Format (Mac OS) menu.
4. Click Save. The Export PNG dialog box opens.
5. Under Export, select the content to export. To export a specific page, enter the page number in the Range field.

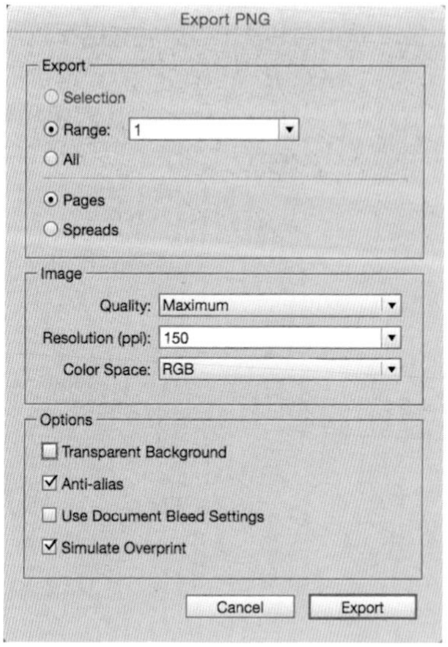

Figure 6.42 Export PNG dialog box

6. Under Image:

   Select the preferred quality setting from the Quality menu. Maximum quality provides the best result, but could result in a larger file size.

   - To specify the Resolution, select an option from the menu or enter a value. For PNG files used in Microsoft Office, for example, 150 ppi works well.
   - From the Color Space menu, select RGB. Remember, that is the color space used for digital media and web publishing.
7. Under Options:
   - Select Transparent Background to create a PNG that supports transparency.
   - Select Anti-Alias to create smoother edges.
   - To restrict the exported page to the page area itself, deselect Use Document Bleed Settings.
   - Select Simulate Overprint if your page contains any transparency effects, such as drop shadows, directional feather, or different opacity levels.
8. Click Export.

The PNG file is now created.

Exporting as JPEG

For photographic pages, or pages that have file size restrictions, you could export to JPEG, which provides a higher level of compression, and thus smaller file sizes.

★ ACA Objective 2.5

To export a page to JPEG (**Figure 6.43**):

1   Choose File > Export.

2   Enter the name for the file in the File Name (Windows) or Save As (Mac OS) field.

3   Select JPEG from the Save As Type (Windows) or Format (Mac OS) menu.

4   Click Save. The Export JPEG dialog box opens.

5   Under Export, select the page to export.

6   Under Image, select a Quality option. Keep in mind that the lower the quality, the more lossy the resulting image will be. Leave the Format Method set to Baseline. In the early days of the Internet, Progressive download was preferred, so the image would be downloaded incrementally. With faster Internet speeds today, that is no longer required.

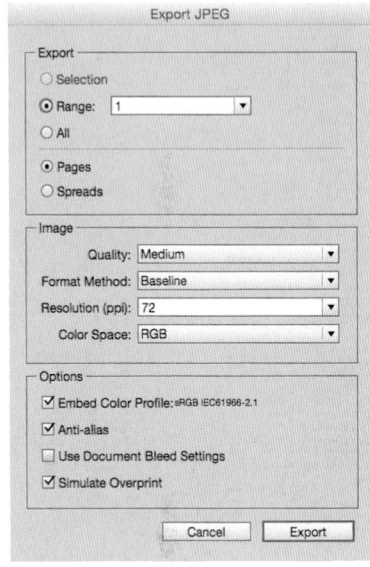

Figure 6.43 Export JPEG dialog box

> **NOTE** *To see the different quality variations when applying a high amount of compression for JPEG export, try exporting the same comic page with different quality settings, leaving the resolution set to 72 ppi. Open the resulting images in a web browser, and see if you can spot the differences.*

7   Under Options, select Simulate Overprint if the page you export contains transparency.

8   Click Export.

Wow, well done! You have completed another project, and you are nearly at the end of the projects covered in this book. For the final project, you'll start by revising previously learned skills to get more practice, and then learn how to add very cool interactive elements such as movies and slideshows to an InDesign project that is exported as an eBook file.

Glossary

Additive color Created by combining light.

Alignment Controls how the text is positioned horizontally within the text frame, for example, left, centered, or right.

Analogous colors Colors that are side by side on the color wheel.

Anchor point A point on a path that connects to a line segment.

Animation Movement or transform of a design element on the page.

All caps Using uppercase letterforms for each letter. All letters are the same size.

Alternate layout Variation of an original layout you created in InDesign that is included in the same document as the original.

Asymmetrical Achieves balance with different elements with different weights on each side (or the top and bottom) of a page.

Attribution Creative Commons licensing indicated with "BY." Requires that you credit the original author when using work, and you are allowed to tweak the work as long as proper credit is given to the author.

Auto-size Automatic growth in depth or width of a text frame dependent on the amount of text it contains.

Balance Evenly distributed, but not necessarily centered or mirrored.

Baseline An imaginary line used to organize text along a horizontal plane.

Blackletter fonts Also known as old English, gothic, or textura. Fonts that feature an overly ornate style, and convey a feeling of rich and sophisticated gravitas.

Cast shadow The shadow cast on any objects that are in the shadow of the form. Shadows fade as they get farther from the form casting the shadow.

Chaotic lines Look like scribbles and feel unpredictable and frantic. Convey a sense of urgency, fear, or explosive energy.

Character formatting Text formatting for selected text, for example, font choice, font style (bold, italic), and size.

Character styles Styles used to format words or phrases within a paragraph differently from the rest of the paragraph.

Client's needs The focus and goals for a design project.

Color The perceived hue, lightness, and saturation of an object or light.

Color harmonies Color rules that are named for their relative locations on the color wheel.

Color stop A color that is a starting color for a gradient blend.

Complementary colors Colors that are opposite each other on the color wheel.

Contrast Creates visual interest and a focal point in a composition. It is what draws the eye to the focal point.

Corporate colors Colors that are part of a company's branding.

Creative Commons Ways that artists can release their works for limited use and still choose the way the works are used and shared: Public Domain, Attribution, ShareAlike, NoDerivs, and NonCommercial.

Curved (lines) Expresses fluidity, beauty, and grace.

Decorative fonts Also known as ornamental, novelty, or display, these fonts don't fall into any of the other categories.

Deliverables A predetermined list of items that will be delivered to the customer.

Design elements The building blocks of art defined by artists to provide a framework for creating art.

Design principles Essential rules or assembly instructions of art.

Diagonal (lines) Lines traveling neither on a vertical nor a horizontal path. Express growth or decline and imply movement or change.

Dingbat fonts Also known as wingdings, they consist of a collection of objects and shapes instead of letters, numerals, and punctuation.

Direction A common way to describe lines, such as vertical, horizontal, diagonal.

Direction line Line attached to an anchor point that controls the curvature of a path.

Docked panels Panels that snap to the side of the document window.

Elements of art The building blocks of creative works. They are the "nouns" of design, such as space, line, shape, form, texture, value, color, and type.

Emphasis Describes the focal point to which the eye is naturally and initially drawn in a design.

Fair use A set of rules that specify how and when copyrighted material can be used and that make sure copyright protection doesn't come at the cost of creativity and freedom.

Feedback loop A system set up to continually encourage and require input and approval from a client on a project's direction.

Flow A category related to the energy conveyed by lines and shapes.

Focal point What the design is all about. The call to action or the primary message you are trying to get across.

Font The whole collection of the typeface in each of its sizes and styles.

Footer rows Bottom row or rows of a table.

Form Describes three-dimensional objects, such as spheres, cubes, and pyramids.

Frame Objects of varying shapes (rectangles, ellipses, etc.) that contain content (such as text or images) or simply reflect a stroke and/or fill color.

Hand-drawn lines Appear to be created through traditional media, such as paints, charcoal, or chalk.

Header rows Top row or rows of a table.

Geometric (lines) Tend to be straight and have sharp angles. Look manmade and intentional. Communicate strength, power, and precision.

Geometric shapes Predictable and consistent shapes, such as circles, squares, triangles, and stars. They are rarely found in nature and convey mechanical and manufactured impressions.

Glyph Each character of a font, whether it is a letter, number, symbol, or swash.

Gradient Blends between different colors or shades of color.

Gradient ramp Preview for a gradient that shows the color blend and color stops.

Gutter The spacing between columns.

Handwritten fonts Also known as hand fonts, they simulate handwriting.

Highlight The area of a form that is directly facing the light and appears lightest.

Horizontal Moving from left to right, and expresses calmness and balance.

Horizontal scale Describes the function of stretching letters and distorting the typeface geometry.

Hyperlinks Interactive links that take you from a source point you click (or tap) to a destination somewhere else.

Hyphenation Determines if and when words should be split with hyphens when wrapping to the next line.

Ideographs (ideograms) Images that represent an idea, such as a heart representing love.

IDML InDesign Markup Language, a file format that provides backward compatibility with earlier versions of InDesign.

Implied lines Lines that don't really exist but are implied by shapes, such as dotted or dashed lines, people waiting in lines, or the margins of a block of text.

Indent Settings that determine how far an entire paragraph or its first line is indented from the edges of the text-frame's columns.

Index A list of topics, also referred to as index entries, that includes page number references and "see also" references.

Index entries Topics listed in the index.

Index markers Hidden characters that provide a page reference for the topics listed in the index.

Iterations New versions of a design that successively become closer to the desired result.

Iterative work Work that is shared as it is completed, allowing the customer to chime in with comments while it is still easy to make changes.

Justified Aligns text to a straight edge on both the right and left edges of a paragraph.

Kerning The space between specific character pairs.

Leading (line spacing) The amount of space between the baselines of two lines of text. In InDesign, leading is set as a character attribute.

Ligatures Special characters used to represent letter combinations, such as "fi."

Light source The perceived location of the lighting in relation to the form.

Line A mark with a beginning and end point.

Line segment Part of a path that joins two anchor points.

Line spacing See Leading.

Licensing A way to legally use copyrighted material for a certain time and in a certain way, usually associated with paying a fee established by the copyright holder.

Lowercase Small letters, the opposite of uppercase.

Margins Define the image area on the page. Headers and footers are positioned in the top and bottom margin area between the page edge and the margins.

Master items Design elements placed on a master page.

Master pages Pages that add common design elements to document pages, such as page numbers, headers, and footers.

Masthead Headline or title for a magazine.

Metadata Information that is included in a document but is hidden, such as copyright, lens information, location via GPS, camera settings, and more.

Metric kerning Kerns letter pairs based on information specified in the font; kerning adjusts space between characters.

Model releases The permission that is required when a person's face is identifiable in a photo and the image will be used to promote something—whether it's a product or idea.

Monochromatic Different shades and tints of the same color. Communicates a relaxed and peaceful feeling.

Monospaced font Fixed-width or nonproportional fonts that use the same amount of horizontal space for each letter.

Motion path Line that an object follows as part of a animation.

Movement Visual movement within a design such as the natural tracking of the eye across a page as the eye moves from focal point to focal point.

Negative space Blank areas in a design, also known as white space.

NoDerivs (ND) Creative Commons licensing. Requires that you not change material when you incorporate it into your own work. It can be used freely, but you must pass it along without change.

NonCommercial (NC) Creative Commons licensing. Means you can use work in your own creative work as long as you don't charge for it.

Object shadow The area of the form that is facing away from the light source and appears darkest.

Object styles Styles that apply basic formatting attributes (such as fill, stroke, corner options, and text-frame options) to selected objects.

Opacity Level by which an object is transparent or see-through; 100% opacity is nontransparent.

Optical kerning More even kerning applied by InDesign that overwrites metric kerning; kerning adjusts the space between characters.

Organic lines Lines that are usually irregular and imperfect. Found in nature.

Organic shapes Shapes that are random or generated by something natural. They are usually asymmetrical and convey natural, homemade, or relaxed feelings.

Overset text Text that does not fit inside a text frame.

Page reference A page number for topics listed in an index that points the reader to a location in a publication where the topic is covered.

Paragraph formatting See Paragraph settings.

Paragraph settings Affect an entire paragraph rather than selected words. These settings include alignment, hyphenation, and so on.

Paragraph spacing Similar to leading, but applies to an entire paragraph instead of lines of type within them. Also includes the spacing above or below paragraphs.

Paragraph style Styles that apply all text formating to a paragraph.

Pasteboard An area surrounding the document pages used to store design elements that don't appear on a page.

Path Shape assembled from anchor points and line segments.

Pattern A repetitive sequence of different colors, shapes, or values.

Pica Old typographical unit of measurement. One pica is made up of 12 points.

Pictograph (pictogram) Graphic symbol that represents something in the real world. Computer icons are pictographs that suggest the function they represent, such as a trash can icon to delete a file.

Points Unit of measurement used for type size.

Poster The image that appears when a media element is first viewed in a digital media publication.

Primary color Red, blue, and green. These can be combined to create every other color in the visible spectrum.

Process color Color made up of multiple color components; generally refers to mixing Cyan, Magenta, Yellow, and Black for offset printing.

Project creep Unplanned changes that increase the amount of work (scope) that a project requires. When the project loses focus and spins out of control, it eats up more and more time and effort.

Project deadlines Dictates when work needs to be completed.

Project scope Outlines the amount and type of work to be completed.

Proportion (scale) Describes the relative size and scale of elements.

Public Domain Creative Commons licensing. When copyright is expired or released and no longer applies to the content, or when an artist releases his or her work. It can be used without worrying about infringement.

Radial Circular type of balance that radiates from the center instead of the middle of a design.

Reflected highlight Area of a form that is lit by reflections from the ground or other objects in a scene.

Repetition Repeating an element in a design.

Representative shapes Shapes used to represent information. They are helpful in communicating with multicultural and multilingual audiences.

Rhythm Creative and expressive, rather than a consistent pattern or repetition in a design.

Rule of thirds A technique for laying out the space of your page to provide a focal point. Two vertical and two horizontal lines evenly divide the space into nine equal boxes, as in a tic-tac-toe board.

Run-in head A heading that is part of the paragraph text itself, rather than a paragraph on its own.

Runt A single word that appears on the last line of a paragraph and is considered typographically undesirable.

Sans serif fonts Font without serifs (the small lines extending from the strokes of a character). Often used for headlines and titles for their strong, stable, modern feel.

Script fonts (formal) Mimic handwriting. They convey a feeling of beauty, grace, or feminine dignity.

Secondary colors Created when you combine primary colors.

Sepia tones Images in which different shades of gray appear in different shades of a reddish-brown color.

Serif fonts Fonts that feature small lines extending from the strokes of the characters. Serif fonts are associated with typewriters, and they convey tradition, intelligence, and class.

Shape An area enclosed or defined by an outline, such as circles, squares, triangles, and even clouds.

ShareAlike Creative Commons licensing. Allows you to use an item in any way you want as long as your creation is shared under the same license as the original work.

Sketches Representative drawings of how to lay out a document or web page. These are sometimes one of the deliverables of a project.

Slab serif fonts Squared-off versions of a typical serif font. Also known as Egyptian, block serif, or square serif, they convey a machine-built feel.

Small caps Uses only uppercase letterforms for each letter, with lowercase letters appearing in a smaller size.

Space The canvas or working area. Its dimensions are determined by the resolution of the page you are creating.

Specifications Detailed written goals and limits for a project. These are sometimes one of the deliverables of a project.

Spread Page layout in which pages face each other.

Spot color Premixed ink created specifically for use in print production.

Stock photo Images for which the author retains copyright but a license for use is available.

Style (line) An effect applied to a line, such as varying width.

Style groups Styles, such as paragraph or object styles, organized in folders.

Style override Extra formatting applied in addition to a style's formatting. For example, an object may have a stroke applied in addition to the formatting specified in its object style.

Subtractive color Created by subtracting light. Printing uses subtractive color while digital devices use additive color.

Swashes Special characters with flowing and elegant endings for the ascenders and descenders.

Symmetrical Occurs when you can divide a page along its middle, and the left side of the page is a mirror image of the right (or the top reflects the bottom). Conveys an intentional, formal, and mechanical feeling.

Tertiary color Created by mixing primary and secondary colors.

Text frame Box-like element that contains text.

Texture The actual, tactile texture in real objects or the appearance of texture in a two-dimensional image.

Tracking Uniform spacing applied to two or more selected characters.

Typeface Specific letterform set, such as Helvetica, Arial, Garamond, and so on. It is the "look" of the characters.

Type size A font's height from the highest ascender to the lowest descender.

Unity (harmony) Also known as harmony and sharing similar traits. Low contrast. Things that go together should look like they belong together. The opposite of variety.

Uppercase Words typed in capital letters.

Value Describes the lightness or darkness of an object. Together with color, value represents the visible spectrum, such as a gradient.

Variety High contrast. The opposite of unity.

Variable width lines Expresses flow and grace.

Vertical Moving from top to bottom. Vertical lines tend to express power and elevation.

Vertical scale Describes the function of stretching letters and distorting the typeface geometry.

Weight (line) The thickness of a line.

Wireframe Rough, representative sketch of how to lay out a document.

Workspace Everything you see onscreen in InDesign, such as the application with its Tools panel, Control panel, and document window containing pages and pasteboard.

Index

+ (plus) sign, 99, 145, 190–191

A
Adobe Capture CC, 86–87
Adobe Color, 86
Adobe Creative Cloud. *See* Creative Cloud libraries
Adobe Illustrator files, 62, 63
Adobe InDesign
    ACA objectives for, 2, 34, 78, 120, 172, 224
    changing screen modes, 6
    compatibility with earlier versions, 115
    Essentials workspace for, 4–5
    importing text files into, 183–184
    modifying preferences in, 45
    opening, 4
    panels for, 15–18
    tools for, 7–14
    using Photoshop and Illustrator files in, 62, 63
Adobe Photoshop files, 62, 63
AI files, 63, 64
aligning text
    with baseline grid, 142–145
    Control panel options for, 71
    tabs for, 157–158
    vertically in text frames, 100
alternate layouts, 118–119
A-Master master page, 125–126
anchor points
    defined, 101
    direction lines for, 252
    repositioning, 251
angle of gradient, 176–177
Application bar, 4, 5, 26
auto leading, 72, 94–95
auto-sizing text frames, 100

B
baseline grid, 143–144
bleed, 38, 39, 122, 123
blending modes, 105–106, 107–108
book files, 220–223. *See also* comic book project; recipe book design
    creating, 220–221
    exporting, 222–223
    opening, 221
    synchronizing settings in, 222
    uses for, 220
borders for tables, 204–205
brochure layouts, 116
bulleted lists, 159–160, 194–196
buttons
    clickable panel, 18
    Create New Page, 127
    interactive PDF, 163, 164, 165–169
    New Library Item, 242–243

C
capital letters
    all text in, 12, 96
    drop caps in, 152–153
cells
    aligning text in, 203
    selecting, 201
    styling, 210–211
    text insets in, 204
chapters. *See* sections
character styles
    applying and editing, 194
    bullet and numbered lists, 194–196
    creating, 193
    modifying hyperlink appearance, 257
    nesting, 196–198
    uses for, 188, 192–193
characters. *See also* character styles; special characters
    adjusting leading for, 71
    changing bullet, 160
    formatting, 70, 71
    hiding/showing, 71
    kerning, 95–97
    tracking, 95–96, 97
    viewing tabs in text, 208
check boxes, 163
Check Spelling dialog box, 239
child objects. *See* parent-child layouts
clear buttons, 166, 167
clearing
    all effects, 108
    Color Theme tool content, 85
    paragraph style overrides, 190, 191
    rotation, 24
CMYK color
    about, 57, 135
    converting color themes to, 85, 86
    creating, 58–59
    selecting swatches of, 60
    viewing color separations for, 138
color. *See also* CMYK color; color themes; RGB color
    adding, 57
    applying in text frames, 98
    color rules, 84, 85
    creating color swatches, 58–59, 83
    editing text, 71
    gradient blends of, 61–62
    methods for applying, 59–60
    process, 57, 136, 137
    removing stroke or fill, 61
    selecting shape without fill, 54
    spot, 58, 135–138
    tint swatches of, 91–92
color rules, 84, 85
color separations, 137–138
color swatches
    adding color theme to, 84–85
    complementary color based on, 88–89
    creating, 58–59, 83
    duplicating and editing, 90–91
    loading from other documents, 92–93
    merging, 90
    saving, 92, 93
    sharing via CC library, 93
    text with gradient, 175–177
    tint swatches, 91–92
color themes
    converting to RGB or CMYK, 85, 86
    selecting, 83–86
    using from Adobe Capture CC, 86–87
columns
    aligning text across, 142–145
    indenting text within, 155–156
    master pages for different layouts, 126–127
    matching text frame width to, 140–141
    number of, 123, 141
    page design using, 122–123, 139–141
    spanning paragraphs across, 142
    threading text between, 145–147, 176
    using as layout guides, 38
columns, table, 201–202
combo boxes, 163
comic book project, 224–261
    about, 225
    ACA objectives for, 224
    checking spelling, 238–239
    exporting in web format, 259–261
    freeform shapes and lines in, 249–256
    grid-based designs for, 226–232
    hyperlinks for, 256–258
    placing and linking content to, 232–238
    text changes in, 238–241
    working with libraries, 241–249
comma-delimited text, 207
commands. *See* menus
content
    checking spelling of, 238–239
    fitting to comic frame, 229–230
    loading into Content Conveyor tool, 233–235
    placing and linking, 232–238
    placing with Content Placer tool, 233, 234
    preserving changes to child objects, 237–238
    searching/replacing text, 240–241
    updating links to, 235
Content Collector tool, 233
Content Conveyor tool, 233–235, 236
Content Placer tool, 233, 234
"continued from" lines, 147